Artificial Intelligence

Turning Data Into Dominance

Herkimer Throckmorton

ISBN: 9781779661722
Imprint: Telephasic Workshop
Copyright © 2024 Herkimer Throckmorton.
All Rights Reserved.

Contents

Introduction 1
The Rise of Artificial Intelligence 1

Understanding Data 13
What is Data? 13
Data Exploration and Visualization 24
Fundamentals of Statistics and Probability 35

Introduction to Machine Learning 53
What is Machine Learning? 53
Machine Learning Algorithms 65
Model Evaluation and Selection 95

Big Data and AI 109
Introduction to Big Data 109
Data Processing and Analysis 120
Data Mining and Predictive Analytics 136

Natural Language Processing 155
Introduction to Natural Language Processing 155
Introduction 164
Speech Recognition and Generation 172
Language Translation 180

Computer Vision 191
Introduction to Computer Vision 191
Convolutional Neural Networks 203
Image Generation and Style Transfer 214

AI and Robotics 221
- Robotics in the Age of AI 221
- Reinforcement Learning for Robotics 231
- Future Directions of AI and Robotics 237

AI in Business 243
- AI Applications in Marketing and Sales 243
- AI Applications in Finance 252
- AI Applications in Healthcare 259

AI Ethics and Social Implications 269
- Bias and Fairness in AI 269
- Privacy and Data Protection 277
- Impact on Employment and Society 290

The Future of AI 299
- New Frontiers in AI Research 299
- AI and Human Augmentation 307
- AI and Creativity 312

Index 323

Introduction

The Rise of Artificial Intelligence

The Evolution of AI Technology

Artificial Intelligence (AI) has come a long way since its inception. In this section, we will explore the fascinating evolution of AI technology, from its early beginnings to the present day. Strap in and get ready for a wild ride!

1. The Birth of AI: It all started in the 1940s when visionary scientists began to dream of creating machines that could mimic human intelligence. In 1956, the Dartmouth Conference marked the official birth of AI as a field of study. The conference brought together pioneers like John McCarthy, Marvin Minsky, and Allen Newell, who laid the foundation for AI research.

2. The Early Years: In the 1950s and 1960s, AI research focused on the development of symbolic AI. This approach aimed to create intelligent systems by representing knowledge in the form of symbols and manipulating them using logical rules. Early AI programs, such as the Logic Theorist and the General Problem Solver, demonstrated the potential of symbolic AI.

3. The AI Winter: Despite the early successes, AI research faced a significant setback in the 1970s. The limitations of symbolic AI, coupled with high expectations and overhyped promises, led to a period known as the AI Winter. Funding for AI research dwindled, and the field entered a phase of stagnation.

4. Expert Systems: In the 1980s, AI research saw a resurgence with the development of expert systems. These systems used knowledge bases and rule-based reasoning to emulate the decision-making capabilities of human experts. Expert systems found practical applications in fields such as medicine, finance, and engineering, but they were limited by their inability to learn from data.

5. Machine Learning Revolution: The 1980s also witnessed the emergence of a new paradigm in AI: machine learning. Machine learning algorithms enabled

computers to learn and improve from experience without being explicitly programmed. The introduction of neural networks, such as the backpropagation algorithm, paved the way for breakthroughs in pattern recognition and data analysis.

6. The Rise of Big Data: In the 21st century, the explosion of digital data has transformed AI research. The availability of massive datasets, coupled with advances in computing power, has fueled the development of data-driven AI techniques. Machine learning algorithms, such as deep neural networks, have achieved remarkable success in areas such as image recognition, natural language processing, and autonomous driving.

7. Reinforcement Learning: Another significant development in AI technology is reinforcement learning. Inspired by the principles of operant conditioning, reinforcement learning enables machines to learn through trial and error. Algorithms like Q-learning and Deep Q-networks have revolutionized fields such as robotics and game playing, with applications ranging from self-driving cars to playing complex games like Go.

8. The AI Renaissance: In recent years, AI has experienced a renaissance, driven by advancements in deep learning and the availability of vast computing resources. Deep learning models, powered by neural networks with many layers, have achieved breakthrough performance in tasks such as speech recognition, machine translation, and image synthesis. The integration of AI into everyday life through virtual assistants, smart home devices, and recommendation systems has made AI technology more accessible and pervasive.

9. Ethical Concerns: As AI technology continues to advance, ethical considerations have become paramount. The potential risks associated with AI, such as bias, privacy invasion, and job displacement, have raised important questions about the responsible development and deployment of AI systems. It is crucial to address these concerns to ensure that AI technology benefits society as a whole.

10. The Future of AI: AI technology holds immense potential for transforming various industries and tackling complex societal challenges. From AI-driven healthcare and autonomous systems to the fusion of AI with emerging technologies like quantum computing and human augmentation, the future of AI promises exciting possibilities. However, we must proceed with caution, ensuring that AI is developed and used in a way that aligns with our values and priorities.

In this section, we have explored the evolution of AI technology, from its birth to the present day. We have witnessed the rise and fall of different AI paradigms, the impact of big data, and the emergence of machine learning and deep learning as key drivers of AI progress. But the journey is far from over. As we continue to push the boundaries of AI, it is essential to consider the ethical implications and guide the development of AI technology to create a future that benefits everyone.

So, buckle up, as we plunge deeper into the realm of AI and discover its inner workings and applications in the following chapters!

AI in Everyday Life

Artificial Intelligence (AI) has become an integral part of our everyday lives, shaping the way we interact with technology, make decisions, and navigate the world. From voice assistants like Siri and Alexa to recommendation algorithms on streaming platforms, AI is all around us, often without us realizing it. In this section, we will explore some of the key areas where AI is present in our daily lives and the impact it has on individuals and society.

AI-powered voice assistants have gained immense popularity in recent years. These virtual companions are capable of recognizing and understanding natural language, allowing users to interact with their devices through voice commands. Whether it's asking for the weather forecast, setting a reminder, or playing music, voice assistants offer convenience and efficiency.

For instance, Amazon's Alexa uses a combination of natural language processing and machine learning algorithms to understand user commands and respond accordingly. It can control smart home devices, answer questions, and even perform tasks like ordering groceries or scheduling appointments. Similarly, Apple's Siri and Google Assistant provide users with personalized assistance, helping them navigate their smartphones and access information effortlessly.

Recommendation algorithms are another area where AI has made significant strides in everyday life. These algorithms collect vast amounts of data on user preferences and behavior to suggest personalized content and products. Platforms like Netflix, Spotify, and Amazon use AI algorithms to analyze user data, such as viewing history and patterns, to provide tailored recommendations.

Netflix, for example, uses a combination of collaborative filtering and content-based filtering techniques to suggest movies and TV shows based on a user's past viewing habits. The more data the algorithm collects, the better it becomes at understanding an individual's taste and providing accurate recommendations. This not only enhances user experience but also drives engagement and customer satisfaction.

Another area where AI has had a transformative impact is in the healthcare sector. Medical professionals can leverage AI-powered tools to expedite diagnosis, improve patient care, and enhance research capabilities. For instance, AI algorithms can analyze medical images and accurately detect abnormalities or identify patterns that may indicate a specific disease or condition.

AI-based cancer screening tools, such as mammography AI, have shown promising results in detecting breast cancer at its early stages. These tools use deep learning algorithms to analyze mammograms and flag suspicious areas that require further examination. By assisting radiologists in their decision-making process, AI can potentially reduce false negatives and improve the overall accuracy of cancer screenings.

In addition to healthcare, AI is also transforming the transportation industry. Self-driving cars, powered by AI and machine learning algorithms, are being developed to enhance road safety and offer autonomous transportation. Companies like Tesla, Waymo, and Uber are investing heavily in developing self-driving technology, with the goal of reducing accidents and improving traffic efficiency.

Self-driving cars rely on a combination of sensors, cameras, and AI algorithms to perceive the environment, make decisions, and navigate their surroundings. The algorithms analyze real-time data to detect and respond to obstacles, traffic signals, and pedestrians. While fully autonomous vehicles are still in the testing phase, the potential impact on everyday life, especially in terms of reducing congestion and providing accessible transportation, is immense.

However, AI in everyday life also raises significant ethical considerations and challenges. The collection and use of personal data for AI algorithms can raise concerns about privacy and security. Additionally, the deployment of AI technologies in critical areas such as healthcare and transportation requires careful consideration of their reliability, accountability, and potential biases.

To fully harness the benefits of AI in everyday life, it is crucial to address these ethical challenges through robust regulations, transparency in AI decision-making processes, and ongoing research on bias mitigation techniques.

In conclusion, AI has seamlessly integrated into our everyday lives, revolutionizing the way we interact with technology, consume content, and access healthcare. From voice assistants to recommendation algorithms, AI has become an essential part of our routines. However, it is important to approach AI deployment with an awareness of its ethical implications and to continuously strive for a balance between technological advancements and social considerations.

Key Takeaways

- AI-powered voice assistants like Siri and Alexa have become popular, providing users with personalized assistance and convenience.

- Recommendation algorithms use AI to analyze user data and provide tailored suggestions for content and products, enhancing user experience.

- AI is transforming healthcare by improving diagnosis accuracy and aiding in early disease detection.

- Self-driving cars, powered by AI algorithms, have the potential to revolutionize transportation by improving road safety and traffic efficiency.

- Ethical considerations such as privacy, security, and bias need to be addressed to fully harness the benefits of AI in everyday life.

Exercises

1. Think about the AI-powered devices you interact with regularly. How do they make your life easier? Can you identify any potential ethical concerns regarding the use of these devices?

2. Research and write a short report on a recent development in AI technology that has impacted everyday life, such as a breakthrough in natural language processing or image recognition.

3. Explore the privacy policies of popular AI-driven platforms. Identify any potential risks associated with the collection and use of personal data. Propose mechanisms that can mitigate these risks.

Additional Resources

- Video: "How AI is Shaping the Future of Everyday Life" by TEDx Talks

- Book: "The Big Nine: How the Tech Titans and Their Thinking Machines Could Warp Humanity" by Amy Webb

- Article: "Ethical Considerations in AI: Addressing Bias and Discrimination" by Harvard Business Review

The Impact of AI on Industries

In the ever-expanding world of artificial intelligence, its impact on various industries cannot be underestimated. AI has become a disruptive force, transforming traditional business models and revolutionizing the way industries operate. From healthcare to finance and everything in between, AI is reshaping industries in ways we could never have imagined.

One area where AI is making a considerable impact is healthcare. The ability of AI systems to analyze vast amounts of medical data, such as patient records and medical images, is revolutionizing the field of diagnostics. AI-powered algorithms can now detect diseases and abnormalities with unmatched accuracy, leading to earlier diagnosis and better patient outcomes. Additionally, AI is accelerating the drug discovery process, allowing researchers to identify potential new drug candidates more efficiently.

Finance is another industry significantly impacted by AI. Intelligent algorithms are being used to detect fraudulent activities and protect consumers from financial crimes. AI-powered chatbots and virtual assistants are providing personalized financial advice to customers, enhancing their experience and increasing customer satisfaction. Moreover, algorithmic trading systems are leveraging AI to make real-time predictions and optimize investment strategies.

The transportation and logistics sector is also being transformed by AI. Self-driving vehicles are becoming a reality, with AI algorithms powering their navigation systems and ensuring safety on the roads. Additionally, AI is optimizing supply chain management by predicting demand patterns, optimizing routes, and reducing inefficiencies in the transportation of goods.

Manufacturing is yet another industry benefiting from AI advancements. AI-driven robots are replacing manual labor in various manufacturing processes, leading to increased productivity, improved quality control, and cost reduction. Intelligent automation systems are also allowing for more flexible and responsive production lines, enabling manufacturers to quickly adapt to changing market demands.

However, AI's impact is not without its challenges and ethical considerations. The widespread adoption of AI technologies raises concerns about privacy, data security, and job displacements. It is crucial to address these ethical issues and ensure that AI is developed and deployed in a responsible and inclusive manner.

As AI continues to evolve, its impact on industries will only grow stronger. It is essential for businesses and industries to embrace AI and harness its potential to stay competitive in the rapidly evolving digital landscape.

To further explore the impact of AI on industries, I recommend reading the following resources:

- "The Industries of the Future" by Alec Ross

- "Machine, Platform, Crowd: Harnessing Our Digital Future" by Andrew McAfee and Erik Brynjolfsson
- "AI Superpowers: China, Silicon Valley, and the New World Order" by Kai-Fu Lee
- "The Fourth Industrial Revolution" by Klaus Schwab

Now that we've covered the impact of AI on industries, let's move on to the ethical considerations in AI development in section 1.1.4. Brace yourselves; it's about to get ethical up in here!

Ethical Considerations in AI Development

As we dive deeper into the world of artificial intelligence (AI), it is essential to explore the ethical considerations surrounding its development. AI technology has the potential to transform industries, improve our lives, and drive economic growth. However, it also poses significant ethical challenges that must be addressed to ensure its responsible and beneficial use.

The Power and Influence of AI

AI systems have the power to make decisions and take actions that can greatly impact individuals and society as a whole. As these systems become more advanced and autonomous, they can have far-reaching consequences. From self-driving cars making split-second decisions on the road to AI algorithms determining loan approvals, the ethical implications of these decisions cannot be underestimated.

Transparency and Explainability

One of the key ethical concerns in AI development is the lack of transparency and explainability. Machine learning algorithms often operate as so-called "black boxes," making it challenging to understand how they arrive at their decisions. This lack of transparency raises concerns about biases, discrimination, and accountability. When an AI algorithm denies someone a loan or recommends certain medical treatments, individuals have a right to know how the AI system arrived at that decision.

To address this issue, researchers and policymakers are working on developing explainable AI (XAI) techniques. These methods aim to make AI systems more transparent and provide insights into their decision-making processes. By understanding the reasoning behind AI decisions, we can better ensure fairness, accountability, and trust in these systems.

Bias and Fairness

AI systems are only as unbiased as the data they are trained on. If the training data contains biases, whether conscious or unconscious, the AI algorithm will also exhibit those biases. This can lead to discriminatory outcomes, perpetuating and amplifying existing societal biases.

For example, facial recognition systems have been shown to have higher error rates for certain ethnicities and genders, leading to potential discrimination. AI algorithms used in hiring processes have also been found to favor certain demographic groups, exacerbating existing inequalities in job opportunities.

Addressing bias in AI requires a multi-faceted approach. It starts with diverse and representative training data, ensuring that underrepresented groups are included. Additionally, AI designers and developers must actively work to identify and mitigate biases in algorithms. Techniques like fairness-aware machine learning and algorithmic auditing can be employed to evaluate the fairness of AI systems and make necessary adjustments.

Data Privacy and Security

AI systems rely heavily on data, often collected from individuals without their explicit consent. This raises concerns about data privacy and security. The misuse or mishandling of personal information can have severe repercussions, such as identity theft, surveillance, and infringements on personal freedoms.

As AI technology advances, it is essential to establish strict regulations and protocols to protect individual privacy rights. Data protection laws, such as the European Union's General Data Protection Regulation (GDPR), are steps in the right direction. AI developers should also implement privacy-enhancing techniques such as data anonymization and differential privacy to minimize risks to individuals' privacy.

Accountability and Governance

With the increasing autonomy of AI systems, questions arise regarding who should be held responsible for their actions. How can we ensure that AI developers, designers, and users are accountable for the outcomes of AI systems? Establishing clear lines of responsibility is crucial to mitigate the potential harms caused by AI technology.

Governance frameworks and regulations are necessary to oversee the development and deployment of AI systems. These frameworks should address issues such as transparency, accountability, and the ethical use of AI. It is also important to involve a diverse group of stakeholders, including experts from various fields, policymakers, and members of the public, in the decision-making process to prevent the concentration of power in the hands of a few.

Human-Centered AI

In designing and developing AI systems, it is paramount to prioritize human well-being and ensure that AI serves human values. AI should augment human capabilities and decision-making, rather than replace or undermine them. Ethical considerations must be integrated into the core design principles of AI systems.

A human-centered approach to AI requires interdisciplinary collaboration, involving experts from fields such as computer science, ethics, sociology, and philosophy. This approach will steer AI development in a direction that aligns with our societal values and respects human dignity.

Case Study: AI in Criminal Justice

One poignant example of the ethical considerations in AI development is its use in the criminal justice system. AI algorithms are increasingly being used to predict reoffending rates, determine parole decisions, and assign prison sentences. However, concerns have been raised about the fairness and accuracy of these algorithms.

In some cases, AI algorithms have been found to disproportionately target marginalized groups and perpetuate biases present in historical data. This can lead to a perpetuation of unjust systems and exacerbate existing disparities in the criminal justice system.

To address these issues, researchers and policymakers are working to develop AI systems that ensure fairness and unbiased decision-making. By improving the transparency of the algorithms, incorporating diverse training data, and involving experts and communities affected by these systems, we can strive for a more just and equitable criminal justice system.

Conclusion

Ethical considerations play a vital role in the development of AI technology. From transparency and fairness to privacy and accountability, addressing these ethical challenges is vital to ensure the responsible and beneficial use of AI. By integrating ethical guidelines into AI development, we can create AI systems that serve humanity and contribute to a more equitable and inclusive future.

In the next chapter, we will dive into the fundamentals of data analysis and exploration, essential for harnessing the power of AI.

The Future of AI

As we delve into the fascinating world of Artificial Intelligence, it's important to consider not just where AI has come from and where it stands today but also the exciting possibilities that lie ahead. The future of AI holds great promise, as well as concerns and challenges that need to be addressed. In this section, we will explore the potential paths that AI may follow and the impact it could have on various aspects of our lives.

Advancements in AI Research

The field of AI is constantly evolving, driven by rigorous research and innovation. One area that holds immense promise is quantum computing and its potential intersection with AI. Quantum computing leverages the principles of quantum mechanics to perform complex computations at unprecedented speeds. This has the potential to revolutionize AI algorithms by enabling the processing of vast amounts of data with exceptionally high speed and accuracy. Imagine the possibilities of training deep neural networks in a fraction of the time it takes today or solving optimization problems with billions of variables in practically no time at all.

Another exciting frontier in AI research is explainable AI. While AI models can achieve remarkable accuracy in many tasks, they often operate as black boxes that lack transparency. Explainable AI aims to develop techniques that can provide insights into how AI models arrive at their decisions. This is particularly important in critical applications such as healthcare and finance, where explainability is crucial for building trust and ensuring ethical decision-making.

Lastly, the integration of AI and space exploration presents a world of possibilities. AI can revolutionize space missions by enabling autonomous navigation, efficient resource management, and intelligent data analysis. For instance, AI-powered rovers can explore distant planets and moons, analyze geological data, and transmit key information back to Earth. The future of space exploration will be greatly enhanced by AI-driven technologies, pushing the boundaries of human knowledge and understanding of the universe.

AI and Human Augmentation

AI has the potential to augment human capabilities and profoundly impact various aspects of our lives. One exciting area is brain-computer interfaces (BCIs), which establish a direct communication pathway between the brain and an external device. BCIs have the potential to revolutionize healthcare by enabling individuals with disabilities to regain mobility, communicate with others, and even control robotic prosthetics through their thoughts. Furthermore, BCIs can enhance cognitive abilities, enabling us to interface directly with AI systems, augmenting our problem-solving capabilities or learning new skills at an accelerated rate.

Additionally, AI can play a crucial role in assisted living for the elderly and people with chronic conditions. Smart home devices equipped with AI algorithms can monitor health parameters, detect emergencies, and provide personalized assistance. For example, an AI system can analyze a person's gait and predict the risk of falling, prompting timely interventions to prevent accidents. AI-driven virtual assistants can also provide companionship and support, enhancing the overall quality of life for individuals who may require additional care.

AI and Creativity

Contrary to the common belief that AI only excels in analytical tasks, it also showcases remarkable creative potential. AI-generated art, for instance, has gained significant attention in recent years. Deep learning models can analyze vast art collections, identify patterns, and generate novel artworks that emulate various artistic styles. This opens up endless possibilities for artists, enabling them to explore new concepts, push boundaries, and collaborate with AI as a creative partner.

Music composition is another domain where AI displays significant potential. AI-powered systems can analyze vast musical libraries, learn patterns, and compose original pieces in different genres and styles. In fact, some AI-generated music has made it onto mainstream platforms, blurring the line between human and AI creativity. This convergence of human and AI artistic expression offers exciting possibilities for musicians to explore new aesthetic landscapes and push the boundaries of musical composition.

Likewise, AI has begun to reshape the film and entertainment industry. AI algorithms can analyze massive amounts of data, including audience preferences, box office trends, and critical reviews, to make data-driven recommendations for content creation and distribution. This deep understanding of audience preferences can help filmmakers and content creators tailor their work to resonate with specific target audiences, enhancing the overall viewing experience and driving the success of their projects.

Conclusion

Artificial Intelligence has come a long way and promises to shape the future in profound ways. From advancements in research, such as quantum computing and explainable AI, to the potential of AI and human augmentation through brain-computer interfaces, the future is filled with exciting possibilities. AI's creative potential in generating art, composing music, and enhancing the film and entertainment industry also offers unique opportunities for collaboration between humans and AI.

However, as we move forward, we must also address the ethical and societal implications of AI. Issues of bias and fairness, privacy and data protection, as well as the impact of automation on employment, must be carefully considered and addressed. With responsible development and thoughtful regulation, we can harness the power of AI for the benefit of humanity and ensure a future where AI combines with human ingenuity to push the boundaries of what is possible. AI truly has the potential to revolutionize our world, and it is up to us to steer its trajectory responsibly.

Understanding Data

What is Data?

Types of Data: Structured vs. Unstructured

Data is the lifeblood of artificial intelligence. It fuels the algorithms that power AI systems and helps machines learn and make intelligent decisions. However, data comes in different forms, and understanding the types of data is crucial for effectively harnessing the power of AI. In this section, we will explore two main types of data: structured and unstructured.

Structured Data

Structured data refers to information that is organized and formatted in a specific way. It is highly organized, making it easy to search, analyze, and process. Structured data is usually stored in databases and can be easily represented as tables with rows and columns.

A common example of structured data is a spreadsheet containing sales data with columns for date, product, quantity, and price. Each row represents a specific sale, and the values in each column are well-defined and consistent.

One of the key advantages of using structured data is that it can be easily queried using database query languages like SQL (Structured Query Language). This allows for efficient retrieval of specific data subsets and performing complex calculations and analysis.

Structured data is prevalent in many industries, including finance, retail, and healthcare. It enables businesses to track sales, monitor inventory, manage customer information, and perform various data-driven operations.

Example: Consider a database of student records in a university. The database contains tables for student information, courses, and grades. Each table has well-defined columns representing specific attributes such as student ID, name, course code, and grade. With structured data, the university could easily generate reports on student performance, track enrollment trends, and identify areas for improvement.

Unstructured Data

Unstructured data, on the other hand, is information that does not have a predefined structure. It does not fit neatly into tables or rows and columns. Unstructured data is typically in the form of text, images, audio, video, social media posts, emails, documents, and sensor data.

Unlike structured data, unstructured data poses unique challenges for analysis and processing. It is often messy, incomplete, and difficult to extract meaningful information from. This makes it a more complex and time-consuming task for machines to understand.

However, unstructured data can also provide valuable insights and context. For example, analyzing customer reviews and comments on social media can help businesses gauge public sentiment and gather feedback on their products or services.

Advancements in natural language processing (NLP) and computer vision have made it possible to extract information from unstructured data. NLP techniques can analyze text and extract entities, sentiments, and relationships, while computer vision algorithms can interpret images and recognize patterns.

Example: Consider a social media platform with millions of user posts. These posts contain text, images, and videos generated by users worldwide. Analyzing the unstructured data from these posts using NLP and computer vision techniques can provide valuable insights about user preferences, sentiment trends, and potential engagement opportunities for businesses.

The Blurred Line: Semi-structured Data

Between structured and unstructured data lies semi-structured data. This type of data is partially organized, with some elements following a structured format while others are unstructured. Semi-structured data may include XML (eXtensible Markup Language) files, JSON (JavaScript Object Notation) documents, and HTML (Hypertext Markup Language) pages.

Semi-structured data is flexible and allows for more versatility than structured data. It can capture complex relationships and hierarchical structures, making it suitable for representing data in applications like web scraping, data exchange, and data integration.

Example: An online shopping website may store product information in XML files. While some elements like the product name, price, and description follow a structured format, other parts, such as customer reviews, can be unstructured text. This combination of structured and unstructured data allows for organizing and presenting product information in a consistent manner while still capturing diverse customer feedback.

Choosing the Right Data Type

When working with AI systems, it is essential to understand the type of data involved. This knowledge helps determine the most appropriate algorithms, methods, and tools for processing and analyzing the data effectively.

Structured data is suitable for tasks that require precise and consistent information, such as business analytics, financial modeling, and database management. On the other hand, unstructured data is useful for tasks like sentiment analysis, image recognition, and natural language understanding.

In many real-world scenarios, AI applications often deal with a combination of structured and unstructured data. By utilizing techniques like data preprocessing, feature engineering, and data fusion, it is possible to integrate and derive insights from both types of data.

Example: A healthcare organization wants to develop an AI system for predicting disease outcomes based on patient records. The patient records contain structured data (e.g., demographics, lab results) and unstructured data (e.g., clinical notes, medical imaging). By combining data from both sources, the AI system can leverage the structured data for statistical modeling and use natural language processing techniques to extract relevant information from the unstructured clinical notes.

Summary and Key Takeaways

In this section, we explored the two main types of data: structured and unstructured. Structured data is highly organized, easily searchable, and represented in tabular form, making it suitable for efficient analysis. Unstructured data, on the other hand, lacks a specific format and requires more advanced techniques to extract valuable insights. Semi-structured data falls in between, combining elements of both structured and unstructured data.

Understanding the type of data is crucial for designing AI systems and selecting appropriate algorithms and tools. In real-world applications, it is common to encounter a mix of structured and unstructured data, necessitating techniques for integrating and leveraging information from both sources.

As AI continues to evolve, advancements in data processing and analysis will play a critical role in unlocking the potential of both structured and unstructured data. The ability to extract meaningful information and derive insights from diverse data sources will pave the way for more intelligent AI systems.

Data Collection Methods

In the world of artificial intelligence, data is the fuel that powers the algorithms and models. Without data, AI would be nothing more than a pipe dream. In this section, we will dive deep into the various methods of collecting data, ranging from traditional approaches to cutting-edge techniques. So, grab your data collection tools and let's embark on this exciting journey!

Traditional Data Collection Methods

Traditionally, data collection involved a lot of manual effort and painstaking attention to detail. Researchers would often rely on surveys, interviews, and observations to gather the necessary information. While these methods are still widely used today, they do have their limitations.

One common method is the survey, where researchers design a set of questions to gather specific information from a target population. Surveys can be conducted through different mediums, such as face-to-face interviews, phone calls, or online forms. However, surveys can suffer from biases, as respondents may not always provide accurate or complete answers.

Another traditional method is interviews, where researchers directly interact with individuals or groups to collect data. Interviews can be structured or unstructured, depending on the research goals. Structured interviews follow a predetermined set of questions, while unstructured interviews allow for more open-ended discussions. However, interviews can be time-consuming and require skilled interviewers to extract meaningful insights.

Observational methods involve researchers observing individuals or events in their natural setting. This can provide valuable information about behavior, patterns, and trends. However, observational studies can be influenced by the observer's bias and may not always capture the complete picture.

Emerging Data Collection Methods

With the advancement of technology, new data collection methods have emerged, revolutionizing the field of AI. These methods leverage the power of modern technology to gather vast amounts of data more efficiently and accurately.

One popular method is web scraping, where automated bots gather data from websites. This technique is particularly useful when collecting data from large online databases or social media platforms. However, web scraping must be done responsibly and within legal boundaries to respect privacy and avoid copyright infringements.

Sensor-based data collection involves using various sensors to capture data from the physical world. For example, smart devices equipped with sensors can collect data on temperature, movement, or even air quality. These sensors enable the collection of real-time data, providing valuable insights for applications such as smart cities or environmental monitoring.

Mobile data collection takes advantage of the ubiquity of smartphones and mobile apps. Mobile apps can collect data on user behavior, location, and preferences. This data can be invaluable for market research, personalized advertising, or improving user experience. However, privacy concerns must be addressed to ensure user consent and protect sensitive information.

Social media data collection focuses on extracting valuable information from social media platforms. The vast amount of user-generated content on platforms like Twitter, Facebook, or Instagram provides a rich source of data for sentiment analysis, trend detection, or brand monitoring. However, ethical considerations like user privacy and data ownership need to be carefully addressed.

Challenges and Ethical Considerations

While data collection methods have evolved and become more sophisticated, challenges and ethical considerations still persist. It is important to address these challenges to ensure responsible and ethical use of data in AI applications.

One challenge is data quality and representativeness. Biases may be introduced if the collected data does not adequately represent the target population. For example, if a facial recognition system is trained primarily on data from light-skinned individuals, it may perform poorly on darker-skinned individuals. Such biases can perpetuate discrimination and unfairness, so diverse and representative data collection is crucial.

Another challenge is privacy and data protection. As AI systems rely on vast amounts of personal data, it is essential to adhere to data protection regulations and ensure user consent. Data breaches and unauthorized access to sensitive information can have severe consequences, eroding trust in AI systems. Therefore, robust security measures and ethical guidelines must be implemented throughout the data collection process.

Moreover, data ownership and consent are critical ethical considerations. Users should have control over their data and be informed about how it will be used. Transparent communication and obtaining explicit consent from individuals are essential steps to ensure ethical data collection.

Real-World Example: Ride-Hailing Apps

To illustrate the importance of data collection methods, let's consider ride-hailing apps like Uber or Lyft. These platforms collect vast amounts of data about their users, drivers, and routes. By analyzing this data, they can optimize driver allocations, estimate arrival times, and enhance user experiences.

Ride-hailing apps collect data through various methods. They gather information about users' pick-up and drop-off locations, trip durations, and feedback ratings. They also utilize sensors in drivers' smartphones to monitor factors like vehicle speed and driver behavior. Additionally, they leverage GPS data to track the location and movement of drivers and riders in real-time.

This comprehensive data collection enables ride-hailing apps to provide personalized recommendations, efficient routing, and predictive analytics. For example, the app can suggest nearby restaurants based on a rider's location, or estimate the arrival time based on historical traffic data.

However, to ensure ethical use of data, ride-hailing apps must address privacy concerns, obtain user consent, and implement robust security measures. They must also continuously evaluate and address any potential biases in their algorithms to ensure fair and unbiased treatment of drivers and riders.

Summary

In this section, we explored various data collection methods, ranging from traditional approaches to emerging technologies. Traditional methods like surveys, interviews, and observations are still widely used, although they have their limitations. Emerging methods such as web scraping, sensor-based data collection, mobile data collection, and social media data collection leverage the power of modern technology to gather data more efficiently and accurately.

We also discussed the challenges and ethical considerations in data collection, including data quality, privacy, and consent. Ensuring diverse and representative

WHAT IS DATA?

data, protecting user privacy, addressing biases, and obtaining explicit consent are crucial steps in responsible data collection.

Data collection is the foundation of AI, and the quality and diversity of the data directly impact the performance and fairness of AI models and systems. As AI technology continues to advance, it is essential to navigate the complex terrain of data collection with caution, responsibility, and a commitment to ethical practices.

Data Cleaning and Validation

Data is the lifeblood of artificial intelligence. Without high-quality and reliable data, AI models cannot make accurate predictions or provide valuable insights. However, data in its raw form often contains errors, inconsistencies, and missing values. To ensure the integrity and reliability of data, a crucial step called data cleaning and validation is necessary. In this section, we will explore the importance of data cleaning and validation, as well as the techniques and tools used to accomplish this task.

The Importance of Data Cleaning

Data cleaning is the process of identifying and correcting or removing errors, inconsistencies, or missing values in a dataset. It is a critical step in preparing data for analysis and modeling. Clean data ensures the accuracy and reliability of the results obtained from AI algorithms, leading to more robust and trustworthy AI applications.

There are several reasons why data cleaning is essential:

- **Improved Accuracy:** Clean data eliminates errors and inconsistencies, leading to more accurate and reliable AI models. With accurate models, organizations can make informed decisions and take appropriate actions based on the insights derived from the data.

- **Enhanced Model Performance:** AI models are trained on clean data, resulting in better performance and higher predictive accuracy. Machine learning algorithms rely heavily on the quality of input data, and cleaning the data ensures that the models learn meaningful patterns and relationships.

- **Consistent and Reliable Results:** When data is clean and free from errors, AI models produce consistent and reliable results. This consistency is essential for making sound business decisions and building trust in the AI applications.

- **Reduced Bias:** Biases can occur in data due to various factors such as sampling biases or human error. Data cleaning helps identify and mitigate these biases, resulting in a more unbiased dataset and fairer AI models.
- **Cost and Time Efficiency:** Cleaning the data at the initial stages of a project saves time and resources in the long run. It minimizes the need to revisit and correct errors later and avoids potential setbacks caused by flawed data.

Techniques for Data Cleaning and Validation

Data cleaning and validation involve a range of techniques and methods to identify and deal with errors, inconsistencies, and missing values in the dataset. Let's explore some common techniques used in the data cleaning process:

1. **Data Profiling:** Data profiling is the initial step in data cleaning, where the structure, quality, and content of the dataset are analyzed. It helps to identify missing values, outliers, and inconsistencies within the dataset. Various statistical measures, such as mean, median, mode, and standard deviation, are calculated to gain insights into the data.

2. **Handling Missing Values:** Missing values are a common issue in datasets and can lead to biased or incomplete results. There are several strategies to handle missing values, such as deletion of rows or columns with missing values, imputing missing values with mean or median values, or using advanced imputation techniques like multiple imputations or predictive modeling.

3. **Removing Duplicates:** Duplicates often occur in datasets and can lead to skewed analysis or modeling results. Removing duplicate records ensures each data instance is unique and prevents oversampling. The identification and removal of duplicates can be done based on a subset of attributes or the entire dataset.

4. **Handling Outliers:** Outliers are extreme values that deviate significantly from the other data points in the dataset. They can impact the performance and accuracy of AI models. Various techniques such as statistical methods, visualization, or clustering algorithms can be used to identify and handle outliers effectively.

5. **Data Transformation:** Data transformation involves converting the data into a suitable format for analysis or modeling. This can include scaling

variables, encoding categorical variables, or transforming skewed variables using logarithmic or power transformations. These transformations help improve the performance and interpretability of AI models.

6. **Data Integration:** In some cases, data may be spread across multiple sources or in different formats. Data integration involves combining data from various sources into a single dataset, ensuring consistency and compatibility. This step is crucial for deriving meaningful insights and accurate modeling.

7. **Quality Assessment:** After the data cleaning process, a final quality assessment is performed. This involves validating the cleaned dataset against predefined quality metrics, such as accuracy, completeness, consistency, and conformity. Any remaining issues or anomalies are addressed before moving forward with analysis or modeling.

Tools for Data Cleaning and Validation

Data cleaning and validation can be a complex and time-consuming process. Fortunately, there are several tools available that simplify and automate this task. Let's explore some popular tools used in data cleaning:

- **OpenRefine:** OpenRefine is an open-source tool that provides a user-friendly interface for cleaning and transforming messy datasets. It allows for efficient handling of missing values, removal of duplicates, and data standardization. OpenRefine also supports advanced operations such as clustering and data reconciliation.

- **Trifacta Wrangler:** Trifacta Wrangler is a highly intuitive data preparation tool that offers a visual interface for cleaning and transforming data. It enables users to easily identify and handle missing values, outliers, and inconsistencies. Trifacta Wrangler's smart suggestions and data quality profiling make the data cleaning process more efficient and accurate.

- **Microsoft Excel:** Microsoft Excel is a widely used spreadsheet tool that also offers basic functionality for data cleaning. It provides features such as filtering, sorting, and conditional formatting, which can be used to identify and remove errors, duplicates, and outliers. Excel also supports simple transformations and data integration.

- **Python Libraries:** Python, a popular programming language for data analysis and machine learning, provides several libraries for data cleaning.

Pandas, a widely used library, offers powerful data manipulation and cleaning capabilities. Other libraries like NumPy and SciPy provide functions for statistical analysis and outlier detection.

- **R Packages:** R, another widely used programming language for data analysis, has several packages dedicated to data cleaning and validation. The 'tidyverse' collection of packages, including 'dplyr' and 'tidyr,' provides functions for data manipulation, cleaning, and transformation. The 'outliers' package offers various methods for detecting and handling outliers.

It is essential to choose the right tool based on your specific data cleaning requirements, dataset size, and available resources.

Data Cleaning in Action: Example and Caveats

To illustrate the importance of data cleaning and validation, let's consider an example in the healthcare domain. Suppose a hospital wants to analyze the relationship between patient demographics and hospital readmission rates. The dataset contains patient records with attributes such as age, gender, ethnicity, medical history, and readmission status.

During the data cleaning process, the following tasks are performed:

- **Handling Missing Values:** Missing values in the medical history attribute are imputed using the mode value, representing the most frequent medical condition observed among patients.

- **Removing Duplicates:** Duplicate records, identified based on the combination of patient ID and admission date, are removed to ensure each patient is represented only once.

- **Handling Outliers:** Outliers in the age attribute, representing patients above 100 years old, are identified and removed as they are unlikely and could skew the analysis.

- **Data Transformation:** Categorical variables such as gender and ethnicity are encoded numerically for modeling purposes. Age is also transformed from years to age groups (e.g., 18-30, 31-45) for easier interpretation.

- **Data Integration:** Additional data sources, such as socioeconomic factors by patient zip code, are integrated into the dataset to provide a more comprehensive analysis.

- **Quality Assessment:** The final cleaned dataset is assessed for accuracy, completeness, and consistency. A validation process is performed to ensure all cleaning tasks were executed correctly.

It is important to note that data cleaning is not a one-time task. As new data is collected or changes occur in existing data, the cleaning process needs to be repeated to maintain data quality. Additionally, data cleaning decisions should be made based on domain knowledge and a deep understanding of the dataset to avoid unintentional biases or errors.

Exercises

To enhance your understanding of data cleaning and validation, here are some exercises for you to try:

1. Download a dataset from a reputable source and perform data cleaning techniques such as handling missing values, removing duplicates, and handling outliers.

2. Identify potential biases in a dataset, both known and unknown. Propose strategies to address and mitigate these biases.

3. Explore a real-world case study where data cleaning played a crucial role in the success or failure of an AI application. Discuss the challenges faced and the lessons learned.

4. Experiment with different data cleaning tools such as OpenRefine, Trifacta Wrangler, or Python libraries. Compare their functionalities and ease of use.

Remember, practice is key to mastering data cleaning techniques. The more you engage with real-world datasets, the more confident and skilled you will become in ensuring data quality for AI applications.

Resources

To further expand your knowledge of data cleaning and validation, here are some recommended resources:

- Books:
    - Dasu, T., & Johnson, T. (2003). Exploratory data mining and data cleaning. John Wiley & Sons.
    - Seltman, H. J. (2020). Modern data science with R. Chapman and Hall/CRC.

- Online Courses and Tutorials:
    - Coursera: Data Cleaning and Analysis by University of California, Davis.
    - DataCamp: Data Cleaning in R Track.
    - Kaggle: Data Cleaning Challenge.
- Websites:
    - Towards Data Science - Data Cleaning section: `https://towardsdatascience.com/tagged/data-cleaning`
    - Data.gov - Data Quality section: `https://www.data.gov/data-quality`

These resources provide comprehensive and practical guidance on data cleaning techniques, best practices, and case studies.

Summary

In this section, we explored the importance of data cleaning and validation in the context of artificial intelligence. We learned that clean and reliable data is crucial for accurate AI models, consistent results, and unbiased insights. Various techniques such as handling missing values, removing duplicates, and handling outliers were discussed. We also explored popular tools like OpenRefine, Trifacta Wrangler, and Python libraries for data cleaning.

Remember, data cleaning is a continuous and iterative process that requires domain knowledge and attention to detail. By mastering data cleaning techniques, you can unlock the true potential of AI and turn raw data into valuable insights.

Data Exploration and Visualization

Exploratory Data Analysis

Ah, exploratory data analysis, the realm of data scientists where they dive headfirst into the vast sea of data, navigating the depths to uncover hidden treasures of knowledge. It's like being a detective, hunting for clues and patterns that can unlock the secrets of the data universe. So, grab your magnifying glass and let's embark on this data-driven adventure!

The Importance of Exploratory Data Analysis

Before we dive into the nitty-gritty details, let's take a step back and understand why exploratory data analysis (EDA) is so damn important. You see, EDA is the compass that guides us in the vast sea of data, helping us make sense of it all. It allows us to understand the shape, structure, and patterns hidden within our data, enabling us to make informed decisions.

EDA is the preliminary step in any data analysis process. It helps us gain insights, identify anomalies, and check for data quality issues. By examining the data visually and statistically, we can develop our intuition and create a solid foundation for further analysis. Think of it as the warm-up before a data workout.

Approaches to Exploratory Data Analysis

Now that we understand the importance of EDA, let's explore some key approaches and techniques that will help us navigate the data maze.

Descriptive Statistics: Just like a good storyteller, descriptive statistics paint a picture of our data. They provide us with a summary of the main characteristics, such as measures of central tendency (mean, median, mode) and measures of dispersion (variance, standard deviation, range). Descriptive statistics give us a bird's-eye view of the data, helping us understand its distribution, spread, and overall flavor.

Data Visualization: Ah, the beauty of visualizing data! Humans are visual creatures, and data visualization allows us to see patterns that our puny little brains might otherwise miss. We can create captivating plots, charts, and graphs that showcase the underlying patterns, relationships, and trends within the data. With the help of visualization libraries like Matplotlib and ggplot, we can create stunning visual masterpieces that would make Picasso proud.

Data Transformations: Sometimes, the raw data doesn't fit our fancy analysis methods. That's where data transformations come in handy. We can apply mathematical operations, such as logarithmic or exponential transformations, to reshape the data into a more suitable form. These transformations can help us address issues like skewness, heteroscedasticity, and outliers, allowing for more robust analysis.

Missing Data Handling: Ah, the bane of every data scientist's existence. Missing data is like that puzzle piece that vanished into thin air, leaving a gaping hole in our analysis. We need to carefully handle missing data to avoid biased or inaccurate results. Techniques like imputation (replacing missing values with estimated ones) or deletion (removing observations with missing data) can help us fill the gaps and move forward with our analysis.

Outlier Detection: Outliers, those rebellious data points that don't conform to the norm, can wreak havoc on our analysis. They can skew our results, violate assumptions, and generally make our lives miserable. That's why we need to identify and deal with them. Outlier detection techniques, such as the z-score or the interquartile range, can help us flag those troublemakers and decide whether to remove them or treat them differently in our analysis.

Real-World Example: Exploring Airbnb Data

To put all these concepts into context, let's embark on a real-world analysis of Airbnb data. Imagine you're planning a trip to a new city and want to find the perfect accommodation. Lucky for you, there's a dataset available with loads of information on Airbnb listings in that city.

Your goal is to explore the data and gain insights that will help you make an informed decision. You start by loading the dataset into your preferred data analysis environment and begin the EDA journey.

First, you calculate descriptive statistics for the price variable to understand its distribution. You find that the mean price is $100 per night, with a standard deviation of $50. Armed with this information, you can now compare individual listings to the average and identify any extreme outliers or unusually cheap options.

Next, you visualize the spatial distribution of Airbnb listings on a map, color-coded by price. This helps you identify areas where prices are higher or lower, giving you an idea of which neighborhoods might suit your budget.

Digging deeper, you decide to explore the relationship between the price and various listing attributes. Using scatter plots, you examine how the number of bedrooms, amenities, and location affect the price. This helps you understand which factors contribute most to the variation in prices.

After analyzing the data, you discover a hidden gem—a listing with a reasonable price, great location, and rave reviews. It's the perfect place for your dream vacation!

Caveats and Challenges

As with any scientific endeavor, exploratory data analysis has its fair share of caveats and challenges. Here are a few common pitfalls to watch out for:

Confirmation Bias: Ah, the sneaky devil called confirmation bias. It tempts us to cherry-pick data that supports our preconceived notions or desired hypotheses.

To avoid this slippery slope, we should maintain an open mind, consider alternative explanations, and let the data speak for itself.

Data Overload: With the abundance of data at our fingertips, it's tempting to indulge in excessive exploration. However, too much of a good thing can be overwhelming and may lead to analysis paralysis. It's important to strike a balance between thorough exploration and efficient decision-making.

Spurious Correlations: Sometimes, we stumble upon relationships that seem significant but are actually just coincidences. Remember the old saying: "Correlation does not imply causation." It's crucial to exercise caution and skepticism when interpreting correlations and to seek out additional evidence before making any bold claims.

Summary

Exploratory data analysis is the compass that guides us through the intricate maze of data. It helps us understand the shape, structure, and patterns hidden within our data, paving the way for thoughtful analysis. By employing descriptive statistics, data visualization, data transformations, and outlier detection techniques, we can gain insights that inform our decision-making. However, we must be mindful of the caveats and challenges, such as confirmation bias, data overload, and spurious correlations, to ensure robust and reliable analysis.

So, my dear data adventurers, sharpen your swords of analysis and embark on this journey of exploratory data analysis. May you uncover hidden treasures of knowledge and navigate the vast sea of data with confidence and curiosity!

Exercises

1. Take a dataset of your choice (e.g., sales data, weather data, social media data) and perform exploratory data analysis. Calculate descriptive statistics, create visualizations, and detect any outliers or missing data.

2. Explore a public dataset from a reputable source, like Kaggle or the UCI Machine Learning Repository. Choose a variable of interest and examine its distribution, relationships with other variables, and any observed patterns or anomalies.

3. Investigate the relationship between educational attainment and income using a relevant dataset. Perform exploratory data analysis to uncover any correlations, visualize the data, and discuss your findings.

4. Challenge yourself to find a real-world dataset with unconventional variables to explore. Think outside the box and aim for an intriguing analysis that sheds light on a unique aspect of the data.

Remember, in the world of exploratory data analysis, curiosity is your best friend. Happy exploring!

Visualization Techniques

In this section, we will explore various visualization techniques that are commonly used in the field of data analysis and artificial intelligence. Effective visualization is crucial for understanding complex data and conveying insights to others. We will discuss different types of visualizations, their applications, and the tools available to create them.

Types of Visualizations

Visualizations are powerful tools that allow us to represent data in a visual form, making it easier to identify patterns, trends, and relationships. Here are some commonly used visualization types:

1. **Bar Charts:** Bar charts are used to compare the values of different categories or groups. They consist of horizontal or vertical bars whose lengths represent the values being compared. Bar charts are effective for visualizing categorical or numerical data.

2. **Line Charts:** Line charts are used to show the relationship between two variables over time or any continuous dimension. They are particularly useful for displaying trends, patterns, and changes in data over a period.

3. **Pie Charts:** Pie charts are circular representations divided into segments that show the proportion of different categories within a whole. They are useful for displaying the composition or distribution of categorical variables.

4. **Scatter Plots:** Scatter plots are used to display the relationship between two numerical variables. Each data point is represented as a dot on the graph, and the position of the dot corresponds to the values of the variables. Scatter plots help identify correlations and outliers.

5. **Heatmaps:** Heatmaps represent data using colors to indicate the magnitude of values in a matrix. They are commonly used to visualize large datasets, such

as gene expression data, where the color intensity shows the level of expression for each gene under different experimental conditions.

6. **Network Diagrams:** Network diagrams show relationships between entities by representing them as nodes (vertices) connected by links (edges). They are used to model complex systems, such as social networks, transportation networks, or biological networks.

7. **Choropleth Maps:** Choropleth maps use color shading or patterns to represent data values for different geographic regions. They are commonly used to display demographic data or other stats at a regional level.

8. **Word Clouds:** Word clouds display words from a text corpus, where the size of each word represents its frequency or importance. They are often used to summarize the main themes or terms in a document or set of documents.

Choosing the Right Visualization

Selecting the appropriate visualization technique for your data is essential for effective communication. Here are some guidelines to help you choose the right visualization:

- Identify the purpose: Determine the goal of your visualization. Are you trying to show comparisons, trends, distributions, or relationships? This will help you narrow down the options.

- Understand the data type: Consider the nature of your data (categorical, numerical, time-series, etc.) and choose a visualization technique that can effectively represent that type of data.

- Consider the audience: Different visualizations may be more meaningful to different audiences. Understand the background and expertise of your audience and choose a visualization that will resonate with them.

- Keep it simple: Stick to simple and intuitive visualizations. Avoid clutter and unnecessary embellishments that can distract from the main message.

- Experiment: Don't be afraid to experiment with different visualizations and iterate until you find the most suitable one. Visualizations are subjective, and sometimes different perspectives can lead to better insights.

Tools for Data Exploration and Visualization

There are several tools available to create visualizations, ranging from basic spreadsheet software to advanced programming libraries. Here are a few popular tools commonly used in the field of artificial intelligence:

- **Microsoft Excel:** Excel is a widely used spreadsheet software that offers basic charting capabilities. It is suitable for simple visualizations and analysis tasks.

- **Tableau:** Tableau is a powerful data visualization tool that provides a wide array of visualization options. It offers a user-friendly interface and supports interactive dashboards.

- **Python:** Python is a popular programming language for data analysis and visualization. Libraries like Matplotlib, Seaborn, and Plotly provide extensive capabilities for creating high-quality visualizations.

- **R:** R is another programming language commonly used for statistical analysis and data visualization. It has several packages, such as ggplot2, that offer a wide range of visualization options.

- **D3.js:** D3.js is a JavaScript library that allows for the creation of highly customizable, interactive visualizations on the web. It is widely used for creating dynamic and engaging visuals.

Best Practices for Visualization

To create effective visualizations, it is important to follow some best practices. Here are a few tips to keep in mind:

- **Simplify the design:** Use a clean and uncluttered design, focusing on the key elements. Avoid excessive decorations or distracting elements that can overshadow the data.

- **Use consistent colors:** Choose a color palette that is visually appealing and ensure consistency across different visualizations. Use colors purposefully to highlight important information.

- **Provide context:** Use labels, titles, and captions to provide context and help the audience understand the visualization. Include relevant units, axes labels, and sources to avoid confusion.

DATA EXPLORATION AND VISUALIZATION

- **Emphasize the main message:** Highlight the main findings or insights by using visual cues like colors, annotations, or callouts. Guide the reader's attention to the most important information.

- **Test and iterate:** Show your visualizations to others and gather feedback. Iterate and refine your visualizations based on the feedback to improve their clarity and effectiveness.

Interactive and Dynamic Visualizations

Interactive and dynamic visualizations allow users to explore the data and gain deeper insights. Here are some techniques to create interactive visualizations:

- **Filters and controls:** Provide interactive filters and controls that allow users to change parameters, select subsets of data, or switch between different views. This empowers users to explore the data from different perspectives.

- **Hover effects and tooltips:** Use hover effects or tooltips to reveal additional information when users interact with elements in the visualization. This helps provide more context and details without cluttering the main view.

- **Animations and transitions:** Use animations and transitions to guide the user's attention and provide a smooth and engaging experience. Animated transitions can be used to show changes over time or highlight specific elements.

- **Drill-down and zooming:** Allow users to drill down into the data by zooming in on specific regions or details. This enables the exploration of data at different levels of granularity.

Real-World Example: Visualizing COVID-19 Data

To illustrate the importance of visualization techniques, let's consider the visualization of COVID-19 data. A line chart can effectively represent the daily number of cases over time, allowing us to identify trends and spikes. By adding a moving average to the visualization, we can smooth out the data and observe the overall trajectory of the pandemic. Using different colors, we can differentiate between different regions or countries and compare their progress.

Additionally, a choropleth map can display the distribution of COVID-19 cases across geographical regions. By using shades of color, we can show the severity of the outbreak in different areas. This allows policymakers to identify hotspots and allocate resources accordingly.

In interactive visualizations, we can incorporate filters to allow users to focus on specific regions or time periods. Hover effects can provide additional information, such as the number of cases or the percentage change, when users interact with specific elements.

These visualizations not only help researchers and policymakers understand the spread of the virus, but also enable the general public to stay informed and make data-driven decisions.

Conclusion

In this section, we explored various visualization techniques used in the field of data analysis and artificial intelligence. We discussed different types of visualizations, their applications, and considerations for choosing the right technique. We also highlighted the importance of best practices in visualization design and introduced tools for creating visualizations. Additionally, we explored interactive and dynamic visualizations and their benefits. Finally, we provided a real-world example of visualizing COVID-19 data to demonstrate the practical application of visualization techniques. Effective visualization is a crucial component of AI and data analysis, enabling us to understand complex data and communicate insights effectively.

Tools for Data Exploration and Visualization

In the world of data analysis, exploration and visualization are invaluable tools that help us make sense of complex datasets. These tools allow us to uncover patterns, identify trends, and communicate insights in a visually compelling way. In this section, we will explore the various tools available for data exploration and visualization, and learn how to leverage them effectively.

Data Visualization Libraries

One of the key components of data exploration and visualization is the ability to create informative and visually appealing graphs, charts, and plots. Fortunately, there are several powerful libraries available in Python that make this task relatively straightforward.

Matplotlib: Matplotlib is a widely used plotting library that provides a flexible and comprehensive set of tools for creating static, animated, and interactive visualizations in Python. It offers a wide range of plot types, including line plots, scatter plots, bar charts, and histograms. With Matplotlib, you can easily customize almost every aspect of your visualizations to suit your needs.

Seaborn: Seaborn is built on top of Matplotlib and provides a high-level interface for creating aesthetically pleasing and informative statistical graphics. It simplifies the process of creating complex visualizations by providing built-in functions for common tasks like grouping data, adding regression lines, and creating heatmaps. Seaborn also integrates well with Pandas, a popular data manipulation library, making it a great choice for exploratory data analysis.

Plotly: Plotly is a modern and interactive data visualization library that allows you to create interactive plots, dashboards, and presentations. It supports a wide range of plot types, including scatter plots, line plots, bar charts, and 3D visualizations. One of the standout features of Plotly is its ability to create interactive plots that respond to user interactions, such as hovering over data points or zooming in on specific regions.

ggplot: Inspired by the highly popular ggplot2 library in R, ggplot provides a powerful and elegant grammar of graphics implementation in Python. It follows a declarative approach, where you specify the relationship between variables and the desired visual representation, and the library takes care of the rest. ggplot allows you to create complex plots with minimal code, making it a favorite among data scientists and statisticians.

Data Exploration Tools

Once we have a grasp of the basic data visualization tools, we can move on to exploring our data in greater detail. Exploratory data analysis (EDA) is a critical step in understanding the characteristics of our dataset and uncovering any relationships or patterns that may exist within it. Here are some popular tools for data exploration:

Pandas: Pandas is a powerful data manipulation library that provides high-performance, easy-to-use data structures and data analysis tools for Python. It allows you to load, manipulate, and analyze structured data using its DataFrame object, which is similar to a table or spreadsheet. With Pandas, you can filter, sort, group, aggregate, and transform your data, enabling you to gain meaningful insights quickly.

NumPy: NumPy is a fundamental library for scientific computing in Python. It provides support for large, multi-dimensional arrays and matrices, along with a collection of mathematical functions to operate on these arrays. NumPy is a popular choice for numerical computations, such as calculating descriptive statistics, performing matrix operations, and generating random numbers. Its integration with other libraries, like Pandas, makes it an essential tool for data exploration.

Jupyter Notebook: Jupyter Notebook is an open-source web application that allows you to create and share documents containing live code, visualizations, and explanatory text. It provides an interactive environment where you can write and execute code, annotate your results, and embed visualizations directly in your analysis. Jupyter Notebook supports multiple programming languages, including Python, R, and Julia, making it a versatile tool for data exploration and analysis.

Tableau: Tableau is a powerful data visualization software that allows you to connect to various data sources, explore data with interactive visualizations, and create engaging dashboards and reports. With its drag-and-drop interface and intuitive design, Tableau makes it easy for non-technical users to explore and analyze data. It also offers advanced features like data blending, forecasting, and geospatial analysis, making it a popular choice among businesses and data professionals.

Proper Data Visualization Practices

While having access to powerful tools is essential, it is equally important to use them correctly to communicate information effectively. Here are some best practices to keep in mind when creating data visualizations:

- **Choose the Right Visualization:** Select a visualization that best represents the relationships or patterns in your data. Bar charts are great for comparing categories, line plots for showing trends over time, and scatter plots for exploring relationships between variables.

- **Keep it Simple:** Avoid cluttering your visualizations with unnecessary elements. Remove excessive gridlines, labels, or decorations that distract from the main message. Simplicity allows your audience to focus on the critical information.

- **Label and Title Everything:** Clearly label your axes, provide a title for your visualizations, and include a legend if necessary. This ensures that viewers understand what they are looking at and can interpret the information correctly.

- **Use Color Intentionally:** Colors can be a powerful tool to convey information, but they can also confuse or mislead your audience if not used properly. Use color deliberately to highlight important elements or distinguish different groups. Be wary of using colors that may be difficult for color-blind individuals to distinguish.

- **Provide Context and Interpretation:** Always accompany your visualizations with clear and concise explanations. Describe what the visualization is showing, provide relevant context, and highlight key insights or trends. Effective storytelling through visualization can enhance understanding and engagement.

Proper data visualization not only helps you gain a deeper understanding of your data but also enables you to communicate your findings to others effectively. By leveraging the right tools and following best practices, you can unlock the full potential of data exploration and visualization.

Summary

Data exploration and visualization are crucial steps in the data analysis process. They allow us to gain insights, identify trends, and communicate complex information more effectively. In this section, we explored various tools for data exploration and visualization, including popular libraries like Matplotlib, Seaborn, Plotly, and ggplot. We also discussed data exploration tools such as Pandas, NumPy, Jupyter Notebook, and Tableau. Lastly, we highlighted some best practices for creating impactful visualizations. With these tools and techniques at our disposal, we can turn raw data into compelling visual stories. Now, let's dive deeper into the fundamentals of statistics and probability in the next section.

Fundamentals of Statistics and Probability

Descriptive Statistics

Descriptive statistics is a branch of statistics that focuses on summarizing and describing the main features of a dataset. It provides us with tools and techniques to analyze and interpret data, allowing us to gain insights and make meaningful interpretations.

Measures of Central Tendency

One of the fundamental aspects of descriptive statistics is understanding measures of central tendency, which help us determine the typical or central value of a dataset. The three most commonly used measures are the mean, median, and mode.

The mean, often referred to as the average, is calculated by summing up all the values in the dataset and dividing it by the total number of observations. It represents the central value around which the data tends to cluster. For example, let's say we have the following dataset: 3, 5, 7, 7, 10. The mean of this dataset is (3 + 5 + 7 + 7 + 10) / 5 = 6.4.

The median is the middle value of a dataset when it is arranged in ascending or descending order. In case of an even number of observations, the median is the average of the two middle values. The median is not affected by extreme values and is often used to represent the typical value of the data. In our previous example, the median of the dataset is 7.

The mode represents the value that occurs most frequently in a dataset. It can be used for both numerical and categorical data. If there are multiple values that occur with the highest frequency, the dataset is considered multimodal. In the dataset from our previous example, 7 is the mode.

Measures of Variability

In addition to central tendency, descriptive statistics includes measures of variability that quantify the spread or dispersion of a dataset. These measures provide insights into how the data points are spread out around the central value.

The range is the simplest measure of variability and is calculated as the difference between the highest and lowest values in the dataset. It provides an idea of the extent of the spread but is influenced by extreme values.

The variance measures the average squared deviation of each data point from the mean. It provides a more precise measure of spread by taking into account the distance of each observation from the mean. However, the variance is not directly interpretable since it is in squared units.

The standard deviation is the square root of the variance and is expressed in the same units as the data. It provides a measure of spread that is easily interpretable and is commonly used. The standard deviation is calculated by taking the square root of the variance.

For example, let's consider the following dataset representing the weights of five students in kg: 55, 58, 60, 63, 65. The mean weight is (55 + 58 + 60 + 63 + 65) / 5 = 60.2 kg. The standard deviation can be calculated by first finding the variance: $[(55-60.2)^2 + (58-60.2)^2 + (60-60.2)^2 + (63-60.2)^2 + (65-60.2)^2]/5 = 8.56$. Taking the square root of the variance gives us a standard deviation of approximately 2.92 kg.

FUNDAMENTALS OF STATISTICS AND PROBABILITY

Skewness and Kurtosis

In addition to measures of central tendency and variability, descriptive statistics also considers skewness and kurtosis, which provide information about the shape of the distribution.

Skewness measures the asymmetry of a distribution. A symmetric distribution has a skewness of 0, while positive skewness indicates that the tail of the distribution is on the right side. Negative skewness suggests a longer tail on the left side. Skewness can be calculated using the following formula:

$$Skewness = \frac{3 \times (Mean - Median)}{StandardDeviation}$$

Kurtosis measures the heaviness of the tails of a distribution. It tells us how much of the distribution's variance is due to extreme values. A positive kurtosis indicates heavy tails and a more peaked distribution compared to the normal distribution. A negative kurtosis suggests lighter tails and a less peaked distribution. Kurtosis can be calculated using the following formula:

$$Kurtosis = \frac{4 \times ((Mean - Median)/StandardDeviation)^4}{SampleSize}$$

It is important to note that both skewness and kurtosis are affected by the sample size. As the sample size increases, estimates of skewness and kurtosis become more reliable.

Summary

Descriptive statistics plays a crucial role in understanding and interpreting data. It provides us with measures of central tendency, such as the mean, median, and mode, which help us determine the typical value of a dataset. Measures of variability, such as the range, variance, and standard deviation, quantify the spread of the data. Skewness and kurtosis provide insights into the shape of the distribution.

By analyzing the descriptive statistics of a dataset, we can gain a deeper understanding of the underlying patterns, trends, and characteristics of the data. This information is invaluable for making informed decisions, drawing meaningful conclusions, and communicating the insights effectively.

Resources

If you want to delve deeper into descriptive statistics, here are some recommended resources:

- *Statistics in Plain English* by Timothy C. Urdan: This book provides a clear and concise introduction to descriptive statistics, explaining concepts in simple language with real-world examples.

- *Descriptive Statistics for Data Science* by Randal S. Olson: This online tutorial offers a comprehensive overview of descriptive statistics, along with practical examples and code snippets for data scientists.

- Khan Academy - Descriptive Statistics (https://www.khanacademy.org/math/statistics-probability/summarizing-quantitative-data) provides free video lessons and practice exercises on descriptive statistics.

Exercises

1. Calculate the mean, median, and mode for the given dataset: 12, 15, 15, 18, 20, 12, 12, 18, 15, 20.

2. Find the range, variance, and standard deviation for the following dataset: 35, 30, 28, 32, 33, 31, 29, 28.

3. Determine the skewness and kurtosis of the dataset: 5, 2, 3, 4, 5, 5, 6, 5, 3, 4, 5, 6.

Solutions

1. The mean of the dataset is (12 + 15 + 15 + 18 + 20 + 12 + 12 + 18 + 15 + 20) / 10 = 15.7. The median is 15, and the mode is 12 and 15.

2. The range of the dataset is 35 - 28 = 7. The variance can be calculated as $[(35 - 31)^2 + (30 - 31)^2 + (28 - 31)^2 + (32 - 31)^2 + (33 - 31)^2 + (31 - 31)^2 + (29 - 31)^2 + (28 - 31)^2]/8 = 4$. The standard deviation is the square root of the variance, approximately 2.

3. The mean is (5 + 2 + 3 + 4 + 5 + 5 + 6 + 5 + 3 + 4 + 5 + 6) / 12 = 4.416. The median is 4.5. To calculate the standard deviation, we first find the variance: $[(5 - 4.416)^2 + (2 - 4.416)^2 + (3 - 4.416)^2 + (4 - 4.416)^2 + (5 - 4.416)^2 + (5 - 4.416)^2 + (6 - 4.416)^2 + (5 - 4.416)^2 + (3 - 4.416)^2 + (4 - 4.416)^2 + (5 - 4.416)^2 + (6 - 4.416)^2]/12 = 1.081$. The standard deviation is approximately 1.039. The skewness can be calculated as (3 * (4.416 - 4.5)) / 1.039,

which is approximately -0.081. To calculate the kurtosis, we use the formula: $(4 * ((4.416 − 4.5)/1.039)^4)/12$, which is approximately -0.805.

Note: It is important to note that the skewness and kurtosis values are approximate.

Inferential Statistics

Inferential statistics is the branch of statistics that focuses on drawing conclusions and making predictions about a population based on a sample of data. It involves using probability theory and statistical models to generalize from a smaller set of observations to a larger population. This section explores the principles and techniques of inferential statistics, providing the foundation for making informed decisions and predictions in various fields.

Sampling Techniques

The process of inferential statistics starts with collecting a representative sample from a population of interest. A sample is a subset of the population that is selected to provide insights into the entire population. The goal is to ensure that the sample is unbiased and accurately reflects the characteristics of the population.

There are different sampling techniques, each with its own advantages and limitations. Some common sampling methods include:

- **Simple random sampling:** In this method, every individual in the population has an equal chance of being selected for the sample. This technique is unbiased and straightforward to implement when a sampling frame is available.

- **Stratified sampling:** This technique divides the population into homogeneous groups called strata and then selects a random sample from each stratum. Stratified sampling ensures that each subgroup is represented in the sample, allowing for more accurate estimations, especially when there are significant differences between the subgroups.

- **Cluster sampling:** Cluster sampling involves dividing the population into clusters or groups and randomly selecting a few clusters to include in the sample. This technique is useful when it is impractical to sample individuals directly, such as in large geographic areas or organizational settings.

- **Systematic sampling:** This method involves selecting every kth individual from the population, where k is a fixed interval calculated based on the desired sample size and the total population size. Systematic sampling is simple to implement and provides a representative sample if there is no systematic pattern in the population ordering.

Choosing an appropriate sampling technique depends on factors such as the research objectives, available resources, and the nature of the population under study. It is crucial to ensure that the selected sample is representative and unbiased to obtain accurate inferences about the larger population.

Estimation

Once a sample is selected, inferential statistics allows us to make estimates and draw conclusions about population parameters based on the information from the sample. Estimation involves quantifying the uncertainty associated with the estimates and providing intervals within which the true population parameters are likely to fall.

Two commonly used techniques for estimation are point estimation and interval estimation:

- **Point estimation:** Point estimation involves using a single value, called a point estimate, to approximate the unknown population parameter. The point estimate is typically computed from the sample data and is used as the best guess for the true value of the parameter. For example, the sample mean is often used as a point estimate for the population mean.

- **Interval estimation:** Interval estimation provides a range of plausible values, called a confidence interval, within which the true population parameter is likely to fall. The confidence interval is constructed using the point estimate along with the margin of error, which is determined by the sample size and the desired level of confidence. For instance, a 95% confidence interval for the population mean represents that, if the sampling process and estimation were repeated many times, 95% of the intervals generated would contain the true population mean.

The choice between point estimation and interval estimation depends on the level of precision required in the estimation. Point estimates provide a single value that may or may not be close to the true population parameter, while interval estimates provide a range of values that capture the uncertainty associated with the estimation process.

FUNDAMENTALS OF STATISTICS AND PROBABILITY

Hypothesis Testing

Another fundamental aspect of inferential statistics is hypothesis testing. Hypothesis testing allows us to assess the strength of evidence in favor of a particular claim or hypothesis about the population. It involves setting up competing hypotheses and using sample data to determine whether the observed evidence supports or contradicts the null hypothesis.

The hypothesis testing process consists of the following steps:

1. **Formulating the hypotheses:** The null hypothesis (H_0) represents the default assumption, while the alternative hypothesis (H_1) contradicts the null hypothesis and represents the claim we want to test.

2. **Choosing the significance level:** The significance level (α) is the maximum probability of making a Type I error, which occurs when we reject the null hypothesis when it is true. Commonly used significance levels are 0.05 and 0.01.

3. **Collecting and analyzing the data:** The sample data is analyzed to calculate a test statistic, which measures the strength of the evidence against the null hypothesis. The choice of the test statistic depends on the type of data and the hypothesis being tested.

4. **Making a decision:** The test statistic is compared to the critical value(s) or the p-value to determine whether there is enough evidence to reject the null hypothesis. If the test statistic falls in the critical region or the p-value is less than the significance level, the null hypothesis is rejected in favor of the alternative hypothesis.

Hypothesis testing is a crucial tool in various fields, from medicine to social sciences, allowing researchers to draw conclusions and make decisions based on evidence from sample data.

Common Errors and Sample Size Determination

When conducting inferential statistics, it is essential to be aware of common errors that can occur during hypothesis testing. These errors include Type I error (rejecting the null hypothesis when it is true) and Type II error (failing to reject the null hypothesis when it is false). The significance level (α) determines the probability of committing a Type I error, while the power of the test ($1 - \beta$) measures the ability to detect a true difference or effect.

Sample size determination plays a crucial role in conducting inferential statistics with sufficient power. A small sample size may lead to a lack of statistical power, making it difficult to detect true differences or effects. On the other hand, a large sample size can increase the precision of estimates and reduce the sampling error, but it may also be costly and time-consuming to collect and analyze a large amount of data.

Various factors influence the determination of sample size, such as the desired level of confidence, effect size, variability in the data, and the statistical power needed. Researchers often use sample size calculators or consult statistical experts to determine an appropriate sample size for their study.

Real-World Example: A/B Testing

One concrete application of inferential statistics is A/B testing, a technique commonly used in the field of marketing. A/B testing is a randomized experiment where two or more variants of a webpage, advertisement, or user interface are compared to determine which one yields better outcomes.

For example, let's consider a scenario where an e-commerce company wants to test two different versions of an email campaign to see which one generates a higher click-through rate (CTR). They randomly divide their subscriber list into two groups: Group A receives Version 1 of the email, while Group B receives Version 2. After the campaign is sent, the data on CTR from both groups are collected and analyzed.

Inferential statistics allow the company to draw conclusions about the effectiveness of the two email versions based on the observed CTR data. They can conduct a hypothesis test to determine whether there is a significant difference in the CTR between the two groups. Additionally, interval estimation can provide a range of plausible values for the difference in CTR, along with the associated uncertainty.

By using inferential statistics, the company can make data-driven decisions and choose the email version that is likely to yield the highest CTR, optimizing their marketing efforts and improving their overall business performance.

Summary

Inferential statistics is a powerful tool for making predictions, drawing conclusions, and testing hypotheses about populations based on sample data. It involves sampling techniques, estimation, hypothesis testing, and the consideration of common errors and sample size determination.

FUNDAMENTALS OF STATISTICS AND PROBABILITY

With the principles and techniques of inferential statistics, we can gain valuable insights from data, make informed decisions, and contribute to advancements in various fields. Whether it's predicting customer behavior, testing the effectiveness of new treatments, or optimizing business strategies, inferential statistics is a critical component of modern data analysis and decision-making processes.

Key Takeaways

- Inferential statistics is concerned with drawing conclusions about populations based on sample data.

- Sampling techniques, such as simple random sampling and stratified sampling, ensure that samples are representative and unbiased.

- Estimation involves point estimation and interval estimation, providing point estimates and confidence intervals for population parameters.

- Hypothesis testing involves formulating competing hypotheses, analyzing sample data, and making decisions based on the evidence against the null hypothesis (H_0).

- Sample size determination is crucial for ensuring sufficient statistical power in inferential statistics.

Resources

For further exploration of inferential statistics and its applications, the following resources are recommended:

- Agresti, A., & Franklin, C. A. (2018). *Statistics: The Art and Science of Learning from Data*. Pearson.

- Freedman, D., Pisani, R., & Purves, R. (2007). *Statistics*. W.W. Norton & Company.

- OpenIntro Statistics: https://www.openintro.org/stat/

- Khan Academy: Inferential statistics: https://www.khanacademy.org/math/ap-statistics/summarizing-quantitative-data-ap

Inferential statistics allows us to make accurate predictions and informed decisions based on limited data. It is a powerful tool that empowers researchers and practitioners across disciplines, driving advancements and innovation in the era of data-driven decision making. So, embrace inferential statistics and let it guide you in turning data into dominance!

Probability Theory

In this section, we will delve into the exciting world of probability theory. Probability is a fundamental concept in artificial intelligence and data analysis. Understanding probability allows us to quantify uncertainty and make informed decisions in AI applications. So, let's roll up our sleeves and dive right in!

Basics of Probability

Probability is the branch of mathematics that studies the likelihood of events occurring. It provides a framework for analyzing and predicting uncertain outcomes. In probability theory, we use the term "experiment" to refer to a specific action or process that produces a particular outcome. The set of all possible outcomes of an experiment is called the sample space, denoted by Ω.

Events and Probability

In probability theory, an event is a subset of the sample space. We use capital letters like A, B, or C to denote events. The probability of an event is a number between 0 and 1, inclusive, that indicates the likelihood of that event occurring. We denote the probability of event A as $P(A)$.

Probability Axioms

Probability theory is built upon a set of axioms that ensure consistency and coherence. These axioms are as follows:

1. Axiom 1: For any event A, $P(A) \geq 0$. The probability of an event is always non-negative.

2. Axiom 2: $P(\Omega) = 1$. The probability of the entire sample space is 1.

3. Axiom 3: For a sequence of mutually exclusive events $A_1, A_2, \ldots$, $P(A_1 \cup A_2 \cup \ldots) = P(A_1) + P(A_2) + \ldots$. The probability of the union of mutually exclusive events is the sum of their individual probabilities.

These axioms provide a solid foundation for probability theory. From these axioms, various theorems and rules can be derived to solve complex probability problems.

Probability Rules

Next, let's explore some essential rules that govern the calculation of probabilities:

1. Rule 1: Complement Rule: The probability of the complement of an event A is given by $P(A^C) = 1 - P(A)$.

2. Rule 2: Addition Rule: For any two events A and B, the probability of their union is given by $P(A \cup B) = P(A) + P(B) - P(A \cap B)$.

3. Rule 3: Multiplication Rule (general case): For any two events A and B, the probability of their intersection is given by $P(A \cap B) = P(A) \cdot P(B|A)$.

4. Rule 4: Multiplication Rule (special case): For independent events A and B, the probability of their intersection is given by $P(A \cap B) = P(A) \cdot P(B)$.

These rules are incredibly useful when solving probability problems involving multiple events.

Conditional Probability

Conditional probability is a fundamental concept that allows us to calculate the probability of an event given that another event has occurred. It is denoted by $P(A|B)$, read as "the probability of A given B." The formula for conditional probability is given by:

$$P(A|B) = \frac{P(A \cap B)}{P(B)}$$

Where $P(A \cap B)$ represents the probability of both events A and B occurring simultaneously, and $P(B)$ is the probability of event B occurring.

Bayes' Theorem

Bayes' Theorem is a powerful tool for updating our beliefs or probabilities based on new evidence. It allows us to calculate the probability of an event given some prior knowledge. The theorem is expressed as follows:

$$P(A|B) = \frac{P(B|A) \cdot P(A)}{P(B)}$$

Where $P(A|B)$ is the probability of event A given event B, $P(B|A)$ is the probability of event B given event A, $P(A)$ is the prior probability of event A, and $P(B)$ is the prior probability of event B.

Bayes' Theorem has wide applications in various areas, including spam filtering, medical diagnosis, and machine learning algorithms like Naive Bayes.

Expected Value and Variance

In probability theory, the expected value, also known as the mean or average, is a measure of the central tendency of a random variable. It represents the long-term average outcome of an experiment. The expected value of a discrete random variable X is denoted by $E(X)$ and is calculated as:

$$E(X) = \sum_{x} x \cdot P(X = x)$$

Where x represents the possible values of X, and $P(X = x)$ is the probability mass function (PMF) of X.

Variance measures the spread or dispersion of a random variable around its expected value. It is denoted by $\text{Var}(X)$ and is calculated as:

$$\text{Var}(X) = E((X - E(X))^2)$$

Standard deviation, denoted by σ, is the square root of the variance and provides a useful measure of the typical distance between each data point and the mean.

Probability Distributions

Probability distributions play a crucial role in probability theory and serve as mathematical models for various random phenomena. Here are a few essential probability distributions:

- **Uniform Distribution:** The uniform distribution assigns equal probability to all outcomes within a specified interval.

- **Binomial Distribution:** The binomial distribution models the number of successes in a fixed number of independent Bernoulli trials.

- **Normal Distribution:** The normal distribution, also known as the Gaussian distribution, is a continuous distribution that is symmetrical and bell-shaped.
- **Poisson Distribution:** The Poisson distribution models the number of events that occur in a fixed interval of time or space.

These distributions have specific probability mass functions (PMFs) or probability density functions (PDFs) that allow us to calculate probabilities or generate random variables.

Common Probability Problems

Probability theory can be applied to a wide range of real-world problems. Here are a few examples:

- **Birthday Problem:** What is the probability that at least two people in a room share the same birthday?
- **Monty Hall Problem:** In a game show, a contestant is presented with three doors. Behind one door is a car, and behind the other two are goats. After the contestant chooses a door, the host reveals one of the doors with a goat. Should the contestant switch their choice?
- **Gambler's Ruin:** Two gamblers, each with a finite amount of money, play a game where they bet against each other. What is the probability that one player goes bankrupt before the other?

These examples illustrate the practical applications of probability theory in solving intriguing puzzles and decision-making scenarios.

Further Resources and Recommendations

Probability theory is a rich and vast field, with applications in nearly every branch of science and technology. Here are a few recommended resources to deepen your understanding and explore the fascinating world of probability:

- **Book:** "Introduction to Probability" by Joseph K. Blitzstein and Jessica Hwang.
- **Online Course:** "Probability - The Science of Uncertainty and Data" by MIT OpenCourseWare.

- **Website:** Khan Academy offers a comprehensive collection of probability tutorials and exercises.

These resources will equip you with the knowledge and skills to tackle complex probability problems and excel in the realm of artificial intelligence.

In Conclusion

Probability theory forms the bedrock of artificial intelligence and data analysis. By understanding probability, we can quantify uncertainty, make informed decisions, and create intelligent systems that turn data into dominance. So embrace the power of probability, and let it guide you on your journey into the exciting world of AI.

Exercises

1. Suppose you have a bag of 10 marbles, of which 3 are red and 7 are blue. What is the probability of selecting a red marble if you pick one at random?

2. A fair six-sided die is rolled. What is the probability of rolling an odd number or a number greater than 4?

3. In a class of 30 students, 18 of them play basketball and 12 play soccer. If a student is selected at random, what is the probability that they play either basketball or soccer?

Note: Solutions to the exercises can be found at the end of the book.

Time to put your probability skills to the test! See how well you can solve these problems and remember, probability is all around us, so keep an eye out for real-life examples too. Enjoy the challenge!

Statistical Modeling

Statistical modeling is a powerful tool in the field of artificial intelligence that allows us to understand and analyze complex relationships between variables. It provides a framework for making predictions and drawing conclusions based on data. In this section, we will explore the principles of statistical modeling and its applications in AI.

Principles of Statistical Modeling

At its core, statistical modeling is about finding patterns and relationships in data. It involves using mathematical functions to represent these relationships and using statistical techniques to estimate the parameters of these functions. The goal is to create a model that accurately represents the underlying structure of the data, allowing us to make predictions or draw conclusions.

One common statistical modeling technique is regression analysis. Regression models the relationship between a dependent variable and one or more independent variables. It helps us understand how changes in the independent variables affect the dependent variable. For example, in a sales context, we could use regression analysis to model how changes in advertising expenditure impact sales revenue.

Another important principle of statistical modeling is inference. Inference refers to the process of drawing conclusions about a population based on a sample of data. By using inferential statistics, we can make predictions or test hypotheses about a larger population using a smaller sample. This is crucial in cases where collecting data from the entire population is impractical or impossible.

Types of Statistical Models

There are various types of statistical models used in AI, each suited for different types of data and research questions. Here are a few commonly used models:

- Linear Regression: This model assumes a linear relationship between the dependent variable and the independent variables. It is widely used for predicting a continuous outcome based on one or more predictors.

- Logistic Regression: Logistic regression is used when the dependent variable is binary or categorical. It models the probability of an event occurring based on one or more independent variables.

- Decision Trees: Decision trees are a flexible and interpretable model that uses a tree-like structure to represent decisions and their possible consequences. They are often used for classification problems.

- Random Forest: Random forests are an ensemble learning method that combines multiple decision trees to make more accurate predictions. They are known for their robustness and ability to handle high-dimensional data.

- Support Vector Machines: Support vector machines are used for both classification and regression problems. They classify data by finding an optimal hyperplane that maximally separates the different classes.

- **Naive Bayes:** Naive Bayes is a probabilistic model that relies on Bayes' theorem. It assumes all features are independent, making it computationally efficient and particularly useful for text classification tasks.

- **Clustering Algorithms:** Clustering algorithms are used to group similar data points together based on their characteristics. They are widely used in unsupervised learning tasks to discover hidden patterns in data.

Applications of Statistical Modeling in AI

Statistical modeling has numerous applications in the field of artificial intelligence. Here are a few examples:

1. **Predictive Analytics:** Statistical models can be used to make predictions about future events or outcomes. For example, a marketing team could use regression analysis to predict customer churn based on various customer attributes and historical data.

2. **Anomaly Detection:** Statistical modeling can help identify unusual patterns or outliers in data, which can be useful in fraud detection or network security.

3. **Risk Assessment:** Statistical models can be used to assess and quantify risk in various domains, such as insurance or finance. For example, a credit scoring model can analyze a borrower's characteristics to predict their creditworthiness.

4. **Personalized Recommendations:** Collaborative filtering models, such as the one used by Netflix to recommend movies, rely on statistical modeling techniques to make personalized recommendations based on user preferences and behavior.

Caveats and Considerations

While statistical modeling is a powerful tool, it is not without its limitations and caveats. Here are a few important considerations:

- **Assumptions:** Statistical models often make assumptions about the underlying data, such as linearity or independence. It is essential to assess if these assumptions hold true for the given problem and data.

- **Overfitting:** Overfitting occurs when a model performs very well on the training data but fails to generalize well to unseen data. Regularization techniques, such as L1 or L2 regularization, can help mitigate overfitting.
- **Interpretability:** Some models, like decision trees, are highly interpretable, while others, like neural networks, are considered black boxes. It's important to choose a model that aligns with the interpretability requirements of the problem at hand.

Real-World Example: Predicting Housing Prices

Let's consider a real-world example to illustrate the use of statistical modeling. Suppose we want to predict housing prices based on various features such as location, square footage, number of bedrooms, etc. We can collect historical data on house prices along with their corresponding features.

Using a linear regression model, we can estimate the relationship between the dependent variable, which is the house price, and the independent variables, such as square footage and number of bedrooms. By fitting the model to the data, we can obtain estimates for the coefficients of each independent variable, indicating the strength and direction of their influence on the house price.

Once the model is trained, we can make predictions on new, unseen data. For instance, given the features of a newly listed house, we can use the model to estimate its price. This can guide potential buyers or sellers in making informed decisions.

Summary

Statistical modeling is an essential tool in the field of artificial intelligence. It allows us to understand complex relationships in data and make predictions or draw conclusions. By leveraging various models and techniques, we can gain valuable insights from data and use them to drive decision-making and develop intelligent systems. Understanding statistical modeling is crucial for aspiring AI practitioners and researchers.

Further Reading

If you're interested in diving deeper into statistical modeling, here are some recommended resources:

- "An Introduction to Statistical Learning" by Gareth James et al.
- "Pattern Recognition and Machine Learning" by Christopher Bishop

- "Elements of Statistical Learning" by Trevor Hastie, Robert Tibshirani, and Jerome Friedman

These books provide in-depth coverage of statistical modeling techniques, their applications, and the underlying theory. Happy modeling!

Introduction to Machine Learning

What is Machine Learning?

Supervised vs. Unsupervised Learning

When it comes to machine learning, there are two primary types of learning paradigms: supervised learning and unsupervised learning. These two approaches play a crucial role in training AI systems and extracting valuable insights from data. In this section, we will explore the key differences between supervised and unsupervised learning and understand their applications in the field of artificial intelligence.

Supervised Learning

Supervised learning is a type of machine learning where the algorithm learns from labeled data. Labeled data refers to input data that has corresponding output labels or target values. The goal of supervised learning is to train a model that can predict the correct output for new, unseen input data.

To illustrate how supervised learning works, let's consider a classic example of email categorization. Suppose we have a dataset of emails, each labeled as either "spam" or "not spam." Our task is to build a model that can accurately classify new incoming emails as spam or not spam.

In supervised learning, we can divide our labeled dataset into two subsets: a training set and a test set. The training set is used to train the model, while the test set is used to evaluate its performance. The model learns from the training set by extracting patterns and relationships between the input features (e.g., email text, sender, subject) and the corresponding output labels (spam or not spam).

There are various algorithms used in supervised learning, such as linear regression, logistic regression, decision trees, random forest, support vector machines (SVM), naive Bayes, and k-nearest neighbors (KNN). Each algorithm has its strengths and weaknesses, and choosing the right one depends on the nature of the problem and the available data.

Once the model is trained, we can use it to make predictions on new, unlabeled data. For example, we can feed an unseen email into the trained model, and it will predict whether the email is spam or not spam based on the patterns it learned during training. This prediction is based on the knowledge gained from the labeled data used for training the model.

Unsupervised Learning

Unlike supervised learning, unsupervised learning deals with unlabeled data. In unsupervised learning, the algorithm is tasked with finding patterns, structure, or relationships within the data without any predefined output labels.

To understand unsupervised learning better, let's consider a clustering problem. Suppose we have a dataset of customer purchase behavior, with no information about customer segments or labels. Our goal is to group similar customers together based on their purchasing habits.

Unsupervised learning algorithms work by exploring the inherent structure in the data. They discover patterns, clusters, or anomalies that may not be immediately apparent to humans. Some popular unsupervised learning techniques include clustering algorithms, dimensionality reduction, and anomaly detection.

Clustering algorithms, such as k-means clustering or hierarchical clustering, aim to group similar data points together based on their proximity in feature space. In our customer purchase behavior example, a clustering algorithm can help identify distinct customer segments with similar purchase patterns.

Dimensionality reduction techniques, like principal component analysis (PCA) or t-SNE (t-Distributed Stochastic Neighbor Embedding), help reduce the dimensionality of high-dimensional data by capturing the most important features or patterns. This can be particularly useful when dealing with complex datasets where visualization or analysis becomes challenging.

Anomaly detection algorithms focus on identifying rare or abnormal instances in the data. These anomalies can represent potential fraud, errors, or outliers. Anomaly detection is particularly valuable in various domains, including cybersecurity, fraud detection, and system monitoring.

The key advantage of unsupervised learning is its ability to discover hidden patterns or structures in data without relying on labeled examples. It allows for

WHAT IS MACHINE LEARNING?

exploratory analysis, data visualization, and gaining insights into the data's intrinsic properties. However, since there are no predefined labels, evaluating the performance of an unsupervised learning model can be more challenging compared to supervised learning.

Supervised vs. Unsupervised Learning

Now let's compare and contrast supervised and unsupervised learning:

- **Target Variable:** In supervised learning, we have labeled data with a target variable that the model aims to predict. In unsupervised learning, there are no predefined output labels, and the goal is to uncover hidden patterns or structures within the data.

- **Training Process:** Supervised learning requires a labeled training dataset, where the model learns from both input features and corresponding output labels. Unsupervised learning, on the other hand, only requires unlabeled data and focuses on learning from the input features alone.

- **Applications:** Supervised learning is well-suited for tasks such as classification, regression, and prediction, where the goal is to predict a specific output based on input features. Unsupervised learning is useful for tasks like clustering, anomaly detection, and dimensionality reduction, where the aim is to discover patterns or structures within the data.

- **Evaluation:** Supervised learning models can be evaluated based on how accurately they predict the target variable on labeled test data. Unsupervised learning, being exploratory in nature, often relies on metrics like clustering stability, silhouette score, or visual inspections to evaluate the quality of discovered patterns or structures.

- **Data Requirements:** Supervised learning heavily relies on labeled data, which may require manual labeling or domain expertise. Unsupervised learning can work with unlabeled data, making it useful when labeled data is scarce or expensive to obtain.

It's worth noting that supervised and unsupervised learning are not mutually exclusive. In some scenarios, a combination of both learning paradigms, known as semi-supervised learning, can be employed. Semi-supervised learning leverages the small amount of labeled data and the larger volume of unlabeled data to improve the performance and generalization of AI models.

Knowing when to use supervised or unsupervised learning depends on the problem at hand, the nature of the available data, and the expected outputs. It's essential to carefully consider the characteristics of the data and the goals of the analysis to select the most appropriate learning approach.

Case Study: Autonomous Vehicle Development

To better understand the practical applications of supervised and unsupervised learning, let's explore how they can be used in the development of autonomous vehicles.

Supervised learning plays a crucial role in training models to recognize and interpret various objects and scenarios on the road. Through labeled data such as images and sensor readings captured during test drives, supervised learning algorithms can learn to identify pedestrians, traffic signs, other vehicles, and different road conditions. This knowledge is essential for making accurate and informed decisions while driving.

On the other hand, unsupervised learning can be used to discover patterns and structure within large datasets collected from autonomous vehicles. By analyzing unlabeled sensor data, unsupervised learning algorithms can identify recurring scenarios, anomalies, or patterns that may have previously gone unnoticed. This can help in understanding complex traffic situations and extracting valuable insights to improve autonomous driving algorithms.

For example, unsupervised learning techniques like clustering can be employed to group similar driving scenarios together based on sensor inputs. This can aid in identifying common patterns, such as specific road configurations or traffic situations, helping autonomous vehicle systems to make better decisions in similar situations.

By combining the strengths of both supervised and unsupervised learning, researchers and engineers in the autonomous vehicle industry can develop more robust and intelligent systems that are capable of dealing with a wide range of real-world driving scenarios.

Summary

In this section, we explored the difference between supervised and unsupervised learning in the context of machine learning. Supervised learning relies on labeled data to train models that can predict specific outputs based on given inputs. On the other hand, unsupervised learning focuses on uncovering hidden patterns or structures within unlabeled data.

While supervised learning is suitable for tasks like classification, regression, and prediction, unsupervised learning shines in tasks such as clustering, anomaly detection, and dimensionality reduction. Both learning paradigms have their unique strengths and play important roles in advancing artificial intelligence.

We also discussed how supervised and unsupervised learning can be applied in the development of autonomous vehicles. Supervised learning helps in training models to recognize and interpret various objects and scenarios on the road, while unsupervised learning aids in discovering patterns and insights from unlabeled sensor data.

As we continue our journey through the world of artificial intelligence and data, it is crucial to understand the different learning approaches and their scope of applications. The next exciting chapter will dive into the fundamental principles and algorithms used in machine learning, providing a solid foundation for building intelligent systems that can turn data into dominance. So buckle up and get ready to explore the exciting world of machine learning!

Reinforcement Learning

Reinforcement learning is like that friend who always takes risks, learns from mistakes, and ultimately becomes a badass. It is a type of machine learning where an agent learns to make decisions by interacting with an environment. The agent receives feedback in the form of rewards or punishments, guiding it in the right direction. This is similar to how we humans learn through trial and error.

The Markov Decision Process (MDP)

To understand reinforcement learning, we need to start with the Markov Decision Process (MDP), which provides a mathematical framework for modeling the interaction between an agent and an environment.

In an MDP, an agent operates in discrete time-steps within an environment. At each time-step, the agent observes the current state of the environment and takes an action. The environment transitions to a new state, and the agent receives a reward based on its action. This process continues until a terminal state is reached.

Formally, an MDP is defined by a tuple (S, A, T, R), where:

- S is the set of possible states in the environment.
- A is the set of possible actions the agent can take.
- T is the state transition function, which specifies the probability of transitioning from one state to another, given an action.

- R is the reward function, which provides a numeric reward for each state-action pair.

The Bellman Equation

The Bellman equation is the foundation of reinforcement learning. It states that the value of being in a particular state s under a policy π can be expressed as the sum of the immediate reward and the discounted value of the expected future states:

$$V^\pi(s) = \sum_a \pi(a|s) \sum_{s',r} p(s',r|s,a) \left[r + \gamma V^\pi(s')\right]$$

Here, $V^\pi(s)$ represents the value of state s under policy π, $\pi(a|s)$ is the probability of taking action a in state s, $p(s',r|s,a)$ is the probability of transitioning to state s' and receiving reward r, and γ is the discount factor that determines the importance of future rewards.

The Bellman equation allows us to estimate the value of each state and make optimal decisions by maximizing the cumulative reward over time.

Q-Learning

Q-Learning is one of the most popular algorithms for solving reinforcement learning problems. It uses a table, known as the Q-table, to store the expected reward for each state-action pair.

The Q-value for a state-action pair (s, a) is updated iteratively using the following equation:

$$Q(s,a) \leftarrow Q(s,a) + \alpha \left[r + \gamma \max_{a'} Q(s',a') - Q(s,a)\right]$$

Here, α is the learning rate, r is the immediate reward received after taking action a in state s, and (s', a') is the next state-action pair.

The Q-Learning algorithm iteratively explores the environment, updates the Q-values, and adjusts the policy accordingly. It eventually converges to an optimal policy that maximizes the expected cumulative reward.

Exploration vs Exploitation

One of the challenges in reinforcement learning is the exploration-exploitation tradeoff. The agent needs to balance the exploration of new actions to discover potentially better rewards, while also exploiting its current knowledge to maximize the cumulative reward.

To tackle this challenge, we can use an epsilon-greedy policy. During exploration, the agent selects a random action with probability ϵ, and selects the action with the highest Q-value otherwise. This ensures a balance between exploration and exploitation.

Applications of Reinforcement Learning

Reinforcement learning has found applications in various fields, showcasing its power and versatility. Let's explore a few examples:

- **Game Playing:** Reinforcement learning has achieved remarkable success in mastering complex games like Chess and Go. AlphaZero, a reinforcement learning algorithm, defeated world-class players in both games using self-play and deep neural networks.

- **Autonomous Driving:** Reinforcement learning is revolutionizing autonomous driving by enabling vehicles to learn optimal driving policies through interactions with the environment. This helps in making intelligent decisions on the road and ensuring passenger safety.

- **Robotics:** Reinforcement learning plays a vital role in training robots to perform various tasks, such as grasping objects, assembly, and locomotion. Robots learn from real-world experiences and continuously improve their performance.

- **Healthcare:** Reinforcement learning is being used to optimize treatment strategies for diseases like cancer and diabetes. By learning from patient data, it helps in identifying personalized treatment plans and improving patient outcomes.

Remember, reinforcement learning is not just about gaming and robots; it offers a wide range of possibilities across industries.

Reinforcement Learning in Real Life

To put things into perspective, let's take a look at a real-life example of reinforcement learning in action.

Suppose you're at the gym, trying to improve your rowing performance. Initially, you row with random intensity and stroke patterns. Over time, your brain, acting as the reinforcement learning agent, receives feedback (reward) based on how fast and efficiently you row. You start to adjust your stroke, increasing the intensity when you receive positive feedback and decreasing it otherwise.

As you continue to practice and refine your rowing technique, your brain learns to make optimal decisions, maximizing your rowing performance.

Resources

To dive deeper into reinforcement learning, I recommend the following resources:

- *Reinforcement Learning: An Introduction* by Richard S. Sutton and Andrew G. Barto.
- *Deep Reinforcement Learning* by Pieter Abbeel and John Schulman.
- OpenAI Gym: a Python library for reinforcement learning experiments.

Remember, learning never stops, and in the world of reinforcement learning, there's always something new and exciting to explore.

WHAT IS MACHINE LEARNING? 61

Exercise

Let's put your knowledge of reinforcement learning to the test with a little exercise.

Suppose you are training an agent to navigate a maze. At each time-step, the agent can move in one of four directions: up, down, left, or right. The goal is to find the shortest path from the start to the goal while avoiding obstacles.

Design a reward function that encourages the agent to reach the goal as quickly as possible, penalizes hitting obstacles, and provides a small negative reward for each time-step taken. Implement Q-Learning to train the agent to navigate the maze using a suitable exploration strategy.

Once your agent is trained, test its performance by randomly generating different maze configurations and evaluate its success rate in finding the shortest path.

Remember, the key is to strike a balance between exploration and exploitation to guide the agent towards achieving optimal performance.

Hint: You can represent the maze as a grid, where each cell represents a state. The agent can take actions to move between adjacent cells.

Deep Learning and Neural Networks

In the world of artificial intelligence, deep learning and neural networks have emerged as powerful tools for solving complex problems. Deep learning is a subfield of machine learning that focuses on training artificial neural networks to learn and make predictions in a manner similar to the human brain. In this section, we'll explore the basics of deep learning, the architecture of neural networks, and some popular deep learning models.

The Basics of Deep Learning

Deep learning is inspired by the structure and function of the human brain. Just like the brain consists of interconnected neurons, deep learning models are built using artificial neural networks. Neural networks are mathematical models that are designed to recognize patterns and relationships in data.

At the core of a neural network are artificial neurons, also known as nodes or units. These neurons are organized into layers, with each layer receiving inputs from the previous layer and generating outputs that are passed to the next layer. The first layer is called the input layer, the last layer is called the output layer, and any layers in between are referred to as hidden layers.

Neural Network Architecture

The architecture of a neural network refers to its structure and organization. It determines how information flows through the network and how it is transformed at each layer. There are several types of neural network architectures, each suited for different types of tasks. Here, we'll focus on two popular architectures: feedforward neural networks and convolutional neural networks.

Feedforward Neural Networks: Feedforward neural networks are the simplest type of neural network architecture. They consist of multiple layers of artificial neurons, with connections only going forward, from one layer to the next. These networks are primarily used for tasks such as classification and regression. A common architecture is the multilayer perceptron (MLP), which consists of an input layer, one or more hidden layers, and an output layer.

Convolutional Neural Networks (CNNs): CNNs are a type of neural network architecture specially designed for image and video processing tasks. They are inspired by the organization of the visual cortex in the human brain. CNNs use a specialized layer called a convolutional layer, which applies a set of learnable filters to input data. This allows the network to automatically learn features and patterns at different spatial scales. CNNs are widely used in tasks such as image classification, object detection, and image generation.

Popular Deep Learning Models

Deep learning has gained popularity due to its ability to solve complex problems with remarkable accuracy. There are several deep learning models that have achieved state-of-the-art performance in various domains. Let's take a look at some of the most popular models:

1. Recurrent Neural Networks (RNNs): RNNs are a type of neural network that can process sequential data, such as time series or text. Unlike feedforward neural networks, RNNs have feedback connections, allowing information to flow in cycles. This enables them to capture temporal dependencies in the data. RNNs have been successfully applied to tasks such as language modeling, machine translation, and speech recognition.

2. Generative Adversarial Networks (GANs): GANs are a type of neural network architecture that can generate new data samples that are similar to a given training dataset. GANs consist of two networks: a generator network that generates fake samples, and a discriminator network that tries to distinguish between real and fake samples. The generator and discriminator are trained simultaneously, playing a min-max game. GANs have been used for various tasks, including image generation, style transfer, and data augmentation.

3. Transformer: The Transformer model, introduced in 2017, revolutionized the field of natural language processing (NLP). It employs a self-attention mechanism, allowing the model to capture contextual relationships between words in a sentence. Transformers have achieved state-of-the-art results in tasks such as machine translation, sentiment analysis, and text summarization.

Training Deep Learning Models

Training deep learning models involves two main steps: forward propagation and backpropagation. During forward propagation, the input data is passed through the layers of the neural network, and the output is computed. This output is then compared to the desired output using a loss function, which measures the difference between the predicted and actual values. The goal is to minimize this loss by adjusting the parameters, or weights, of the neural network.

Backpropagation is the process of calculating the gradient of the loss function with respect to each weight in the network. This gradient is then used to update the weights using an optimization algorithm, such as gradient descent. The process of forward propagation followed by backpropagation is repeated iteratively until the model converges to the optimal set of weights.

Applications of Deep Learning

Deep learning has revolutionized many industries and has a wide range of applications. Here are a few examples:

1. Image Recognition: Deep learning models, especially CNNs, have achieved remarkable performance in image recognition tasks. They can classify images into different categories, detect objects in images, and even generate realistic images.

2. Natural Language Processing: Deep learning models have greatly improved the performance of various natural language processing tasks, such as text classification, sentiment analysis, and machine translation.

3. Healthcare: Deep learning is being used in the healthcare industry for tasks such as medical imaging diagnosis, drug discovery, and personalized medicine.

4. Autonomous Vehicles: Deep learning plays a crucial role in enabling autonomous vehicles to perceive and understand their environment. It is used in tasks such as object detection, lane recognition, and path planning.

Challenges and Future Directions

Although deep learning has achieved remarkable success in various domains, it still faces several challenges. One major challenge is the need for large amounts of labeled training data. Deep learning models are data-hungry and require massive datasets for effective training. Another challenge is the interpretability of deep learning models. They are often referred to as "black boxes" because it is difficult to understand how they make predictions.

In the future, researchers are exploring ways to make deep learning models more interpretable and explainable. They are also working on developing new architectures and algorithms to address the limitations of existing models. Additionally, there is a growing focus on ethics and responsible AI, as deep learning models have the potential to amplify existing biases and have real-world consequences.

Exercises

1. Consider a feedforward neural network with one input layer, two hidden layers with 50 neurons each, and one output layer. What is the total number of trainable parameters in this network?

2. Explain the concept of backpropagation in training deep learning models.

3. Research and explain one recent application of deep learning in a field of your interest. Discuss the impact and potential challenges of this application.

4. Discuss the limitations of deep learning and propose a possible solution for one of the challenges.

5. Imagine you are developing a deep learning model to classify different species of flowers from images. What architecture and training strategies would you use for this task? Explain your reasoning.

Additional Resources

1. Goodfellow, I., Bengio, Y., & Courville, A. (2016). *Deep Learning*. MIT Press.

2. Chollet, F. (2018). *Deep Learning with Python*. Manning Publications.

3. LeCun, Y., Bengio, Y., & Hinton, G. (2015). *Deep learning*. Nature, 521(7553), 436-444.

4. Karpathy, A. (2016). *Deep Learning for Computer Vision*. Stanford University, CS231n course notes.

5. Ng, A. (2017). *Deep Learning Specialization*. Coursera.

6. Colah, C. (2015). *Understanding LSTM Networks*. Retrieved from https://colah.github.io/posts/2015-08-Understanding-LSTMs/

7. TensorFlow Documentation. *https://www.tensorflow.org/*

Remember, the key to mastering deep learning and neural networks is practice and experimentation. The more you dive into hands-on projects and explore real-world data, the better you'll become at turning data into dominance!

Machine Learning Algorithms

Linear Regression

Linear regression is a fundamental statistical technique used to model the relationship between a dependent variable and one or more independent variables. It is one of the simplest and most widely used methods in machine learning and data analysis. In this section, we will explore the principles behind linear regression, understand its assumptions, learn how to interpret the results, and discuss its applications.

Principles of Linear Regression

The goal of linear regression is to find the best-fitting line that represents the relationship between the independent variable(s) X and the dependent variable Y. The line is defined by the equation:

$$Y = \beta_0 + \beta_1 X$$

where β_0 is the y-intercept, β_1 is the slope of the line, and X is the independent variable. The y-intercept represents the value of Y when X is equal to zero, and the slope represents the change in Y for every unit change in X.

The parameters β_0 and β_1 are estimated from the data using a method called the method of least squares. This method minimizes the sum of the squared differences between the actual values of Y and the predicted values from the line.

Assumptions of Linear Regression

Linear regression makes several assumptions about the data:

1. **Linearity**: The relationship between the independent variable(s) and the dependent variable is linear. If the relationship is nonlinear, other regression models are more appropriate.

2. **Independence**: The observations are independent of each other. In the case of time series data, autocorrelation should be considered.

3. **Homoscedasticity**: The variance of the errors is constant across all levels of the independent variable(s). If the variance is not constant (heteroscedasticity), a transformation of the variables or the use of weighted least squares may be necessary.

4. **No multicollinearity**: The independent variables are not highly correlated with each other. Multicollinearity can lead to unstable estimates of the regression coefficients.

Interpreting the Results

Once the linear regression model is fitted to the data, we can interpret the results to understand the relationship between the independent variable(s) and the dependent variable. The key results include:

1. **Intercept** (β_0): It represents the estimated mean value of the dependent variable when all independent variables are equal to zero.

2. **Slope** (β_i): The slope coefficients represent the change in the dependent variable for a one-unit change in the corresponding independent variable, holding all other variables constant.

3. **Significance tests**: Hypothesis tests can be performed to determine if the slope coefficients are significantly different from zero. The p-values associated with these tests provide a measure of the strength of evidence against the null hypothesis.

4. **R-squared** (R^2): It measures the proportion of variance in the dependent variable that can be explained by the linear regression model. Higher values of R^2 indicate a better fit of the model to the data.

Applications of Linear Regression

Linear regression has a wide range of applications across various fields:

1. **Economics**: In economics, linear regression is used to model the relationship between economic variables, such as GDP and unemployment rates.

2. **Finance**: In finance, linear regression is used to estimate the relationship between a stock's returns and the returns of a market index, helping investors make informed decisions.

3. **Marketing**: Linear regression is used to analyze customer behavior, such as the relationship between advertising expenditure and sales revenue, to optimize marketing strategies.

4. **Healthcare**: Linear regression is utilized to analyze the impact of variables like age, BMI, or blood pressure on predicting the risk of developing certain diseases.

Example: Predicting House Prices

Let's consider an example of predicting house prices based on various features such as the number of rooms, the location, and the size of the house. We collect data on several houses, including these features and their actual selling prices. By fitting a linear regression model, we can estimate the relationship between these features and the house prices.

Suppose we have a dataset with the following variables:
- Y (dependent variable): Selling price of the house - X_1 (independent variable): Number of rooms - X_2 (independent variable): Location (categorical variable) - X_3 (independent variable): Size of the house

We can estimate the coefficients β_0, β_1, β_2, and β_3 using the method of least squares. These coefficients will help us predict the selling price of a house based on its characteristics.

In summary, linear regression is a powerful tool that allows us to model and analyze the relationship between variables in a simple and interpretable way. By understanding its principles and assumptions, we can apply linear regression to a wide range of real-world problems, gaining valuable insights and making informed decisions.

Logistic Regression

In the world of machine learning, there are numerous algorithms and models that can make sense of complex datasets and provide valuable insights. One such algorithm is logistic regression, a powerful tool for classification problems. In this section, we will explore the principles, applications, and limitations of logistic regression.

Principles of Logistic Regression

At its core, logistic regression is a form of regression analysis that is used to model the relationship between a dependent variable and one or more independent variables. However, unlike linear regression, which predicts continuous values, logistic regression is specifically designed for binary classification tasks.

To understand how logistic regression works, let's start with its basic principle: the logistic function. The logistic function, also known as the sigmoid function, transforms any real-valued input into a range between 0 and 1. It is defined as:

$$\sigma(z) = \frac{1}{1 + e^{-z}}$$

where z is the linear combination of the independent variables and their respective coefficients. The logistic function allows us to map the continuous input space into a probability space, where the output represents the probability of the event occurring.

In logistic regression, we aim to find the optimal coefficients that minimize the difference between the predicted probabilities and the actual binary labels in the training data. This process involves estimating the coefficients through an optimization algorithm, such as gradient descent.

Applications of Logistic Regression

Logistic regression has found applications in various domains, including healthcare, finance, marketing, and social sciences. Let's explore some examples to illustrate its versatility.

Example 1: Medical Diagnosis

Suppose a hospital wants to develop a model to predict whether a patient has a certain disease based on their symptoms. By collecting data on patients with and without the disease, they can train a logistic regression model to estimate the probability of a patient having the disease given their symptoms. This model can assist doctors in making accurate diagnoses and potentially save lives.

Example 2: Customer Churn Prediction

A telecommunications company wants to identify customers who are likely to cancel their service. By analyzing customer data, including factors like average monthly bill, tenure, and customer complaints, they can build a logistic regression model to predict the probability of a customer churning. Using this information, the company can proactively reach out to high-risk customers and offer them incentives to retain their business.

Example 3: Credit Risk Assessment

A bank wants to evaluate the creditworthiness of loan applicants. By considering factors such as income, credit score, and employment history, they can use logistic regression to estimate the probability of a loan default. This helps the bank make informed decisions about loan approvals and set appropriate interest rates based on the level of risk.

Limitations of Logistic Regression

While logistic regression is a valuable tool, it has its limitations. Here are a few important considerations:

Linearity Assumption: Logistic regression assumes a linear relationship between the independent variables and the log-odds of the dependent variable. If the relationship is non-linear, logistic regression may not perform well without appropriate transformations or interactions.

High Multicollinearity: Logistic regression is sensitive to multicollinearity, which is the presence of strong correlations among independent variables. When multicollinearity exists, it becomes challenging to interpret the impact of individual variables on the outcome accurately.

Imbalanced Data: Logistic regression may struggle when dealing with imbalanced datasets, where one class significantly outweighs the other. In such cases, the model may be biased towards the majority class, resulting in poor performance for the minority class.

Tips and Tricks

Here are some tips and tricks to enhance the performance and interpretability of logistic regression models:

Feature Scaling: To ensure fair treatment of features with different scales, it is often beneficial to standardize or normalize the independent variables before fitting the logistic regression model.

Regularization: Regularization techniques, such as L1 (Lasso) and L2 (Ridge), can help mitigate overfitting and improve the model's generalization ability by adding penalty terms to the cost function.

Feature Engineering: Transforming or combining features can uncover non-linear relationships and boost the predictive power of a logistic regression model. This involves techniques like polynomial expansion, interaction terms, or encoding categorical variables appropriately.

Conclusion

Logistic regression is a versatile and widely-used algorithm in the field of machine learning. Its ability to handle binary classification problems, interpretability, and ease of implementation make it a valuable tool for data scientists across industries. By understanding the principles, applications, and limitations of logistic regression, you can leverage its power and make informed decisions in your own data analysis endeavors.

Summary

- Logistic regression is a form of regression analysis specifically designed for binary classification tasks. - It uses the logistic function to map the linear combination of independent variables and their coefficients to a probability space. - Logistic regression has a wide range of applications, including medical diagnosis, customer churn prediction, and credit risk assessment. - It has limitations, such as the linearity assumption, sensitivity to multicollinearity, and challenges with imbalanced data. - Feature scaling, regularization, and feature engineering techniques can enhance the performance and interpretability of logistic regression models.

Decision Trees

Decision trees are powerful and popular machine learning algorithms that can be used for both classification and regression tasks. They are simple yet effective models that can handle both numerical and categorical data. The key idea behind decision trees is to create a model that predicts the target variable by learning simple decision rules inferred from the data. In this section, we will explore the fundamentals of decision trees, their construction, and their evaluation.

Understanding Decision Trees

At its core, a decision tree is a flowchart-like structure in which internal nodes represent feature or attribute tests, branches represent the outcomes of those tests, and leaf nodes represent the predicted target variable. The tree is built by recursively partitioning the data based on the values of the features, aiming to create homogeneous subsets of data in terms of the target variable within each leaf node.

To make predictions using a decision tree, we start at the root node and traverse down the tree by following the appropriate branches based on the feature values of the data. We continue this process until we reach a leaf node, where we predict the target variable based on the majority class or the average value of the target variable in that leaf node.

Building Decision Trees

The construction of decision trees involves two key steps: feature selection and tree pruning.

MACHINE LEARNING ALGORITHMS

Feature Selection: The goal is to determine the best feature to split the data at each node. Various algorithms can be used for feature selection, such as Gini impurity and information gain. Gini impurity measures the impurity or disorder of a node's class distribution, while information gain measures the reduction in entropy (a measure of disorder) achieved by the split.

Tree Pruning: Decision trees have a tendency to overfit the training data, creating overly complex trees that do not generalize well to unseen data. Pruning is a technique used to address this issue. It involves removing unnecessary branches or nodes from the tree to improve its simplicity and predictive accuracy on unseen data. Common pruning techniques include cost complexity pruning and reduced-error pruning.

Advantages and Limitations of Decision Trees

Advantages:

1. Easy to understand and interpret: Decision trees provide a transparent and intuitive representation of the decision-making process.

2. Able to handle both numerical and categorical data: Decision trees can handle a mix of continuous and discrete data, making them versatile for various types of problems.

3. Interpretability: The decision rules inferred from a decision tree can be easily visualized and understood.

4. Good performance: Decision trees can achieve high accuracy with relatively little data preparation.

Limitations:

1. Overfitting: Decision trees have a tendency to overfit the training data, resulting in poor generalization to unseen data. Pruning techniques can mitigate this issue to some extent.

2. Lack of robustness: Decision trees are sensitive to small changes in the data, which can lead to different tree structures and possibly different predictions. Ensemble methods like random forests can address this limitation.

3. Difficulty in capturing complex relationships: Decision trees struggle to capture complex relationships between features, especially when interactions between features are important.

Example: Predicting Loan Default

To illustrate the use of decision trees, let's consider a common real-world example of predicting loan default. Suppose we have a dataset containing information about loan applicants, such as their income, credit score, employment status, and loan approval status (defaulted or not defaulted).

We can use a decision tree to predict whether a new loan applicant will default on their loan based on the available information. The decision tree will learn decision rules based on the historical data and use them to make predictions for new applicants.

For example, a decision rule in the tree might be "If the applicant's credit score is less than 600 and their income is less than $30,000, then predict loan default." By following these decision rules, the decision tree can effectively classify new loan applicants as either low risk or high risk.

Resources and Further Reading

- Hastie, T., Tibshirani, R., & Friedman, J. (2009). *The Elements of Statistical Learning: Data Mining, Inference, and Prediction*. Springer.

- Breiman, L., Friedman, J., Olshen, R., & Stone, C. (1984). *Classification and Regression Trees*. CRC Press.

- Scikit-learn documentation: Decision Trees. Available at: https://scikit-learn.org/stable/modules/tree.html

- Kaggle Titanic competition: In this popular competition, participants use decision trees to predict the survival of passengers on the Titanic. Available at: https://www.kaggle.com/c/titanic

Quiz

1. What are the advantages of decision trees? a) Can handle both numerical and categorical data b) Easy to interpret and understand c) Good performance with little data preparation d) All of the above

2. How are decision trees constructed? a) By recursively partitioning the data based on feature tests b) By randomly selecting features for splits c) By minimizing the impurity of each split d) By removing unnecessary branches from the tree

3. What is the main limitation of decision trees? a) Overfitting the training data b) Difficulty in capturing complex relationships between features c) Lack of robustness to small changes in the data d) All of the above

4. What is the purpose of tree pruning? a) To remove unnecessary branches or nodes from the tree b) To prevent the tree from overfitting the training data c) To improve the simplicity and predictive accuracy of the tree d) All of the above

5. What is a real-world example where decision trees can be applied? a) Predicting loan default b) Sentiment analysis of social media posts c) Image recognition d) Speech recognition

Random Forest

Random Forest is a powerful machine learning algorithm that belongs to the family of ensemble methods. It is widely used for both classification and regression tasks, and often outperforms many other algorithms, thanks to its ability to handle high-dimensional data and complex relationships.

The Basics

At its core, a Random Forest is composed of multiple decision trees. Each tree is built using a random subset of the training data and a random subset of the features. This randomness in data sampling and feature selection is what gives Random Forest its name and strength.

To understand how a Random Forest works, let's first explore the concept of a decision tree. A decision tree is a flowchart-like structure where each internal node represents a feature or attribute, each branch represents a decision rule, and each leaf node represents an outcome or prediction. The goal is to split the data based on the features and create the most accurate prediction at each leaf node.

Random Forest takes advantage of the diversity of decision trees. By randomly selecting subsets of the data and features, each decision tree in the forest is trained on different aspects of the overall problem. This diversity reduces the risk of overfitting and results in a more accurate and robust prediction.

Building a Random Forest

To build a Random Forest, we follow these steps:

1. Randomly select "m" samples from the dataset with replacement. This is known as bootstrap sampling, or bagging. Each selected sample becomes a training set for an individual decision tree.

2. Randomly select "k" features from the total "n" features. This ensures that each decision tree considers different features. The value of "k" is typically calculated using the square root or logarithm of "n".

3. Construct each decision tree using the selected samples and features. The tree is built using various splitting criteria, such as Gini impurity or information gain, to determine the optimal splits at each node.

4. Repeat the above steps to create a specified number of decision trees.

5. For classification tasks, the final prediction is determined by a majority vote of all decision trees. For regression tasks, the final prediction is the average of all individual tree predictions.

The Random Forest algorithm has several advantages over other machine learning algorithms:

- **Robustness:** Random Forest can handle missing data and outliers in the dataset. It also performs well with categorical and numerical features without requiring extensive pre-processing.

- **Feature Importance:** Random Forest can provide information about feature importance. By analyzing the frequency and depth of feature usage within the forest, we can understand which features have the most influence on the prediction.

- **Overfitting Prevention:** The randomness in Random Forest reduces the risk of overfitting compared to individual decision trees.

- **Versatility:** Random Forest can handle both classification and regression tasks, making it a versatile algorithm.

Applications of Random Forest

Random Forest has a wide range of applications across various industries:

- **Finance:** Random Forest can be used for credit scoring, fraud detection, and predicting stock market trends.

- **Healthcare:** It can aid in diagnosing diseases, predicting patient outcomes, and drug discovery.

- **Marketing:** Random Forest can be utilized for customer segmentation, personalized marketing, and campaign response prediction.

- **Environmental Science:** It can assist in predicting climate change patterns, analyzing ecological systems, and identifying endangered species.

- **Image and Speech Recognition:** Random Forest can be used for object recognition, emotion detection, and speech-to-text conversion.

Limitations and Considerations

While Random Forest is a powerful and versatile algorithm, it has a few limitations and considerations to keep in mind:

- **Interpretability:** The interpretability of Random Forest can be challenging due to the complexity of multiple decision trees. Understanding the exact decision-making process of the model can be challenging.
- **Computational Complexity:** Building and training multiple decision trees can be computationally expensive, especially for large datasets. However, modern hardware and parallel computing techniques have mitigated this issue to some extent.
- **Feature Correlation Impact:** Random Forest tends to underperform when there are strong correlations between features in the dataset. In such cases, other ensemble methods like Gradient Boosting might be more appropriate.

Summary

In conclusion, Random Forest is a powerful ensemble learning algorithm that combines multiple decision trees to make accurate predictions. Its ability to handle complex relationships and high-dimensional data makes it a popular choice for various machine learning tasks. By introducing randomness in data sampling and feature selection, Random Forest reduces the risk of overfitting and improves robustness. While it has some limitations, Random Forest remains an essential tool in the field of artificial intelligence.

Resources

To deepen your understanding of Random Forest and explore further, below are some recommended resources:

- **Books:**
    - "The Elements of Statistical Learning" by Trevor Hastie, Robert Tibshirani, and Jerome Friedman.
    - "Applied Predictive Modeling" by Max Kuhn and Kjell Johnson.

- **Online Courses:**
  - Coursera: "Machine Learning" by Andrew Ng.
  - edX: "Practical Deep Learning for Coders" by Jeremy Howard.
- **Websites:**
  - Towards Data Science: https://towardsdatascience.com/
  - Kaggle: https://www.kaggle.com/

Exercises

Before we conclude, here are some exercises to test your understanding of Random Forest:

1. Explain the concept of bootstrap sampling and its role in Random Forest.
2. Discuss how Random Forest handles missing data and outliers in the dataset.
3. What are the advantages of Random Forest over other machine learning algorithms?
4. Name three real-world applications where Random Forest can be useful.
5. What are the limitations of Random Forest, and how can they be addressed?

Take your time to answer these questions and feel free to refer back to the explanations provided earlier in this section. Remember, practice is crucial to mastering any algorithm, so don't hesitate to experiment with Random Forest using real-world datasets. Good luck on your journey to becoming an AI expert!

Support Vector Machines

In this section, we will delve into the world of Support Vector Machines (SVMs), a powerful machine learning algorithm for classification and regression tasks. SVMs have gained immense popularity in recent years due to their ability to efficiently handle high-dimensional data and achieve remarkable accuracy. With their intuitive geometric interpretation and elegant mathematical framework, SVMs have emerged as a go-to tool for solving complex real-world problems.

The Intuition Behind SVMs

At the heart of SVMs lies the concept of finding an optimal hyperplane that separates data points of different classes in the feature space. The goal is to identify the hyperplane that maximizes the margin, or the distance between the hyperplane and the closest data points called support vectors. By maximizing the margin, SVMs effectively find the best decision boundary, leading to robust and accurate predictions.

To better understand the intuition behind SVMs, let's consider a simple example involving two classes. Imagine we have a dataset of cats and dogs, with each data point representing an animal and its corresponding features like weight, height, and age. Our objective is to classify new animals as either cats or dogs based on these features.

A linear SVM seeks to find the optimal hyperplane that separates the data points of cats and dogs in the feature space. The hyperplane can be represented by the equation $w \cdot x + b = 0$, where w is the weight vector perpendicular to the hyperplane and b is the offset term. Thus, given a new animal feature vector x, we can determine its class by evaluating the sign of $w \cdot x + b$.

Formulating the SVM Optimization Problem

To find the optimal hyperplane, we need to define an objective function that captures the goal of maximizing the margin while minimizing classification errors. SVM achieves this by formulating a convex optimization problem.

Let's assume we have n training samples (x_i, y_i), where x_i denotes the feature vector and y_i represents the corresponding class labels (+1 for cats and -1 for dogs). Our objective is to find the weight vector w and offset term b that minimize the following expression:

$$\frac{1}{2}||w||^2 + C \sum_{i=1}^{n} \max(0, 1 - y_i(w \cdot x_i + b))$$

The first term in the expression represents the margin maximization by minimizing the norm of the weight vector. The second term is the hinge loss function, which penalizes misclassified points and encourages correct classification with a trade-off parameter C.

Solving the SVM Optimization Problem

Solving the SVM optimization problem involves finding the values of w and b that minimize the objective function. This can be achieved using various optimization techniques, such as quadratic programming or gradient descent methods.

One popular approach is the Sequential Minimal Optimization (SMO) algorithm, which iteratively solves subproblems to update the weight vector w and offset term b until convergence. SMO is known for its efficiency and ability to handle large-scale datasets.

Once the optimization problem is solved, we can use the weight vector w to determine the class of new data points by evaluating $w \cdot x + b$.

Advantages and Limitations of SVMs

Support Vector Machines offer several advantages that make them a popular choice for many machine learning tasks:

- SVMs work well with high-dimensional data where the number of features exceeds the number of samples. They can effectively handle complex patterns in large feature spaces.

- SVMs are robust to outliers, as they focus on maximizing the margin and are less influenced by individual data points.

- SVMs provide a good balance between bias and variance, reducing the risk of overfitting.

However, SVMs also have their limitations:

- SVMs can be computationally expensive, especially for large datasets. The training time complexity is $O(n^3)$, where n is the number of samples.

- SVMs are sensitive to the choice of hyperparameters, such as the regularization parameter C and the kernel function. Careful tuning is required to achieve optimal performance.

- SVMs are primarily designed for binary classification tasks. Extending them to multi-class problems requires additional techniques, such as one-vs-all or one-vs-one.

MACHINE LEARNING ALGORITHMS

SVMs in Real-World Applications

Support Vector Machines have found wide-ranging applications in various domains. Here are a few examples:

- **Image Classification:** SVMs have been used extensively in computer vision tasks, such as image classification, object detection, and facial recognition. They can effectively categorize images into different classes based on their features.

- **Text Classification:** SVMs have proven to be valuable in natural language processing tasks, including text classification, sentiment analysis, and spam detection. They can analyze textual data and make accurate predictions based on features extracted from the text.

- **Finance:** SVMs are utilized in financial applications, such as stock market prediction, credit risk assessment, and fraud detection. They can identify patterns and anomalies in financial data to make informed decisions.

Further Reading

To enhance your understanding of Support Vector Machines, the following resources are highly recommended:

- *The Elements of Statistical Learning* by Trevor Hastie, Robert Tibshirani, and Jerome Friedman provides a comprehensive introduction to SVMs and other machine learning techniques.

- *Pattern Recognition and Machine Learning* by Christopher Bishop offers an in-depth exploration of SVMs with a focus on statistical learning theory.

- The scikit-learn documentation (`https://scikit-learn.org`) provides practical examples and code implementations of SVMs in Python.

Exercise: Cats vs Dogs

To test your understanding of Support Vector Machines, try solving the following exercise:

Consider a dataset of cats and dogs, with each data point represented by two features: weight and height. Given this dataset, use an SVM to classify new animals as either cats or dogs based on their weight and height. Evaluate the performance of your SVM using appropriate evaluation metrics and interpret the results.

Hint: You can use the scikit-learn library in Python to implement the SVM algorithm.

Conclusion

Support Vector Machines are a powerful tool for data classification and regression, offering an elegant mathematical foundation and impressive performance. With their ability to handle high-dimensional data and achieve accurate predictions, SVMs have become an essential part of the modern AI landscape. By understanding the principles and techniques behind SVMs, you can leverage their potential to solve complex real-world problems. So go ahead, embrace the power of SVMs, and let your data-driven dominance begin!

Naive Bayes

Naive Bayes is a popular and simple classification algorithm that is based on Bayes' theorem. It is widely used in various machine learning applications, including spam detection, sentiment analysis, and document classification. In this section, we will explore the principles and workings of Naive Bayes, its assumptions, and how it can be used to solve classification problems.

Bayes' Theorem

Before delving into Naive Bayes, let's first understand Bayes' theorem. Bayes' theorem is a fundamental concept in probability theory and provides a way to calculate conditional probabilities.

Bayes' theorem is stated as follows:

$$P(A|B) = \frac{P(B|A) \cdot P(A)}{P(B)}$$

where:

- $P(A|B)$ is the probability of event A given event B has occurred,
- $P(B|A)$ is the probability of event B given event A has occurred,
- $P(A)$ is the prior probability of event A,
- $P(B)$ is the prior probability of event B.

MACHINE LEARNING ALGORITHMS

Bayes' theorem allows us to update our beliefs about an event based on new evidence. In the context of machine learning, we can use it to update the probability of a class label given the observed features.

Assumptions of Naive Bayes

Naive Bayes is based on the assumption of conditional independence between the features given the class label. This means that the presence or absence of a particular feature does not affect the presence or absence of any other feature. Although this assumption may not hold in reality for all datasets, Naive Bayes still performs well in practice and is widely used due to its simplicity and efficiency.

Working of Naive Bayes

Naive Bayes works by calculating the posterior probability of each class label given the observed features and selecting the class label with the highest probability.

Let's consider a binary classification problem with two class labels, C_1 and C_2, and a set of features $X = \{x_1, x_2, ..., x_n\}$. Naive Bayes calculates the probability of each class label given the features as follows:

$$P(C_1|X) = \frac{P(X|C_1) \cdot P(C_1)}{P(X)}$$

$$P(C_2|X) = \frac{P(X|C_2) \cdot P(C_2)}{P(X)}$$

To calculate the probability $P(X|C_i)$, Naive Bayes assumes that the features are conditionally independent given the class label. This allows us to express $P(X|C_i)$ as the product of the probabilities of each individual feature given the class label:

$$P(X|C_i) = \prod_{i=1}^{n} P(x_i|C_i)$$

Now, to determine the class label, we compare the values of $P(C_1|X)$ and $P(C_2|X)$ and select the class label with the higher probability.

Example: Email Spam Detection

Let's illustrate the working of Naive Bayes with an example of email spam detection. Suppose we have a dataset of emails labeled as either "spam" or "not spam" and want to classify new incoming emails.

We can represent each email as a set of features, such as the presence of certain keywords, the frequency of certain words, or the length of the email. We assume that these features are conditionally independent given the class label.

To train our Naive Bayes model, we calculate the probabilities $P(x_i|C_i)$ for each feature given each class label, as well as the prior probabilities $P(C_i)$ for each class label. Then, for a new incoming email, we calculate the posterior probabilities $P(C_1|X)$ and $P(C_2|X)$ using Bayes' theorem, and classify the email as "spam" or "not spam" based on the higher probability.

Advantages and Limitations of Naive Bayes

Naive Bayes has several advantages that contribute to its popularity in machine learning applications:

- **Simplicity**: Naive Bayes is a simple algorithm that is easy to understand and implement. It is particularly suitable for problems with high-dimensional feature spaces.

- **Efficiency**: Naive Bayes has low computational cost compared to other algorithms, making it efficient for large-scale datasets.

- **Good performance**: Despite its simplicity and the assumption of feature independence, Naive Bayes often performs well in practice and produces accurate results.

However, Naive Bayes also has some limitations:

- **Assumption of feature independence**: The assumption of feature independence may not hold in real-world scenarios, which can lead to suboptimal results.

- **Sensitive to irrelevant features**: Naive Bayes treats all features equally, which means it can be sensitive to irrelevant features that have no predictive power.

- **Requires sufficient training data**: Like other machine learning algorithms, Naive Bayes requires a sufficient amount of training data to accurately estimate the probabilities.

Despite these limitations, Naive Bayes remains a popular and effective choice for classification tasks, especially in cases where the assumptions of the algorithm hold reasonably well.

MACHINE LEARNING ALGORITHMS

Further Resources and Exercises

If you want to dive deeper into Naive Bayes and explore more advanced topics, here are some resources to check out:

- Knight, K. and Nair, H., *Probability and Naive Bayesian Learning*. 2020.

- Manning, C.D., Raghavan, P. and Schütze, H., *Introduction to Information Retrieval*, Chapter 13: *Text Classification*.

- Kaggle: https://www.kaggle.com/learn/naive-bayes (Includes exercises and example datasets for Naive Bayes)

To further enhance your understanding, here are a few exercises:

1. Consider a spam detection problem where you have the following features: the presence of the word "free" (F), the presence of the word "discount" (D), and the email length in words (L). Assume that these features are conditionally independent. Use Naive Bayes to calculate the probabilities $P(\text{spam}|F, D, L)$ and $P(\text{not spam}|F, D, L)$ given the following information:

$$P(F|\text{spam}) \& = 0.9, \quad P(F|\text{not spam}) = 0.1$$
$$P(D|\text{spam}) \& = 0.8, \quad P(D|\text{not spam}) = 0.2$$
$$P(L|\text{spam}) \& = 0.6, \quad P(L|\text{not spam}) = 0.4$$
$$P(\text{spam}) \& = 0.5, \quad P(\text{not spam}) = 0.5$$

2. Explore a real-world dataset and apply Naive Bayes to solve a classification problem. For example, you can use the SMS Spam Collection dataset available on Kaggle (https://www.kaggle.com/uciml/sms-spam-collection-dataset). Preprocess the dataset, train a Naive Bayes model, and evaluate its performance using appropriate evaluation metrics.

By completing these exercises, you will gain a better understanding of Naive Bayes and its practical applications.

K-Nearest Neighbors

In the vast world of machine learning algorithms, there are many tools at our disposal. One of the most simple yet effective algorithms is called K-Nearest Neighbors (K-NN). This algorithm falls under the category of supervised learning, which means that it relies on labeled training data to make predictions. K-NN is particularly useful for classification tasks, where we aim to assign an instance to one of several predefined classes based on its features.

The underlying principle behind K-NN is fairly intuitive. It assumes that similar instances or data points will be close to each other in the feature space. So, when we encounter a new data point, we can compare it to its K nearest neighbors and assign the majority class label of those neighbors to the new point. The value of K, usually an odd number, determines how many neighbors are considered.

How K-NN Works

Let's walk through a simple example to understand how K-NN works. Suppose we have a dataset of animal sightings in a national park, with each data point representing an animal and its corresponding features such as height, weight, and fur color. The dataset also includes the class label indicating whether the animal is a carnivore, herbivore, or omnivore.

Now, let's say we spot a new animal in the park and want to determine its type based on its features. We could use K-NN to help us make this classification. We would begin by calculating the distance between the features of the new animal and all the animals in our dataset. The most commonly used distance metric in K-NN is the Euclidean distance or the Minkowski distance.

Once we have the distances, we select the K nearest neighbors (K animals with the smallest distances) to the new animal. For example, if we set K to 5, we would consider the five animals that are most similar to the new animal in terms of their feature values.

Next, we count the number of animals from each class among the K nearest neighbors. The class with the highest count becomes the predicted class for the new animal. In case of a tie, we can use a voting mechanism or other tie-breaking strategies to determine the final prediction.

Choosing the Value of K

The choice of K is crucial in K-NN since it determines the influence of the neighbors on the classification. If we choose a small K, the classification may be more sensitive

MACHINE LEARNING ALGORITHMS

to noise in the data, resulting in higher variance. On the other hand, a large K may lead to over-generalization and lower flexibility.

To determine the optimal value of K, we can perform a hyperparameter tuning process. This involves splitting the labeled data into training and validation sets, and training multiple models with different values of K. We then select the value of K that produces the best performance on the validation set, such as the highest accuracy or F1 score.

Strengths and Weaknesses of K-NN

There are several advantages of using the K-NN algorithm. Firstly, it is easy to understand and implement, making it a good choice for beginners in machine learning. Additionally, K-NN can handle both binary and multiclass classification problems.

However, K-NN also has some limitations. Firstly, it can be computationally expensive when dealing with large datasets or high-dimensional feature spaces since it requires calculating distances for each data point. Furthermore, K-NN is sensitive to the choice of distance metric and the scaling of features. Therefore, it is crucial to preprocess the data and normalize the features to ensure accurate results.

Real-World Applications

K-NN has found numerous applications in various fields. Let's explore a few examples:

- **Healthcare:** K-NN can be used in medical diagnosis by classifying patients based on their symptoms and medical history. It can help identify diseases and suggest appropriate treatments.

- **Recommendation Systems:** K-NN is utilized in recommendation systems to suggest products, movies, or music to users based on their preferences and similarities with other users.

- **Image Recognition:** K-NN can be employed in image recognition tasks to classify images into different categories, such as face recognition, object detection, and image clustering.

- **Text Classification:** K-NN is applied in natural language processing tasks, such as sentiment analysis, spam detection, and topic classification. It can classify text documents based on their word frequencies or semantic similarities.

Conclusion

K-Nearest Neighbors is a powerful and intuitive algorithm for classification tasks. By leveraging the concept of proximity in feature space, it provides a simple yet effective method for making predictions. Although it has certain limitations, K-NN finds wide-ranging applications across various industries and domains. Whether you're classifying animals or diagnosing diseases, K-NN can be a valuable tool in your machine learning toolkit.

So, next time you encounter a new data point and want to predict its class, remember to trust your nearest neighbors, because sometimes in this complex world of artificial intelligence, the answers are just a stone's throw away.

Exercises

1. Consider a dataset of online movie ratings, with features such as genre, duration, and user ratings. Using K-NN, build a classification model to predict whether a user will like a particular movie based on the given features.

2. Research and discuss other distance metrics commonly used in K-NN, such as Manhattan distance and cosine similarity. How do they differ from the Euclidean distance?

3. Explore the concept of weighted K-NN, where the influence of each neighbor is determined by their distance from the new data point. Implement and compare the performance of weighted and non-weighted K-NN on a classification problem of your choice.

Resources

- Raschka, S., & Mirjalili, V. (2017). *Python Machine Learning*. Packt Publishing.

- Hastie, T., Tibshirani, R., & Friedman, J. (2009). *The elements of statistical learning: data mining, inference, and prediction*. Springer Science & Business Media.

- Cover, T., & Hart, P. (1967). Nearest neighbor pattern classification. *IEEE Transactions on Information Theory*, 13(1), 21-27.

Remember, in the world of K-Nearest Neighbors, the distance between you and success can be narrowed down by the wisdom of your neighbors!

Clustering Algorithms

Clustering is a fundamental technique in machine learning and data analysis that aims to group similar data points together based on their characteristics. In this section, we will explore various clustering algorithms, their principles, and applications. Clustering algorithms play a crucial role in pattern recognition, anomaly detection, customer segmentation, and many other fields. So, buckle up and get ready to dive into the exciting world of clustering!

Introduction to Clustering

Clustering is the process of dividing a dataset into groups, called clusters, where data points within each cluster are more similar to each other than to those in other clusters. This unsupervised learning approach helps identify hidden patterns and structures in data without the need for predefined labels or categories. Clustering is widely used in exploratory data analysis and is often one of the first steps in understanding a dataset.

K-Means Clustering

One of the most popular and widely used clustering algorithms is the K-means clustering algorithm. The goal of K-means is to partition the data into K clusters, where K is a predefined number. The algorithm starts by randomly choosing K cluster centroids, which are the centers of the clusters. It then iteratively assigns each data point to the nearest centroid and updates the centroids based on the newly assigned data points. This process continues until the centroids no longer move significantly.

Let's take an example to understand how K-means clustering works. Suppose we have a dataset of customer transactions, and we want to group similar customers based on their purchase behavior. We can apply K-means clustering by considering each customer as a data point and their purchase history as features. The algorithm will identify clusters with similar purchasing patterns, allowing us to target specific customer segments with personalized marketing campaigns.

However, there are a few things to keep in mind when using K-means clustering. First, the algorithm is sensitive to the initial selection of centroids, which may lead to different results. To mitigate this issue, the algorithm is often run multiple times with different random initializations. Second, the number of clusters, K, needs to be predefined, which can be challenging if there is no prior knowledge about the data. Various methods, such as the elbow method or silhouette analysis, can help determine an optimal value for K.

Hierarchical Clustering

Another popular clustering algorithm is hierarchical clustering, which creates a tree-like structure, called a dendrogram, to represent the relationships between data points. There are two types of hierarchical clustering: agglomerative and divisive. Agglomerative clustering starts with each data point as a separate cluster and then repeatedly merges the closest pairs of clusters until only one cluster remains. Divisive clustering, on the other hand, begins with all the data points in a single cluster and progressively splits them into smaller clusters.

Hierarchical clustering has numerous applications, such as analyzing DNA sequences, social network analysis, and image segmentation. One advantage of hierarchical clustering is that it does not require the number of clusters to be predefined. Instead, the dendrogram provides a visual representation of the clustering structure, allowing users to choose the desired number of clusters by cutting the dendrogram at a specific level.

Density-Based Clustering

Density-based clustering algorithms, such as DBSCAN (Density-Based Spatial Clustering of Applications with Noise), focus on identifying areas of high density in the data and separating them from areas of low density. Unlike K-means and hierarchical clustering, density-based algorithms can discover clusters of arbitrary shape and handle noise effectively. DBSCAN, for example, defines clusters as areas of the data space where there is a sufficient density of data points.

DBSCAN works by defining two parameters: epsilon (ε), which specifies the distance within which data points are considered neighbors, and minPts, the minimum number of neighbors required for a point to be considered a core point. Points that do not meet the criteria are classified as noise. DBSCAN starts by randomly selecting a data point and expanding the cluster by connecting neighboring points within ε distance. This process continues until no more neighbors can be added to the cluster.

Density-based clustering is useful for detecting clusters of varying shapes and sizes, making it applicable to a wide range of domains. For instance, it can be used to analyze network traffic to identify abnormal patterns that may indicate cyber attacks or to cluster tweets based on their content to discover emerging topics in social media.

Clustering Evaluation

Evaluating the quality of clustering results is essential to assess the algorithm's performance and choose the most suitable approach for a given dataset. There are various metrics to measure the effectiveness of clustering algorithms, such as the Silhouette coefficient and the Davies-Bouldin index.

The Silhouette coefficient quantifies how well each data point fits into its assigned cluster compared to other clusters. It ranges from -1 to 1, with values closer to 1 indicating that data points are well clustered and values close to -1 suggesting that data points might be assigned to the wrong clusters.

The Davies-Bouldin index, on the other hand, measures the similarity between clusters based on their centroids and scatter. A lower index value indicates better separation between clusters.

When evaluating clustering results, it is also important to consider domain-specific knowledge and understand the context in which the clustering is performed. Visualizing the clusters, analyzing cluster characteristics, and interpreting the results in the context of the problem domain can provide valuable insights.

Clustering in Action

Let's explore a real-world example to see how clustering algorithms can be applied in practice. Imagine you are working for a ridesharing company, and you want to identify user segments based on their travel patterns. By clustering user data, you can tailor your marketing strategies, offer personalized incentives, and improve customer experience.

You start by collecting data on users' trip history, including distance traveled, total fare, and number of rides taken. You then apply K-means clustering to group users into segments based on these features. The clustering algorithm identifies four distinct segments: frequent riders, long-distance travelers, budget-conscious users, and occasional riders. Armed with this knowledge, you can now design targeted marketing campaigns for each segment, such as offering discounts to frequent riders or promoting luxury rides to long-distance travelers.

It is worth noting that clustering is an iterative process, and the results may need refinement based on domain knowledge and continuous experimentation. It is crucial to regularly update and reevaluate the clustering algorithm's performance to ensure that it adapts to changes in user behavior and business objectives.

Conclusion

Clustering algorithms provide powerful tools for analyzing and discovering hidden patterns in data. From K-means to hierarchical and density-based clustering, each algorithm offers unique features and advantages. Understanding the principles, pros, and cons of different clustering techniques is essential for choosing the most appropriate approach for a given problem.

In this section, we have explored the fundamentals of clustering algorithms, their applications, and evaluation metrics. However, this is just the tip of the iceberg. Clustering is a vast field with ongoing research and advancements. So, if you are intrigued by the fascinating world of clustering, keep exploring, experimenting, and pushing the boundaries of what is possible with data and artificial intelligence!

MACHINE LEARNING ALGORITHMS

Dimensionality Reduction

Dimensionality reduction is a crucial technique in machine learning and data analysis. It addresses the challenge of working with high-dimensional data by reducing the number of input variables while retaining important information. In this section, we will discuss the concepts, methods, and applications of dimensionality reduction.

Motivation

High-dimensional data poses several challenges. As the number of variables or features increases, the complexity of the data increases exponentially. This can lead to overfitting, increased computational complexity, and difficulty in visualizing and interpreting the data. Moreover, many machine learning algorithms struggle to perform well when the number of features is larger than the number of observations.

Dimensionality reduction techniques aim to alleviate these challenges by transforming the data into a lower-dimensional space while preserving essential information. This reduction in dimensionality provides several benefits, including improved model performance, faster computation, better data visualization, and enhanced interpretability.

Principal Component Analysis (PCA)

One of the most widely used dimensionality reduction techniques is Principal Component Analysis (PCA). PCA finds a new set of variables, called principal components, that are a linear combination of the original features. These components are orthogonal and ordered in terms of the explained variance, with the first component capturing the most variance in the data.

The process of PCA involves the following steps:

1. Standardize the features to have zero mean and unit variance. This step ensures that each feature contributes equally to the PCA.

2. Compute the covariance matrix of the standardized data. The covariance matrix describes the relationships between features.

3. Calculate the eigenvectors and eigenvalues of the covariance matrix. The eigenvectors represent the directions of maximum variance, while the eigenvalues indicate the amount of variance captured by each eigenvector.

4. Select the top k eigenvectors based on their corresponding eigenvalues. These eigenvectors form the new lower-dimensional space.

5. Project the original data onto the selected eigenvectors to obtain the transformed feature space.

PCA has numerous applications, including data compression, feature extraction, and data visualization. It is particularly useful when dealing with highly correlated features or when the dimensions represent noise or redundancy in the data.

Multidimensional Scaling (MDS)

Multidimensional Scaling (MDS) is another dimensionality reduction technique that emphasizes the preservation of pairwise distances between data points. MDS aims to represent high-dimensional data in a lower-dimensional space while retaining the original pairwise dissimilarity or similarity relationships.

The steps involved in MDS are as follows:

1. Define a dissimilarity measure between pairs of data points. This measure could be based on Euclidean distance, correlation, or any other suitable metric.

2. Construct a dissimilarity matrix that represents the pairwise distances between all data points.

3. Compute the low-dimensional embedding that best approximates the dissimilarity matrix. This embedding can be achieved by minimizing an objective function, such as the stress function.

4. Visualize the low-dimensional representation of the data, typically in two or three dimensions.

MDS is commonly used in fields such as psychology, sociology, and marketing research, where the focus is on understanding and visualizing relationships among objects or entities based on their similarities or dissimilarities.

t-Distributed Stochastic Neighbor Embedding (t-SNE)

t-Distributed Stochastic Neighbor Embedding (t-SNE) is a nonlinear dimensionality reduction technique that is particularly effective at visualizing

MACHINE LEARNING ALGORITHMS

high-dimensional data in two or three dimensions. It is especially useful for exploring complex structures and identifying clusters or patterns in the data.

The key idea behind t-SNE is to model the similarity between high-dimensional data points using a t-distribution, which enables the preservation of local structures in the low-dimensional representation. The algorithm iteratively minimizes the divergence between the joint distributions of the high-dimensional and low-dimensional data.

The steps involved in t-SNE are as follows:

1. Compute pairwise similarities between data points in the high-dimensional space. Gaussian similarity measures, such as the perplexity-based approach, are commonly used.

2. Initialize the low-dimensional representation of the data randomly.

3. Define the similarity between data points in the low-dimensional space using a t-distribution.

4. Optimize the locations of the low-dimensional points to minimize the divergence between the high-dimensional and low-dimensional similarity distributions.

t-SNE is widely used in various domains, including image recognition, natural language processing, and bioinformatics. It has the advantage of preserving both global and local structures, making it ideal for visualizing complex data sets.

Applications and Considerations

Dimensionality reduction techniques find applications in various domains, such as image and video processing, genomics, text mining, and recommendation systems. By reducing the dimensionality, these techniques enable faster processing, improved model performance, and enhanced interpretability.

However, it is important to consider several factors when applying dimensionality reduction:

- Loss of information: Dimensionality reduction inevitably leads to some loss of information. It is essential to assess the impact of this loss and ensure that critical information is not discarded.

- Interpretability: While dimensionality reduction improves interpretability, it is crucial to strike a balance between interpretability and performance.

Highly complex data may require more advanced techniques that sacrifice some interpretability.

- Choosing the right technique: Different dimensionality reduction techniques have specific assumptions and limitations. It is crucial to understand the characteristics of the data and select the most appropriate technique accordingly.

In conclusion, dimensionality reduction is a powerful tool for managing high-dimensional data in machine learning and data analysis. Techniques such as PCA, MDS, and t-SNE enable us to transform and visualize complex data, ultimately leading to better understanding and decision-making.

Key Takeaways:

- Dimensionality reduction reduces the number of variables in high-dimensional data while preserving essential information.
- Principal Component Analysis (PCA) is a widely used technique that finds a new set of variables, called principal components, capturing the most variance in the data.
- Multidimensional Scaling (MDS) focuses on preserving pairwise distances between data points, useful for understanding relationships and visualizing similarities or dissimilarities.
- t-Distributed Stochastic Neighbor Embedding (t-SNE) is a nonlinear technique that excels at visualizing high-dimensional data in two or three dimensions while preserving complex structures.
- Considerations when applying dimensionality reduction include loss of information, interpretability, and choosing the appropriate technique based on the data characteristics.

Resources:

- Bishop, C.M. (2006). Pattern Recognition and Machine Learning. Springer.
- Hastie, T., Tibshirani, R., & Friedman, J. (2009). The Elements of Statistical Learning: Data Mining, Inference, and Prediction. Springer.
- VanderPlas, J. (2016). Python Data Science Handbook. O'Reilly Media.

Exercises:

1. Explain why high-dimensional data can lead to overfitting and why dimensionality reduction is useful in mitigating this problem.

2. Suppose you have a dataset with 100 features. How would you decide on the appropriate number of principal components to retain in PCA? Discuss any relevant evaluation techniques.

3. Give an example of a domain where MDS would be a suitable dimensionality reduction technique and explain why.

4. Compare and contrast PCA and t-SNE in terms of their objectives, assumptions, and applications.

Remember, the key to mastering dimensionality reduction is practice and exploration. So get your hands dirty, try different techniques on diverse datasets, and uncover the underlying patterns in your data. Happy reducing, folks!

Model Evaluation and Selection

Evaluation Metrics

Evaluation metrics are essential in assessing the performance and effectiveness of machine learning models. They allow us to measure how well a model is performing and compare different models to select the best one for a specific task. In this section, we will explore some common evaluation metrics used in machine learning and discuss their interpretation and significance.

Accuracy

Accuracy is perhaps the most intuitive and commonly used metric for evaluating the performance of a classification model. It measures the proportion of correctly predicted instances out of the total number of instances in the dataset. Mathematically, accuracy is defined as:

$$\text{Accuracy} = \frac{\text{Number of Correct Predictions}}{\text{Total Number of Predictions}}$$

While accuracy is easy to understand, it can be misleading in some cases, especially when the dataset is imbalanced. For example, if we have a dataset with 90% of instances belonging to class A and 10% belonging to class B, a model that always predicts class A will achieve an accuracy of 90%. However, this model fails to capture the minority class, class B, effectively. Therefore, accuracy alone may not provide a complete picture of a model's performance.

Precision, Recall, and F1 Score

Precision, recall, and F1 score are commonly used evaluation metrics for imbalanced datasets or when the cost of false positives and false negatives differs. These metrics are derived from a confusion matrix, which summarizes the number of true positives (TP), false positives (FP), true negatives (TN), and false negatives (FN) produced by a classification model.

Precision measures the proportion of correctly predicted positive instances out of all instances predicted as positive. It is defined as:

$$\text{Precision} = \frac{TP}{TP + FP}$$

Recall, also known as sensitivity or true positive rate, measures the proportion of correctly predicted positive instances out of all actual positive instances. It is defined as:

$$\text{Recall} = \frac{TP}{TP + FN}$$

The F1 score is the harmonic mean of precision and recall, providing a balanced measure that combines both metrics into a single value. It is defined as:

$$\text{F1 score} = 2 \times \frac{\text{Precision} \times \text{Recall}}{\text{Precision} + \text{Recall}}$$

Precision and recall are particularly useful when dealing with imbalanced datasets, as they focus on the actual positive instances. For example, in medical diagnosis, where the occurrence of rare diseases is low, we are often more concerned with the ability of a model to correctly identify positive instances rather than overall accuracy.

Receiver Operating Characteristic (ROC) Curve

The Receiver Operating Characteristic (ROC) curve is a graphical representation of the performance of a binary classification model across a range of classification thresholds. The ROC curve is created by plotting the true positive rate (TPR) against the false positive rate (FPR) at various threshold settings.

The TPR, also known as recall or sensitivity, is defined as:

MODEL EVALUATION AND SELECTION

$$\text{TPR} = \frac{TP}{TP + FN}$$

The FPR is defined as:

$$\text{FPR} = \frac{FP}{FP + TN}$$

The ROC curve provides a visual representation of the trade-off between the true positive rate and the false positive rate. A perfect model would have an ROC curve that passes through the point (0,1), indicating a high true positive rate and a low false positive rate across all threshold settings. The area under the ROC curve (AUC-ROC) is commonly used as a metric to quantify the overall performance of a model. A higher AUC-ROC value indicates a better-performing model.

Mean Squared Error (MSE)

Mean Squared Error (MSE) is a common metric used to evaluate regression models. It measures the average squared difference between the predicted and actual values. Mathematically, MSE is defined as:

$$\text{MSE} = \frac{1}{n} \sum_{i=1}^{n} (y_i - \hat{y}_i)^2$$

where y_i is the actual value and $\hat{y}_i$ is the predicted value for the ith instance. Since the squared differences are summed up, larger errors are penalized more than smaller errors. MSE is sensitive to outliers, and if the dataset contains outliers, it may not be the best evaluation metric.

Mean Absolute Error (MAE)

Mean Absolute Error (MAE) is another metric commonly used for regression models. It measures the average absolute difference between the predicted and actual values. Mathematically, MAE is defined as:

$$\text{MAE} = \frac{1}{n} \sum_{i=1}^{n} |y_i - \hat{y}_i|$$

MAE is less sensitive to outliers than MSE since it takes the absolute differences rather than squaring them. However, it does not penalize large errors as heavily as MSE.

Root Mean Squared Error (RMSE)

Root Mean Squared Error (RMSE) is a variant of the MSE metric commonly used in regression models. It represents the square root of the mean squared difference between the predicted and actual values. Mathematically, RMSE is defined as:

$$\text{RMSE} = \sqrt{\frac{1}{n}\sum_{i=1}^{n}(y_i - \hat{y}_i)^2}$$

RMSE is often preferred over MSE as it is in the same units as the target variable, making it more interpretable.

Coefficient of Determination (R-squared)

The Coefficient of Determination, also known as R-squared or the coefficient of multiple determination, is a metric used to assess the goodness of fit of a regression model. It measures the proportion of the variance in the dependent variable that can be explained by the independent variables. R-squared ranges from 0 to 1, with higher values indicating a better fit. Mathematically, R-squared is defined as:

$$R^2 = 1 - \frac{\sum_{i=1}^{n}(y_i - \hat{y}_i)^2}{\sum_{i=1}^{n}(y_i - \bar{y})^2}$$

where y_i is the actual value, $\hat{y}_i$ is the predicted value, and $\bar{y}$ is the mean of the actual values.

R-squared is a useful metric to understand how well the regression model captures the variation in the dependent variable. However, it is important to note that R-squared alone does not indicate the quality of the model in predicting new data. It is always advisable to consider other evaluation metrics, such as RMSE, in conjunction with R-squared.

Cross-Validation

Cross-validation is a crucial technique in machine learning for assessing the performance of a predictive model. It is used to estimate how well the model is likely to perform on unseen data. In this section, we will explore the concept of cross-validation, its different variants, and how to implement it effectively.

The Need for Cross-Validation

When developing a machine learning model, it is important to evaluate its performance accurately. The traditional approach is to train the model on a subset of the available data, known as the training set, and then test its performance on a separate subset, known as the test set. However, this approach has some limitations.

Firstly, the performance of the model on the test set may not accurately represent its performance on new, unseen data. This is because the test set is just one randomly chosen subset of the data, and the model's performance may be overly optimistic or pessimistic depending on the specific data points in the test set.

Secondly, when working with limited data, splitting it into two separate sets may lead to a significant reduction in the amount of data available for training the model. This can result in suboptimal performance and a less reliable evaluation of the model's performance.

Cross-validation addresses these issues by using the available data more efficiently and providing a more robust estimate of the model's performance.

K-Fold Cross-Validation

One of the most commonly used variants of cross-validation is K-fold cross-validation. In K-fold cross-validation, the data is divided into K subsets of approximately equal size, called folds. The model is then trained and tested K times, with each fold being used as the test set once, while the remaining folds are used as the training set. The performance of the model is evaluated by averaging the results across all K iterations.

The steps involved in K-fold cross-validation are as follows:

1. Shuffle the data randomly to ensure that the folds are representative of the entire dataset.

2. Divide the data into K folds.

3. For each iteration:

    a) Use K-1 folds for training and the remaining fold for testing.

    b) Train the model using the training data.

    c) Evaluate the model's performance on the test fold.

4. Calculate the average performance metric across all K iterations to obtain the final performance estimate.

K-fold cross-validation provides a more reliable estimate of the model's performance because it uses multiple test sets, each of which contains a different combination of data points. This helps to mitigate the impact of any particular subset of data on the model's performance.

Benefits and Limitations of K-Fold Cross-Validation

K-fold cross-validation offers several benefits over traditional train-test splitting. Firstly, it allows for a more efficient use of the available data by utilizing all data points for both training and testing. This leads to a more reliable performance estimate, especially when working with limited data.

Secondly, K-fold cross-validation provides a more robust assessment of the model's performance by averaging the results across multiple test sets. This helps to reduce the impact of random variability in the test set on the performance estimate.

However, it is important to note that K-fold cross-validation is not without its limitations. Firstly, it can be computationally expensive, especially for large datasets or complex models. Training and evaluating the model K times can significantly increase the computational cost.

Additionally, in some cases, the data may contain inherent dependencies or temporal patterns that are not captured by random shuffling. In such situations, K-fold cross-validation may not provide an accurate estimate of the model's performance.

Stratified Cross-Validation

Stratified cross-validation is a variant of K-fold cross-validation that addresses the issue of imbalanced class distributions in the data. In imbalanced datasets, where the number of instances in different classes is significantly different, traditional cross-validation may result in inaccurate performance estimates.

Stratified cross-validation ensures that the class distribution is preserved in each fold by randomly sampling instances from each class. This helps to ensure that each fold is representative of the overall distribution of classes in the data.

Nested Cross-Validation

Nested cross-validation is a technique used to tune model hyperparameters while still obtaining an unbiased estimate of the model's performance. It involves using an outer loop of K-fold cross-validation to evaluate the model's performance on the test set and an inner loop of K-fold cross-validation to tune the hyperparameters.

In each iteration of the outer loop, the model is trained and tuned using the inner loop. The performance of the tuned model is then evaluated on the test set, providing an unbiased estimate of how well the model will generalize to new, unseen data.

Nested cross-validation is particularly useful when the model's performance is sensitive to the choice of hyperparameters. It helps to avoid overfitting the hyperparameters to the test set and provides a more reliable estimate of the model's performance.

Conclusion

Cross-validation is a powerful technique for assessing the performance of machine learning models. It addresses the limitations of traditional train-test splitting and provides a more reliable estimate of the model's performance on unseen data.

K-fold cross-validation is a commonly used variant that uses multiple test sets to evaluate the model's performance. It offers several benefits, such as efficient data utilization and robust performance estimation. Stratified cross-validation and nested cross-validation are additional variants that are useful in specific scenarios.

By using cross-validation, machine learning practitioners can make more informed decisions about model selection, hyperparameter tuning, and ultimately, the deployment of AI systems. It is an essential tool in the toolkit of any data scientist or machine learning engineer.

Exercises

1. Discuss the advantages and disadvantages of K-fold cross-validation compared to hold-out validation.
2. What are the potential problems associated with using traditional cross-validation on imbalanced datasets? How does stratified cross-validation address these problems?
3. Explain the difference between model selection and hyperparameter tuning. How does nested cross-validation help in both of these tasks?
4. Can you think of a real-world example where cross-validation would be valuable in assessing the performance of a machine learning model?

Resources

1. Machine Learning Mastery: Jason Brownlee's blog provides a comprehensive guide to machine learning techniques, including cross-validation. Available at: `https://machinelearningmastery.com/`

2. Scikit-learn documentation: Scikit-learn is a popular machine learning library that provides built-in support for cross-validation. The documentation includes examples and explanations of various cross-validation techniques. Available at: https://scikit-learn.org/stable/

3. "Hands-On Machine Learning with Scikit-Learn, Keras, and TensorFlow" by Aurélien Géron: This book offers a practical approach to machine learning, including a detailed explanation of cross-validation. It provides examples and code snippets to help you implement cross-validation effectively.

Model Selection Techniques

In machine learning, model selection plays a crucial role in ensuring that the chosen model performs well on new, unseen data. In this section, we will explore various techniques used for model selection and discuss their advantages and disadvantages. We will also delve into the concept of overfitting and regularization, which are important considerations in model selection.

Evaluation Metrics

Before we dive into model selection techniques, let's first understand evaluation metrics that are used to assess the performance of machine learning models. These metrics provide a quantitative measure of how well a model is performing.

One commonly used evaluation metric for classification tasks is accuracy, which calculates the proportion of correctly classified instances over the total number of instances in the dataset. Accuracy is a simple and intuitive metric; however, it may not be the best choice when dealing with imbalanced datasets.

Another useful metric is precision and recall. Precision measures the proportion of true positive predictions out of all positive predictions, while recall calculates the proportion of true positive predictions out of all actual positive instances. These metrics are particularly useful when the cost of false positives and false negatives is significantly different.

For regression tasks, the mean squared error (MSE) is often used as an evaluation metric. It measures the average squared difference between the predicted and actual values. The lower the MSE, the better the model performance.

It is worth noting that the choice of evaluation metric depends on the specific problem domain and the associated costs of different types of errors.

Cross-Validation

Cross-validation is a technique used to evaluate the performance of machine learning models. It involves splitting the dataset into multiple subsets, called folds. The model is trained on a subset of the data (training set) and evaluated on the remaining data (validation set). This process is repeated several times by changing the folds, and the average performance across all iterations is used as an estimate of how well the model will perform on new, unseen data.

The most common type of cross-validation is k-fold cross-validation, where the data is divided into k equal-sized folds. The model is trained on k-1 folds and tested on the remaining fold. This process is repeated k times, with each fold being used as the validation set exactly once. The final performance metric is the average of the metrics obtained in each iteration.

One advantage of cross-validation is that it provides a more robust estimate of model performance compared to a single train-test split. It also helps in detecting overfitting, as a model that performs well on the training set but poorly on the validation set indicates overfitting.

Model Selection Techniques

Now that we have a better understanding of evaluation metrics and cross-validation, let's explore some model selection techniques:

1. Grid Search: Grid search is a brute-force approach to model selection. It involves defining a grid of hyperparameters and exhaustively searching through all possible combinations using cross-validation. The combination that yields the best performance metric is selected as the optimal set of hyperparameters.

2. Randomized Search: Randomized search is similar to grid search, but instead of exhaustively searching through all combinations, it randomly samples hyperparameters from a predefined search space. This approach can be more efficient when dealing with a large number of hyperparameters and reduces the computational cost compared to grid search.

3. Bayesian Optimization: Bayesian optimization is a sequential model-based optimization technique that incorporates prior knowledge of hyperparameter performance. It uses a probabilistic surrogate model to model the hyperparameter space and performs guided exploration based on the expected improvement. Bayesian optimization requires fewer iterations compared to exhaustive search methods and can handle noisy evaluations.

4. Ensemble Methods: Ensemble methods combine multiple models to achieve better predictive performance. Instead of selecting a single model,

ensemble methods create an ensemble of models and make predictions by aggregating the individual predictions. Techniques like bagging and boosting are commonly used in ensemble learning. Ensemble methods tend to be more robust and less prone to overfitting.

Overfitting and Regularization

Overfitting occurs when a model is overly complex and captures the noise or random fluctuations in the training data, leading to poor generalization on unseen data. Regularization techniques are used to mitigate overfitting by introducing additional constraints on the model.

One commonly used regularization technique is L1 and L2 regularization, also known as LASSO and Ridge regression, respectively. L1 regularization adds a penalty term to the loss function that encourages sparsity by shrinking some of the model coefficients to zero. On the other hand, L2 regularization adds a penalty term that shrinks the magnitude of the model coefficients without enforcing sparsity.

Another technique is early stopping, which stops the training process when the performance on the validation set starts to degrade. Early stopping helps prevent overfitting by avoiding unnecessary iterations that may lead to over-optimization on the training set.

Dropout regularization is a technique commonly used in neural networks. It randomly drops out a fraction of the network units during training, forcing the remaining units to learn more robust and generalizable features.

Summary

In this section, we have explored various model selection techniques and discussed the importance of evaluation metrics and cross-validation. We have also delved into regularization techniques to mitigate overfitting. Remember that the choice of model selection technique depends on the problem domain, the available resources, and the desired trade-offs. By carefully selecting and evaluating models, we can harness the power of machine learning to make informed decisions and unleash the full potential of artificial intelligence.

Now that you've mastered model selection techniques, let's move on to the exciting world of big data and its applications in AI. Buckle up and get ready for some data-driven dominance!

Overfitting and Regularization

When we train a machine learning model, our goal is to find a balance between fitting the training data well and not overfitting to it. Overfitting occurs when a model becomes too complex and starts to memorize the training data instead of learning general patterns. This can lead to poor performance on new, unseen data.

The Problem of Overfitting

To understand overfitting, let's consider a classic example: predicting house prices based on features such as square footage, number of bedrooms, and location. If we fit a linear regression model to the training data, it might look something like this:

$$\hat{y} = w_0 + w_1 x_1 + w_2 x_2 + \ldots + w_n x_n$$

where $\hat{y}$ is the predicted house price, $x_1, x_2, \ldots, x_n$ are the input features, and $w_0, w_1, w_2, \ldots, w_n$ are the weights of the model.

Now, if we have a small training dataset, our model might not capture all the complexities of the real world. In an attempt to fit the data perfectly, it may end up creating a wiggly line that passes through each data point. This is a classic example of overfitting, as the model fails to capture the true underlying patterns and instead fits the noise in the training data.

Why Overfitting is a Problem

Overfitting is a problem because it leads to poor generalization. When a model overfits, it becomes very specific to the training data, and when faced with new, unseen data, it fails to make accurate predictions. In other words, it doesn't understand the underlying patterns well enough to make reliable predictions on unseen examples.

This is especially problematic in machine learning applications where the goal is to make accurate predictions on unseen data. For example, in our housing price prediction problem, the goal is to accurately predict the price of a new house that wasn't in the training data. If our model overfits, it won't be able to make accurate predictions on this new house.

Regularization Techniques

Regularization is a set of techniques used to prevent overfitting and improve the generalization performance of machine learning models. By introducing additional constraints on the model, we can reduce its complexity and force it to focus on the most important features.

L2 Regularization (Ridge Regression): One common regularization technique is L2 regularization, often referred to as ridge regression. It works by adding a penalty term to the loss function that discourages the weights from growing too large.

The L2 regularization term is calculated as the sum of the squares of the weights multiplied by a regularization parameter λ:

$$L2 \text{ regularization term} = \lambda \sum_{i=1}^{n} w_i^2$$

where w_i are the weights of the model. The regularization parameter λ controls the amount of regularization applied, with larger values resulting in more regularization.

By adding the L2 regularization term to the loss function, we encourage the model to find a balance between fitting the data and keeping the weights small. This helps prevent overfitting by reducing the complexity of the model.

L1 Regularization (Lasso Regression): Another commonly used regularization technique is L1 regularization, also known as lasso regression. Like L2 regularization, it adds a penalty term to the loss function, but instead of the sum of squared weights, it uses the sum of the absolute values of the weights:

$$L1 \text{ regularization term} = \lambda \sum_{i=1}^{n} |w_i|$$

L1 regularization promotes sparsity by encouraging some of the weights to become exactly zero, effectively selecting a subset of the most important features. This can be useful in feature selection, as it helps identify the most relevant variables.

Regularization Strength: Finding the Right Balance

When applying regularization, it's important to find the right balance. Too much regularization, and the model becomes too simple and underfits the data. Too little regularization, and the model remains too complex and overfits the data.

The choice of the regularization parameter λ determines the strength of regularization. A common approach is to use cross-validation to tune the value of λ that gives the best performance on validation data. By trying different values of λ

MODEL EVALUATION AND SELECTION

and evaluating the model's performance, we can find the optimal level of regularization.

Other Regularization Techniques

In addition to L2 and L1 regularization, there are other regularization techniques that can be used to prevent overfitting:

Elastic Net Regularization: Elastic Net regularization combines L1 and L2 regularization. It adds both the sum of squares of weights and the sum of absolute values of weights to the loss function. Elastic Net offers a compromise between the feature selection ability of L1 regularization and the ability of L2 regularization to handle correlated features.

Dropout: Dropout is a technique commonly used in neural networks to prevent overfitting. During training, randomly selected neurons are ignored or "dropped out" with a certain probability. This forces the network to learn redundant representations and prevents it from relying too heavily on any particular neuron.

Summary and Key Points

Overfitting occurs when a model becomes too complex and starts to memorize the training data instead of learning general patterns, leading to poor performance on new data.

Regularization techniques such as L2 regularization (ridge regression) and L1 regularization (lasso regression) help prevent overfitting by adding penalty terms to the loss function.

The choice of the regularization parameter determines the strength of regularization, and it can be tuned using techniques like cross-validation.

Other regularization techniques include Elastic Net regularization, which combines L1 and L2 regularization, and dropout, which is commonly used in neural networks.

Finding the right balance of regularization is crucial to obtain a model that generalizes well to unseen data.

Exercises

1. Imagine you are tasked with predicting whether a customer will churn or not based on their past behavior. Design a regularization strategy to train a logistic regression model on this problem.

2. You are given a dataset with 50 features and 1000 examples. How would you use regularization to identify the most relevant features for the task at hand?

3. Take a look at a real-world example of overfitting in any machine learning application you are interested in. Describe how the model's performance deteriorates on new, unseen data.

Additional Resources

If you want to dive deeper into the topic of overfitting and regularization, here are some recommended resources:

- "The Elements of Statistical Learning" by Trevor Hastie, Robert Tibshirani, and Jerome Friedman - "Pattern Recognition and Machine Learning" by Christopher M. Bishop - "Hands-On Machine Learning with Scikit-Learn and TensorFlow" by Aurélien Géron - Online courses on machine learning and regularization on platforms like Coursera and Udemy.

Big Data and AI

Introduction to Big Data

Characteristics of Big Data

Big data is a term that has gained significant attention in recent years, and for good reason. It refers to the vast and complex sets of data that are too large and diverse to be effectively managed and analyzed using traditional data processing techniques. In this section, we will explore the characteristics that define big data and set it apart from other types of data.

Volume

One of the primary characteristics of big data is its sheer volume. Big data sets often involve massive amounts of information that exceed the capacity of traditional data processing systems. This could be in the form of petabytes (one million gigabytes), exabytes (one billion gigabytes), or even zettabytes (one trillion gigabytes) of data. The exponential growth of digital information, fueled by advancements in technology and the increasing interconnectivity of devices, has contributed to the explosion of data volume.

To put this into perspective, consider the following examples:

- Social media platforms generate an enormous amount of data every second, with billions of users sharing posts, photos, and videos.

- E-commerce websites record vast amounts of customer information, including purchase history, preferences, and browsing behavior.

- Scientific research institutions collect massive datasets from experiments, simulations, and observations in fields such as genomics, astronomy, and particle physics.

Dealing with such large volumes of data presents challenges for data storage, processing, and analysis. Traditional database management systems often struggle to handle the scale and complexity of big data, necessitating the use of specialized technologies and tools.

Velocity

In addition to volume, big data is characterized by its velocity, which refers to the speed at which data is generated, captured, and processed. With the advent of real-time data streams and Internet of Things (IoT) devices, data is now being produced at an unprecedented rate.

Consider the following scenarios:

- Sensor networks in smart cities continuously collect data on various environmental parameters, such as temperature, air quality, and traffic flow.

- Financial institutions receive a constant stream of data on stock market transactions and financial news.

- Online platforms monitor user activity in real-time, capturing clicks, searches, and interactions.

To gain actionable insights from big data, it is crucial to process and analyze the data in near real-time. This requires efficient data processing techniques, scalable infrastructure, and powerful algorithms capable of handling high data velocities.

Variety

Another defining characteristic of big data is its variety. Big data is not limited to structured data, such as numerical or categorical values stored in traditional databases. Instead, it encompasses a wide range of data types, including text, images, audio, video, social media posts, sensor data, and more. These diverse data formats may be structured, semi-structured, or unstructured, requiring different approaches for storage, processing, and analysis.

Consider the following examples of varied data sources:

- Textual data from emails, documents, social media feeds, and customer reviews.

- Image and video data from surveillance cameras, drones, and medical imaging devices.

- Sensor data from IoT devices, such as temperature sensors, accelerometers, and GPS trackers.

The ability to handle and make sense of such diverse data sources is crucial for extracting valuable insights. It requires advanced techniques and algorithms to process unstructured data, such as natural language processing for text data or computer vision for image and video data.

Veracity

Veracity refers to the quality and trustworthiness of the data. In the context of big data, this characteristic becomes particularly relevant, as the sheer volume and variety of data can introduce uncertainties and inaccuracies. Big data sets often contain noise, outliers, missing values, and inconsistencies, which need to be addressed to ensure reliable analyses and decision-making.

Data veracity can be compromised by various factors, including:

- Data collection errors or sensor malfunctions, leading to erroneous or incomplete data.

- Inconsistencies and redundancies across different data sources or data silos.

- Data tampering or manipulation, intentionally or unintentionally, by human actors or automated processes.

- Privacy concerns and restrictions that limit access to certain data sources.

To ensure data quality and improve veracity, data cleaning and preprocessing techniques, such as outlier detection, imputation, and data fusion, are applied. Additionally, data governance practices, including data lineage tracking, audit trails, and data quality monitoring, play a crucial role in maintaining the integrity and trustworthiness of big data.

Value

The final characteristic of big data is its inherent value. The vast amount of data being generated has the potential to deliver valuable insights and drive informed decision-making across various domains. However, realizing this value is not automatic. It requires data analytics and machine learning techniques to extract actionable knowledge and derive meaningful interpretations from the data.

By uncovering patterns, relationships, and trends within big data, organizations can gain a competitive advantage, improve operational efficiency, and create new business opportunities. For instance:

- Retail companies can analyze customer purchase data to personalize marketing campaigns and recommend relevant products.
- Healthcare providers can leverage patient data to improve diagnostics, treatment plans, and public health interventions.
- Financial institutions can detect fraud patterns in real-time and enhance risk management strategies.

However, extracting value from big data is not without its challenges. The volume, velocity, and variety of data pose significant computational and analytical hurdles. Additionally, ensuring data privacy, security, and ethical use are essential considerations when dealing with sensitive or personal information.

Summary

In summary, big data is characterized by its volume, velocity, variety, veracity, and inherent value. The immense scale and complexity of big data present challenges and opportunities for data management, processing, and analysis. To harness the power of big data, organizations need to leverage advanced technologies, including distributed computing, machine learning, and data visualization. By doing so, they can unlock valuable insights, drive innovation, and gain a competitive edge in today's data-driven world.

Big Data Technologies and Tools

In today's data-driven world, the volume of data being generated is growing at an unprecedented rate. Organizations across various industries are grappling with the challenge of managing and analyzing massive amounts of data to extract meaningful insights. This has given rise to the need for big data technologies and tools that can handle the velocity, variety, and volume of data. In this section, we will explore the key technologies and tools used in the big data ecosystem.

Hadoop: Distributed File System

One of the foundational technologies in the big data landscape is Apache Hadoop. Hadoop is an open-source framework that enables the distributed storage and

INTRODUCTION TO BIG DATA 113

processing of large datasets across clusters of computers. At the core of Hadoop is the Hadoop Distributed File System (HDFS). HDFS breaks down large files into smaller blocks and distributes them across multiple machines in the cluster, providing fault tolerance and high availability.

Hadoop's distributed computing model allows for parallel processing of data across the cluster, making it ideal for handling big data workloads. Hadoop also provides a programming model called MapReduce, which allows developers to write distributed processing logic that can be executed in parallel across the cluster.

Spark: In-Memory Processing

Apache Spark is another powerful tool in the big data ecosystem that addresses the limitations of Hadoop's disk-based processing. Spark leverages in-memory processing to achieve faster data analysis and iterative machine learning algorithms. The core abstraction in Spark is the Resilient Distributed Dataset (RDD), which represents a fault-tolerant collection of elements that can be operated on in parallel.

Spark provides a rich set of libraries, including Spark SQL for SQL-based querying, Spark Streaming for real-time processing of data streams, and MLlib for scalable machine learning. By caching data in memory, Spark avoids the need to read and write data to disk, resulting in significant performance improvements.

NoSQL Databases

Traditional relational databases often struggle to handle the scale and variety of big data. NoSQL databases offer an alternative approach to data storage and retrieval that is better suited for big data workloads. These databases are designed to be horizontally-scalable, providing high-performance access to large volumes of data.

There are several types of NoSQL databases, including key-value stores, columnar databases, document databases, and graph databases. Each type has its own strengths and use cases. For example, key-value stores like Redis and Cassandra excel at handling high-volume writes and reads, making them suitable for real-time applications and caching. Document databases like MongoDB are well-suited for flexible and schema-less data models. Graph databases like Neo4j are optimized for storing and querying highly connected data, making them ideal for social networks and recommendation systems.

Data Processing Frameworks

To process and analyze big data efficiently, various data processing frameworks have emerged in recent years. These frameworks provide high-level abstractions and APIs that simplify the development of distributed data processing pipelines.

Apache Flink and Apache Beam are among the popular choices for stream processing, which involves continuously processing and analyzing data in real-time. Stream processing frameworks are essential for applications such as fraud detection, real-time monitoring, and sentiment analysis.

Apache Kafka, on the other hand, is a distributed messaging system that provides a scalable and fault-tolerant way to stream data between systems and applications. It acts as a publish-subscribe messaging system, enabling the decoupling of data producers and consumers.

Data Visualization Tools

Data visualization plays a crucial role in making sense of big data. It allows analysts and business users to explore and understand large datasets quickly. There are several powerful data visualization tools available that enable the creation of informative and visually-appealing dashboards and reports.

One popular tool is Tableau, which provides a user-friendly interface for creating interactive visualizations and dashboards. With Tableau, users can connect to various data sources, create visualizations using a drag-and-drop interface, and easily share insights with others.

Another widely-used tool is Power BI from Microsoft. Power BI offers similar capabilities to Tableau, allowing users to connect to different data sources, build interactive reports, and collaborate with colleagues. Power BI also integrates seamlessly with other Microsoft products like Excel and SharePoint.

Data Governance and Security

With the increasing concerns around data privacy and security, proper data governance and security practices are critical in the big data landscape. Organizations need to ensure that sensitive data is protected and accessed only by authorized personnel.

Tools like Apache Atlas provide metadata management and data lineage capabilities, allowing organizations to track the origin and flow of data. Apache Ranger, on the other hand, offers centralized security management for the Hadoop ecosystem, enabling fine-grained access control and policy enforcement.

Additionally, encryption techniques such as data masking and tokenization can be employed to protect sensitive data at rest and in transit. Data anonymization techniques like k-anonymity and differential privacy can help preserve privacy while still allowing for analysis.

INTRODUCTION TO BIG DATA   115

Cloud-based Big Data Services

To address the challenges of managing and scaling big data infrastructures, cloud-based services have emerged as a popular choice. Cloud platforms like Amazon Web Services (AWS), Google Cloud Platform (GCP), and Microsoft Azure provide a wide range of managed big data services that abstract away the complexities of infrastructure management.

For example, AWS offers services like Amazon S3 for scalable object storage, Amazon Redshift for data warehousing, and Amazon EMR for running big data frameworks like Hadoop and Spark. GCP provides services like BigQuery for ad hoc querying and analysis, and Cloud Dataflow for both stream and batch processing. Azure offers services like Azure Blob Storage for object storage and Azure Data Lake Analytics for scalable data processing.

By leveraging cloud-based big data services, organizations can focus on data analysis and application development without worrying about the underlying infrastructure.

Summary

In this section, we explored the key technologies and tools used in the big data ecosystem. We started with Hadoop and its distributed file system, which enables parallel processing of large datasets. We then discussed Spark, a powerful tool for in-memory data processing and analysis.

We also explored NoSQL databases, which provide scalable and flexible storage solutions for big data. We covered the different types of NoSQL databases, including key-value stores, columnar databases, document databases, and graph databases.

Next, we discussed data processing frameworks like Apache Flink and Apache Beam, which are critical for stream processing and real-time data analysis. We also mentioned Apache Kafka, a distributed messaging system that enables the reliable and scalable streaming of data.

Data visualization tools like Tableau and Power BI were highlighted, emphasizing their importance in presenting data insights effectively. We also touched upon data governance and security practices, including technologies like Apache Atlas and Apache Ranger.

Lastly, we explored the benefits of cloud-based big data services offered by AWS, GCP, and Azure, enabling organizations to leverage scalable and managed infrastructure for their big data workloads.

With the ever-growing volume of data, it is essential to stay up-to-date with the latest technologies and tools in the big data landscape. By harnessing the power of these technologies, organizations can unlock valuable insights and gain a competitive edge in today's data-driven world.

Exercises

1. Research and compare different NoSQL databases such as MongoDB, Cassandra, and Neo4j. What are their strengths and weaknesses? Provide real-world examples of applications for each type of database.

2. Explore the capabilities of Apache Flink and Apache Beam for stream processing. Develop a simple streaming application using either framework and analyze a real-time data stream of your choice.

3. Choose a data visualization tool of your preference (e.g., Tableau, Power BI) and create a dashboard that visualizes a dataset of your choice. Focus on creating informative and visually-appealing visualizations.

4. Investigate the data governance and security features offered by cloud-based big data services like AWS, GCP, and Azure. Compare and contrast the capabilities of these services in ensuring data privacy and compliance.

5. Brainstorm and discuss potential ethical considerations and societal implications associated with big data technologies and tools. Consider issues related to data privacy, algorithmic bias, and the impact on employment and society as a whole.

Applications of Big Data in AI

Big data has become a driving force behind the advancement of artificial intelligence (AI) techniques. With the enormous amount of data being generated every day, organizations and researchers are leveraging big data to develop innovative AI solutions that are transforming industries and pushing the boundaries of what is possible. In this section, we will explore some of the key applications of big data in AI and how they are revolutionizing various fields.

Predictive Analytics

Predictive analytics is one of the most prevalent applications of big data in AI. By analyzing large volumes of historical data, organizations can uncover patterns and trends that can help them make accurate predictions about future events or outcomes. This powerful capability has significant implications across different industries.

For example, in finance, big data analytics combined with AI algorithms can be used to predict stock market trends and make informed investment decisions. By analyzing past stock prices, trading volumes, financial statements, news sentiment, and other relevant data, AI models can identify patterns and make predictions on stock performance.

In marketing, predictive analytics allows organizations to better understand consumer behavior and preferences. By analyzing customer data such as purchase history, browsing behavior, demographics, and social media interactions, AI models can predict which products or services a customer is likely to purchase in the future. This information can be used to create personalized marketing campaigns and targeted advertisements, ultimately improving customer engagement and increasing sales.

Fraud Detection

Big data plays a crucial role in fraud detection, particularly in industries such as banking, insurance, and e-commerce. Traditional rule-based systems for fraud detection have limitations when it comes to handling large volumes of data and complex patterns. By leveraging big data and AI techniques, organizations can build robust fraud detection systems that can analyze vast amounts of transactional data in real time.

For instance, banks can use AI algorithms to analyze customer transactions and detect any suspicious activities. By comparing each transaction to historical data patterns, AI models can identify unusual patterns indicative of fraudulent activities, such as large withdrawals, transactions in foreign countries, or multiple small transactions within a short span of time.

Similarly, e-commerce platforms can use big data analytics and AI to detect fraudulent transactions. By analyzing various data points, such as user behavior, purchase history, IP addresses, and shipping addresses, AI models can identify patterns associated with fraudulent activities, such as identity theft or credit card fraud.

Healthcare Analytics

The healthcare industry generates vast amounts of data, including electronic health records, medical imaging, sensor data, and genomics data. Big data analytics combined with AI techniques have the potential to revolutionize healthcare by enabling better diagnosis, treatment, and patient care.

For example, big data analytics can be used to analyze patient data, including medical history, lab results, vital signs, and lifestyle data, to identify patterns and predict health risks. AI models can assist healthcare providers in early detection of diseases, recommending preventive measures, and developing personalized treatment plans.

Furthermore, AI algorithms can analyze medical imaging data, such as X-rays, MRIs, and CT scans, to assist radiologists in detecting abnormalities and diagnosing diseases accurately. By comparing imaging data with large databases of annotated images, AI models can provide more accurate diagnoses and reduce the risk of human error.

Supply Chain Optimization

Managing a complex supply chain involves handling vast amounts of data related to inventory levels, supplier performance, transportation logistics, and customer demand. Big data analytics and AI can help organizations optimize their supply chain operations by predicting demand, managing inventory, and improving delivery schedules.

For instance, by analyzing historical sales data, weather conditions, and other external factors, AI models can predict future demand for products. This information can then be used to optimize the inventory levels and ensure that the right products are available at the right time and in the right quantities.

AI algorithms can also analyze real-time data from transportation systems, such as GPS data, traffic information, and delivery routes, to optimize routing and scheduling. By dynamically adjusting routes based on traffic conditions and other factors, organizations can reduce transportation costs, improve delivery times, and enhance overall efficiency.

Social Media Analytics

Social media platforms generate an incredible amount of data in the form of user-generated content, including text, images, and videos. Big data analytics combined with AI techniques can provide valuable insights into consumer sentiment, trends, and behavior.

For example, organizations can use sentiment analysis to analyze social media posts and comments to understand customer opinions and perceptions about their products or services. By automatically categorizing sentiments as positive, negative, or neutral, organizations can quickly identify potential issues and take proactive measures to address them.

Furthermore, social media analytics can help organizations identify emerging trends and patterns. By analyzing social media conversations, hashtags, and user interactions, AI models can predict trends and help organizations make data-driven decisions, such as product development, marketing strategies, and customer engagement approaches.

Overall, the application of big data in AI has the potential to revolutionize industries and bring about significant advancements in various domains. By leveraging the power of big data analytics and AI techniques, organizations can gain valuable insights, make accurate predictions, improve operational efficiencies, and deliver better products and services to their customers. However, it is important to address ethical considerations, such as privacy and data protection, bias, and the societal impact of AI, to ensure responsible and ethical use of big data in AI applications.

Key Takeaways

- Predictive analytics is a key application of big data in AI, enabling organizations to make accurate predictions about future events or outcomes.

- Big data and AI techniques play a crucial role in fraud detection by analyzing large volumes of transactional data and identifying patterns indicative of fraudulent activities.

- In healthcare, big data analytics combined with AI can revolutionize diagnosis, treatment, and patient care by analyzing patient data, medical imaging, and genomics data.

- Big data analytics and AI can optimize supply chain operations by predicting demand, managing inventory, and improving delivery schedules.

- Social media analytics can provide valuable insights into consumer sentiment, trends, and behavior by analyzing user-generated content on social media platforms.

Further Reading

- Provost, F., & Fawcett, T. (2013). *Data Science for Business: What You Need to Know About Data Mining and Data-Analytic Thinking.* O'Reilly Media.

- Davenport, T. H., & Patil, D. J. (2012). *Data Scientist: The Sexiest Job of the 21st Century.* Harvard Business Review.

- Mayer-Schönberger, V., & Cukier, K. (2013). *Big Data: A Revolution That Will Transform How We Live, Work, and Think*. Houghton Mifflin Harcourt.

Exercises

1. Consider a retail company that wants to optimize its inventory management using big data analytics and AI. Describe the data sources and AI techniques that can be used to achieve this goal.

2. How can big data analytics and AI be applied to improve customer service in the telecommunications industry? Provide examples of AI-powered solutions that can enhance customer experience and satisfaction.

3. Discuss the ethical considerations and challenges associated with using big data in AI applications. How can organizations address these concerns and ensure responsible and ethical use of big data in AI?

Data Processing and Analysis

Data Warehousing

In the realm of artificial intelligence and data analytics, the collection and storage of vast amounts of data are crucial. This is where data warehousing comes into play. A data warehouse is a central repository that stores and organizes data from different sources, making it easily accessible for analysis and decision-making processes. In this section, we will explore the concept of data warehousing, its components, and its significance in the era of big data and AI.

What is Data Warehousing?

Data warehousing involves the process of gathering, integrating, and organizing data from various sources into one centralized location. It serves as a foundation for business intelligence, data analysis, and reporting. By providing a unified view of data, data warehousing enables organizations to make informed decisions based on accurate and comprehensive information.

The data stored in a data warehouse is typically structured, meaning it is organized into predefined formats such as tables, columns, and rows. This organized structure allows for efficient storage, retrieval, and analysis of data.

Components of Data Warehousing

A data warehouse consists of several key components that work together to ensure the effective management and utilization of data. Let's explore these components:

1. **Data Sources:** These are the systems or applications that generate or capture the raw data. Data sources can include databases, spreadsheets, transactional systems, social media platforms, and more.

2. **Data Extraction:** The process of extracting data from various sources is known as data extraction. This involves identifying relevant data, transforming it into a consistent format, and moving it to the data warehouse.

3. **Data Transformation:** Once the data is extracted, it undergoes a transformation process that standardizes, cleans, and integrates it into a consistent structure. This step ensures that the data is compatible with the data warehouse schema and can be easily analyzed.

4. **Data Loading:** Data loading refers to the process of loading transformed data into the data warehouse. This can be done through batch processing, where data is loaded periodically, or in real-time, where data is loaded immediately as it becomes available.

5. **Data Storage:** The data storage component is responsible for efficiently storing the data in the data warehouse. It includes various technologies and techniques, such as indexing, partitioning, and compression, to optimize storage and retrieval performance.

6. **Data Management:** Data management encompasses activities such as data security, access control, backup, and recovery. These ensure the integrity, privacy, and availability of the data stored in the data warehouse.

7. **Data Access and Querying:** Users and analysts interact with the data warehouse through data access tools and query languages. These tools allow for retrieving, analyzing, and visualizing data to gain insights and make data-driven decisions.

Benefits of Data Warehousing

Data warehousing offers numerous benefits for organizations seeking to harness the power of big data and AI. Here are some key advantages:

- **Data Integration and Consistency:** By consolidating data from disparate sources, a data warehouse provides a unified and consistent view of the organization's data. This eliminates data silos and enables efficient analysis and reporting.

- **Improved Decision-making:** With a data warehouse, organizations can access real-time or near-real-time data, allowing for faster and more informed decision-making. Decision-makers can analyze historical patterns, identify trends, and make predictions based on accurate and up-to-date information.

- **Enhanced Data Quality:** Data transformation and cleansing processes in a data warehouse help improve data quality by identifying and correcting errors or inconsistencies. This ensures that the data used for analysis and decision-making is reliable and trustworthy.

- **Scalability and Performance:** Data warehouses are designed to handle large volumes of data and support complex queries. They employ optimization techniques and indexing mechanisms to deliver efficient data retrieval and analysis, even as data volumes grow.

- **Advanced Analytics:** By providing a centralized and structured view of data, data warehousing enables advanced analytics techniques such as data mining, predictive modeling, and machine learning. These techniques can uncover hidden patterns, relationships, and insights that drive innovation and competitive advantage.

Challenges and Considerations

While data warehousing offers immense potential, it also presents challenges that organizations must address. Here are a few considerations in implementing and managing a data warehouse:

- **Data Governance:** Establishing data governance policies and practices ensures the quality, security, and compliance of data in the warehouse. It involves defining data ownership, access controls, data usage policies, and auditing mechanisms.

- **Data Integration Complexity:** Integrating data from heterogeneous sources with varying formats and structures can be complex and time-consuming. Organizations need to develop robust data integration strategies and tools to streamline the process.

- **Data Security:** Protecting sensitive and confidential data stored in the data warehouse is of utmost importance. Organizations must implement stringent security measures, such as encryption, access controls, and data masking, to safeguard against unauthorized access and data breaches.

- **Scalability and Performance Optimization:** As the volume and complexity of data increase, organizations need to ensure that their data warehouse can scale to accommodate growing demands. This may involve adopting technologies like distributed data processing or cloud-based data warehousing solutions.

- **Change Management:** Implementing a data warehouse often requires organizational change, including training employees on new tools and processes and developing a data-driven culture. Change management strategies are crucial to ensure successful adoption and utilization of the data warehouse.

Real-World Example: Retail Analytics

To illustrate the importance of data warehousing, let's consider a real-world example in the retail industry. A large retail chain wants to optimize its inventory management and customer engagement. By implementing a data warehouse, they can gather data from various sources, such as sales transactions, customer demographics, and inventory levels.

With the data warehouse, the retailer can analyze historical sales patterns, identify popular products or trends, and optimize inventory stocking. They can also personalize customer experiences by analyzing customer preferences and buying behaviors.

For instance, the retailer can use the data warehouse to identify customers who frequently purchase baby products. They can then target these customers with personalized marketing campaigns, offering discounts or recommendations on related products.

By leveraging the insights provided by the data warehouse, the retailer can make data-driven decisions, maximize sales, and improve customer satisfaction.

Summary

In this section, we explored the concept of data warehousing, its components, and its significance in the era of big data and AI. We discussed how data warehousing enables organizations to integrate, organize, and analyze large volumes of data, leading to improved decision-making, enhanced data quality, and advanced analytics capabilities.

However, implementing and managing a data warehouse comes with challenges, including data governance, data integration complexity, data security, scalability, and change management. Overcoming these challenges is essential to fully harnessing the potential of data warehousing.

Data warehousing plays a vital role in various industries, such as retail, finance, and healthcare, allowing organizations to gain a competitive edge by leveraging the power of data and AI. As organizations continue to generate and collect massive amounts of data, the importance of data warehousing will only grow, supporting innovation, growth, and success in today's data-driven world.

Key Takeaways

- Data warehousing involves the collection, integration, and organization of data from different sources into a centralized repository.

- The components of data warehousing include data sources, data extraction, data transformation, data loading, data storage, data management, and data access tools.

- Data warehousing offers benefits such as data integration, improved decision-making, enhanced data quality, scalability, and advanced analytics.

- Challenges in data warehousing include data governance, data integration complexity, data security, scalability, and change management.

- Real-world examples, such as retail analytics, highlight the practical applications and benefits of data warehousing.

Further Reading

For more information on data warehousing, explore the following resources:

- Kimball, R., Ross, M., Thornthwaite, W., Mundy, J., & Becker, B. (2013). *The Data Warehouse Toolkit: The Definitive Guide to Dimensional Modeling*. Wiley.

- Inmon, W., Strauss, D., & Neushloss, G. (2005). *DW 2.0: The Architecture for the Next Generation of Data Warehousing*. Morgan Kaufmann.

- Chaudhuri, S., & Dayal, U. (1997). An overview of data warehousing and OLAP technology. *ACM SIGMOD Record*, 26(1), 65-74.

Exercise:
Consider a retail company that wants to increase customer satisfaction by personalizing their marketing campaigns. How can data warehousing assist the company in achieving this goal? Provide a step-by-step plan, including the data sources, data transformation processes, and analysis techniques.

Challenge:
Research and analyze a case study of a company that successfully implemented a data warehouse to improve its operations or gain a competitive advantage. Present your findings, highlighting the specific benefits and challenges faced by the company.

Fun Fact:
Did you know that the concept of data warehousing originated in the late 1980s and early 1990s? It was introduced by pioneers such as Bill Inmon and Ralph Kimball, who developed different approaches to building data warehouses. Their work laid the foundation for modern data warehousing practices.

Stream Processing

In the world of big data and AI, stream processing plays a crucial role in handling and analyzing continuous streams of data in real-time. While batch processing is suitable for processing large volumes of data offline, stream processing allows us to ingest, process, and analyze data as it is generated or received. This enables faster decision-making, real-time monitoring, and the ability to respond to events as they happen.

Introduction to Stream Processing

Stream processing deals with processing continuous, unbounded streams of data, where data items (also known as events or records) are generated and processed one at a time. A data stream consists of a sequence of records, each containing a timestamp and a set of attributes. These attributes represent meaningful information that we want to extract and analyze.

Real-world examples of data streams include social media feeds, stock market tick data, sensor data from IoT devices, and log files generated by web servers. The challenge of stream processing lies in handling an infinite flow of data and extracting valuable insights in real-time.

Stream Processing Frameworks and Technologies

To effectively process and analyze data streams, we need specialized tools and frameworks. Here are a few popular stream processing technologies:

- Apache Kafka: A distributed streaming platform that enables real-time data streaming and processing. Kafka provides fault-tolerant, scalable, and highly available data pipelines, making it a preferred choice for stream processing applications.

- Apache Flink: A powerful open-source stream processing framework that supports both batch and stream processing. Flink provides excellent fault tolerance, low-latency processing, and supports event time processing for handling out-of-order events.

- Apache Samza: A lightweight distributed stream processing framework built on top of Apache Kafka. Samza provides fault tolerance, scalability, and stateful processing of data streams.

- Apache Storm: A distributed real-time stream processing system that is highly scalable and fault-tolerant. Storm enables real-time data processing at large scale and supports multiple programming languages.

These frameworks offer various features and capabilities to handle different aspects of stream processing, such as data ingestion, event processing, state management, fault tolerance, and scalability. Choosing the right framework depends on the specific requirements of your stream processing application.

Stream Processing Concepts

To understand stream processing, let's explore some key concepts:

Event Time and Processing Time When dealing with data streams, it is essential to differentiate between event time and processing time. Event time refers to the time at which an event actually occurred, as indicated by the timestamp in the data record. Processing time, on the other hand, is the time at which the system processes the event.

In stream processing, we often rely on event time for accurate analysis, especially when dealing with out-of-order events and late arrivals. However, processing time is also important, particularly for real-time monitoring and making immediate decisions.

DATA PROCESSING AND ANALYSIS

Windowing Stream processing often involves grouping events into time-based windows to perform aggregations and computations. Windowing allows us to create logical boundaries and process a specific set of events within a defined time interval.

There are different types of windows in stream processing, such as tumbling windows, sliding windows, and session windows. Tumbling windows divide the stream into fixed-size, non-overlapping time intervals, while sliding windows create overlapping intervals. Session windows group events based on gaps in their timestamps, representing periods of activity.

Windowing enables stream processing applications to summarize and analyze data over specific time intervals, providing valuable insights and patterns in real-time.

Streaming Operations In stream processing, we perform various operations on data streams to transform, filter, and aggregate the incoming events. Some common streaming operations include:

- Filtering: Selecting events that meet specific criteria, allowing us to focus on relevant data.

- Mapping: Transforming events by applying functions or rules to modify their attributes or structure.

- Aggregation: Summarizing data within a window by performing operations like counting, averaging, or finding the maximum/minimum value.

- Joining: Combining multiple data streams based on common attributes or keys to derive meaningful insights.

These operations are the building blocks of stream processing applications, allowing us to extract useful information and make timely decisions.

Use Cases and Real-World Examples

Stream processing has a wide range of use cases across industries. Here are a few examples:

- Fraud Detection: Banks and financial institutions use stream processing to analyze transactions in real-time, detecting fraudulent activities and triggering immediate alerts.

- Internet of Things (IoT): Streaming data from sensors in IoT devices allows for real-time monitoring of environmental conditions, predictive maintenance, and anomaly detection.

- Social Media Analytics: Processing social media streams helps understand trends, sentiment analysis, and identifying influencers for targeted marketing campaigns.

- Network Monitoring: Stream processing can analyze network data in real-time, identifying potential security threats, network congestion, and performance issues.

These examples highlight the power of stream processing in handling continuous data streams and deriving insights in real-time.

Challenges and Considerations

While stream processing has numerous benefits, it comes with its own set of challenges. Here are some key considerations:

Scalability As data streams can be voluminous and continuous, stream processing systems need to scale horizontally to handle increasing data rates and accommodate future growth. This requires distributed systems that can efficiently parallelize computations and distribute the workload across multiple nodes.

Fault Tolerance Stream processing systems must handle failures gracefully to ensure continuous operation and prevent data loss. A fault-tolerant system can recover from failures and resume processing without losing processed data or disrupting the pipeline.

Processing Guarantees Depending on the use case, stream processing applications may require different processing guarantees. For example, some applications may prioritize low latency and best-effort processing, while others may require exactly-once processing semantics for data consistency.

State Management Stream processing often involves maintaining and updating the state (e.g., aggregates, counts, session information) of ongoing computations. Managing state efficiently and reliably across distributed systems is critical for accurate analysis and reliable results.

Windowing and Late Arrivals   Handling out-of-order events and late arrivals is a common challenge in stream processing. Windowing mechanisms must be designed to accommodate these scenarios and produce correct and accurate results.

Conclusion

Stream processing plays a vital role in real-time data analysis and decision-making, allowing us to extract valuable insights from continuous data streams. With the right tools and frameworks, stream processing enables businesses to gain a competitive edge by responding promptly to events, detecting anomalies, and capitalizing on emerging trends. Understanding the concepts, challenges, and considerations of stream processing is essential for building efficient and scalable AI systems that harness the power of real-time data.

Batch Processing

Batch processing is a crucial component of data analysis and plays a significant role in handling large volumes of data in various industries. In this section, we will explore the concept of batch processing, its benefits, and its practical applications in the context of artificial intelligence.

Understanding Batch Processing

Batch processing refers to the execution of a series of tasks or jobs together as a group. These tasks are typically performed without any user intervention and are processed sequentially. In the context of data analysis, batch processing involves the execution of data processing tasks on a set or batch of data simultaneously.

Batch processing allows organizations to process large volumes of data efficiently. Instead of processing data in real-time, which can be time-consuming for datasets that are too large to handle at once, batch processing allows for the simultaneous processing of multiple datasets in separate batches. This enables data analysts and AI systems to work on other tasks while data processing is taking place.

One of the common practical scenarios where batch processing is used is in retail companies where large volumes of sales data are processed at the end of the day or week to generate reports on sales performance, inventory management, and customer behavior. By processing the data in batches, the system can handle large datasets more efficiently and provide insights and reports in a timely manner.

Benefits of Batch Processing

Batch processing offers several benefits in the context of data analysis and artificial intelligence:

- **Data Volume Handling:** Batch processing allows organizations to handle large volumes of data without overwhelming the data processing systems. By breaking down the data into manageable batches, it becomes easier to process and analyze the data efficiently.

- **Parallel Processing:** Batch processing enables parallel processing of multiple datasets. This means that different batches of data can be processed simultaneously by different processors or computing resources, speeding up the overall processing time.

- **Resource Management:** By scheduling data processing tasks as batches, organizations can better manage their computing resources. The resources can be allocated to different batches based on their priority and importance, ensuring optimal utilization of available resources.

- **Flexibility:** Batch processing allows for flexibility in scheduling tasks. Organizations can choose to execute data processing jobs during off-peak hours or when the system load is low, minimizing the impact on system performance during peak operating times.

- **Error Handling:** With batch processing, error handling becomes more manageable. If an error occurs during the processing of a batch, it can be isolated and rectified without affecting other batches in the queue. This helps in maintaining data integrity and reliability.

Practical Applications of Batch Processing

Batch processing finds applications in various industries and domains. Here are a few practical examples:

- **Financial Institutions:** Banks and financial institutions often use batch processing to handle large volumes of financial transactions and generate reports for account statements, credit card transactions, and fraud detection. Batch processing enables these organizations to process and reconcile transactions efficiently.

- **E-commerce:** E-commerce companies employ batch processing to analyze customer behavior, process transactions, update inventory, and generate personalized recommendations. By processing data in batches, they can provide real-time insights to customers and improve operational efficiency.

- **Healthcare:** In the healthcare industry, batch processing is used to analyze patient data, manage medical records, and generate reports for clinical research. By processing data in batches, healthcare organizations can ensure compliance with privacy regulations and optimize resource utilization.

- **Supply Chain Management:** Batch processing is utilized in supply chain management to handle inventory management, logistics, and demand forecasting. By processing data on a batch basis, organizations can optimize their supply chain operations and make data-driven decisions.

Challenges and Considerations

While batch processing offers several benefits, there are also challenges and considerations to keep in mind:

- **Latency:** Batch processing is not suitable for real-time applications that require immediate processing and response. The delay between data being received and processed can be a limitation in certain scenarios where real-time decision-making is critical.

- **Data Consistency:** In batch processing, data consistency is crucial. When processing data in batches, it's essential to ensure that the data remains consistent throughout the entire processing cycle. Any inconsistencies or errors can propagate across the entire batch, leading to inaccurate results.

- **Batch Scheduling:** Efficient batch scheduling is a critical aspect of batch processing. Scheduling the right jobs at the right time, considering resource availability and task dependencies, can optimize processing time and ensure timely delivery of results.

- **Error Handling and Recovery:** Dealing with errors during batch processing can be challenging. It's important to have robust error handling mechanisms in place to identify and rectify errors without impacting the entire batch. Additionally, proper data backup and recovery processes should be in place to handle unforeseen situations.

Summary

Batch processing is a fundamental concept in data analysis and artificial intelligence. It allows for the simultaneous processing of multiple datasets, enabling organizations to handle large volumes of data efficiently. With benefits such as data volume handling, parallel processing, resource management, flexibility, and error handling, batch processing finds applications across various industries. However, challenges related to latency, data consistency, batch scheduling, and error handling should be carefully considered and addressed. By understanding and effectively implementing batch processing techniques, organizations can leverage the power of AI in analyzing large datasets and gaining valuable insights for better decision-making.

Real-time Data Analysis

Real-time data analysis is a critical component of modern artificial intelligence systems. As the name suggests, it involves the processing and analysis of data in real-time, enabling organizations to make timely and informed decisions. In this section, we will explore the principles and techniques behind real-time data analysis and its applications in various industries.

The Importance of Real-time Data Analysis

In today's fast-paced world, the ability to analyze data in real-time is of utmost importance. Traditional batch processing methods, where data is collected over a period of time and then analyzed, are no longer sufficient for many applications. With the advent of technologies like the Internet of Things (IoT) and the increasing availability of high-speed networks, enterprises can now collect massive amounts of data in real-time.

Real-time data analysis allows organizations to react swiftly to changing conditions, identify trends, and detect anomalies as they happen. It empowers businesses to make data-driven decisions promptly, giving them a competitive edge in the market. For example, in the financial industry, real-time analysis of market data enables traders to seize profitable opportunities before they vanish.

Architectures for Real-time Data Analysis

To perform real-time data analysis, organizations require robust and scalable architectures that can handle large volumes of data and provide timely insights. Here are two common architectural patterns used for real-time data analysis:

DATA PROCESSING AND ANALYSIS

1. **Lambda Architecture:** The Lambda architecture combines batch and real-time processing to provide near real-time analytics. In this architecture, data is ingested in parallel into both a batch processing system and a real-time processing system. The batch processing system performs complex analysis on historical data, while the real-time processing system provides low-latency analysis on incoming data. The results from both systems are then merged to provide a cohesive view of the data.

2. **Kappa Architecture:** The Kappa architecture simplifies the complexities of the Lambda architecture by eliminating the need for separate batch and real-time processing systems. In this architecture, all data is ingested into a single real-time processing system, which performs both real-time analytics and batch processing on historical data. The Kappa architecture leverages stream processing frameworks, such as Apache Kafka or Apache Flink, to achieve low-latency and scalable processing.

Both architectures have their advantages and trade-offs, and the choice depends on the specific requirements of the application and the available infrastructure.

Tools for Real-time Data Analysis

To enable real-time data analysis, organizations rely on a variety of tools and technologies. Here are some popular ones:

1. **Apache Kafka:** Apache Kafka is a distributed streaming platform that allows organizations to build real-time data pipelines and process high volumes of data in a fault-tolerant manner. It provides durable storage, high throughput, and low-latency messaging capabilities, making it an ideal choice for real-time data analysis.

2. **Apache Flink:** Apache Flink is an open-source stream processing framework that enables high-throughput, fault-tolerant processing of real-time data streams. It supports event-time processing, stateful computations, and offers powerful streaming APIs and libraries. Apache Flink is widely used for real-time analytics, fraud detection, and machine learning applications.

3. **Elasticsearch:** Elasticsearch is a distributed search and analytics engine known for its real-time data indexing and search capabilities. It can ingest data from various sources, perform near real-time analysis, and provide

sub-second search results. Elasticsearch's scalability and robustness make it suitable for real-time log analysis, security monitoring, and operational analytics.

4. **Apache Spark**: Apache Spark is a unified analytics engine that supports both batch processing and real-time streaming analytics. It provides high-level APIs in Java, Scala, Python, and R, making it easy to develop real-time data analysis applications. Apache Spark's in-memory processing capability enables fast and efficient analysis of large datasets.

Challenges in Real-time Data Analysis

While real-time data analysis offers immense benefits, it also poses several challenges that organizations must address. Some of the key challenges include:

- **Data Volume and Velocity**: Dealing with high volumes of data in real-time requires scalable infrastructure and efficient data processing techniques. Organizations must design systems that can handle the velocity of incoming data without sacrificing performance or accuracy.

- **Data Quality and Integrity**: Real-time data may contain errors, missing values, or outliers, which can affect the accuracy of analysis. Implementing data cleansing and validation techniques is crucial to ensure the quality and integrity of real-time data.

- **Latency and Throughput**: Real-time analysis demands low-latency and high-throughput processing. Meeting these requirements often requires distributed computing and optimization techniques to minimize processing time.

- **Security and Compliance**: Real-time data analysis involves processing sensitive information, such as customer data or financial transactions. Organizations must implement proper security measures, including encryption and access controls, to protect data privacy and comply with regulations.

Real-world Applications

Real-time data analysis finds applications in various industries, revolutionizing the way organizations operate. Here are a few examples:

- **Transportation and Logistics:** Real-time analysis of GPS data from vehicles enables companies to optimize routes, improve delivery times, and reduce fuel consumption.

- **Healthcare:** Real-time analysis of patient vital signs and electronic health records allows healthcare providers to detect and respond to critical conditions promptly.

- **Retail:** Real-time analysis of customer transactions and behavior helps retailers personalize marketing campaigns, recommend products, and effectively manage inventory.

- **Energy Management:** Real-time analysis of sensor data from power grids enables energy companies to optimize energy distribution, monitor equipment health, and detect anomalies that may lead to outages.

Conclusion

Real-time data analysis has become a critical component in the age of artificial intelligence. It enables organizations to gain insights, make informed decisions, and respond swiftly to rapidly changing conditions. By leveraging robust architectures, cutting-edge tools, and addressing the associated challenges, organizations can unlock the true potential of real-time data analysis and drive innovation in various industries.

So, don't wait for tomorrow, analyze your data in real-time today and dominate the world of AI!

Data Mining and Predictive Analytics

Association Rule Mining

Association rule mining is a powerful technique in data mining and machine learning that allows us to discover interesting relationships or associations between items in large datasets. In this section, we will explore the principles and methodologies behind association rule mining and its applications in various fields.

Introduction to Association Rule Mining

Association rule mining aims to discover associations or relationships between items in a dataset. These associations are represented as rules of the form 'If X, then Y', where X and Y are sets of items or itemsets. For example, in a retail dataset, an association rule might be 'If a customer purchases bread and milk, then they are likely to purchase eggs'.

The goal of association rule mining is to identify these rules that have high support and confidence. Support is a measure of how frequently an itemset appears in the dataset and confidence measures the strength of the association rule. These measures help us identify the most relevant and interesting rules.

Apriori Algorithm

One of the most popular algorithms for association rule mining is the Apriori algorithm. Developed by Rakesh Agrawal and Ramakrishnan Srikant in 1994, the Apriori algorithm efficiently discovers frequent itemsets and generates association rules.

The Apriori algorithm follows a bottom-up approach, starting with single items and progressively extends the itemsets until no further extension is possible. It operates on a crucial property known as the Apriori property, which states that any subset of a frequent itemset must also be frequent.

The algorithm consists of the following steps:
1. **Generating Frequent Itemsets:** The algorithm starts by scanning the dataset to find the frequent individual items. These items are then used to generate candidate itemsets of size two. 2. **Pruning Infrequent Itemsets:** The algorithm prunes the candidate itemsets by removing those that do not meet the minimum support threshold. 3. **Joining and Pruning:** The algorithm joins the frequent itemsets to generate candidate itemsets of larger sizes. It then prunes the candidate itemsets that do not meet the minimum support threshold. 4. **Repeat Steps 2 and**

3: The algorithm repeats steps 2 and 3 until no further frequent itemsets can be generated.

By iteratively applying these steps, the Apriori algorithm efficiently discovers frequent itemsets that meet the minimum support threshold. These frequent itemsets can be used to derive association rules with high confidence.

Measuring Rule Interestingness

Once we have identified frequent itemsets, we can generate association rules based on these itemsets. However, not all rules are equally interesting or useful. Various measures can be used to evaluate the interestingness of association rules:

1. **Support:** Support measures the frequency of occurrence of an itemset in the dataset. Rules with higher support are considered more interesting as they reflect stronger relationships between items.

2. **Confidence:** Confidence measures the conditional probability of the consequent item(s) given the antecedent item(s) in a rule. Rules with higher confidence are considered more reliable.

3. **Lift:** Lift measures the ratio of the observed support to the expected support of the consequent item(s) given the antecedent item(s). Lift values greater than 1 indicate positive association, while values less than 1 indicate negative association.

4. **Conviction:** Conviction measures the ratio of the expected support to the observed support of the consequent item(s) given the antecedent item(s). Conviction values greater than 1 indicate that the consequent item(s) is highly dependent on the antecedent item(s).

These measures help us evaluate the strength and reliability of association rules, allowing us to filter out less interesting or irrelevant rules.

Applications of Association Rule Mining

Association rule mining has numerous applications in various domains. Let's explore a few examples:

1. **Market Basket Analysis:** In retail, association rule mining is commonly used for market basket analysis. By analyzing customer purchase patterns, retailers can identify product associations and optimize store layout, product placement, and targeted marketing campaigns.

2. **Healthcare:** Association rule mining can be applied to healthcare datasets to discover associations between medical conditions, symptoms, and treatments. This information can help in disease diagnosis, personalized medicine, and treatment recommendation systems.

3. **Customer Behavior Analysis:** E-commerce and online platforms leverage association rule mining to understand customer behavior and preferences. By analyzing clickstream data, they can recommend relevant products, personalize user experiences, and optimize marketing strategies.

4. **Fraud Detection:** Association rule mining can be used in fraud detection systems to identify patterns and associations among fraudulent transactions. By detecting anomalous transactions and suspicious behaviors, organizations can minimize financial losses.

Challenges in Association Rule Mining

While association rule mining is a powerful technique, it does come with its own challenges:

1. **Curse of Dimensionality:** As the size and dimensionality of the dataset increase, finding frequent itemsets becomes computationally expensive. The search space grows exponentially, requiring efficient algorithms and optimization techniques.

2. **Data Sparsity:** In large datasets, itemsets might occur infrequently, leading to sparse data. Sparse datasets can result in fewer frequent itemsets, making it challenging to discover meaningful associations.

3. **Multiple Testing Problem:** When evaluating a large number of association rules, there is a higher chance of finding spurious associations due to random chance. Proper statistical techniques and adjustments are required to address this issue.

4. **Interpretability:** Association rules can be complex and difficult to interpret. It is essential to strike a balance between generating high-confidence rules and ensuring their interpretability to make them actionable.

Despite these challenges, association rule mining continues to be a valuable tool in data mining and machine learning, enabling us to uncover hidden patterns, improve decision-making, and gain valuable insights from large datasets.

Conclusion

Association rule mining is a versatile technique for discovering associations and relationships in large datasets, allowing us to extract valuable insights and make informed decisions. By leveraging the Apriori algorithm and measuring rule interestingness, we can identify relevant patterns and associations. With applications ranging from retail to healthcare, association rule mining plays a significant role in driving business success and scientific advancements.

By incorporating association rule mining into our data analysis toolbox, we enable ourselves to turn raw data into actionable knowledge, unlocking the potential for increased efficiency, personalized experiences, and improved decision-making across various domains. As the field of artificial intelligence continues to advance, association rule mining will undoubtedly play an essential role in turning data into dominance.

Text Mining

Text mining, also known as text analytics, is a fundamental technique in the field of artificial intelligence that focuses on extracting valuable insights and information from unstructured text data. It involves various processes such as natural language processing, information retrieval, and machine learning to analyze and understand the textual content.

Natural Language Processing

Natural Language Processing (NLP) is a subfield of AI that deals with the interaction between computers and human language. It enables computers to understand, interpret, and generate human language. NLP techniques form the foundation of text mining and provide the capabilities to preprocess, analyze, and extract meaningful information from text data.

Tokenization: Tokenization is the process of breaking down text into smaller units called tokens. These tokens can be individual words or phrases, sentences, or even larger segments. Tokenization is crucial because it helps in organizing and structuring the text data for further analysis.

Stop Words Removal: Stop words are common words that do not carry much meaning, such as "the," "a," "is," etc. They are usually removed from the text data during the preprocessing stage as they can introduce noise and hinder accurate analysis. Stop words removal helps in reducing the dimensionality of the data and improving the performance of text mining algorithms.

Stemming and Lemmatization: Stemming and lemmatization are techniques used to reduce words to their base form. Stemming involves reducing words to their root or stem form by removing prefixes or suffixes, while lemmatization maps words to their base form using vocabulary or morphological analysis. Both techniques help in reducing the variations of words and improving the accuracy of text mining algorithms.

Information Retrieval

Information retrieval involves the process of retrieving relevant information from large collections of text data. This is achieved through various techniques such as indexing and querying.

Indexing: Indexing is the process of creating an index, which is a data structure that enables efficient searching and retrieval of specific information. In the context of text mining, an index can be built based on words or phrases present in the text data, allowing for faster retrieval of relevant documents.

Keyword Extraction: Keyword extraction is the process of identifying and extracting the most important words or phrases from a given text document. These keywords can be used to summarize the content of the document or classify it into relevant categories. Various techniques such as TF-IDF (Term Frequency-Inverse Document Frequency) and TextRank can be used for keyword extraction.

Document Similarity: Document similarity measures the similarity between two or more documents based on their textual content. It is useful in tasks such as document clustering, document classification, and recommendation systems. Similarity can be computed using techniques such as cosine similarity, Jaccard similarity, or edit distance.

Machine Learning for Text Mining

Machine learning plays a crucial role in text mining by enabling the development of models and algorithms that can automatically learn patterns and relationships from text data. These models can be used for various tasks such as sentiment analysis, topic modeling, and text classification.

Sentiment Analysis: Sentiment analysis, also known as opinion mining, is the process of determining the sentiment or emotional tone expressed in a piece of text. It can be used to analyze customer feedback, social media posts, or product reviews. Machine learning algorithms such as support vector machines, Naive Bayes, or recurrent neural networks can be used for sentiment analysis.

Topic Modeling: Topic modeling is a technique used to automatically uncover the hidden topics present in a collection of documents. It aims to divide the documents into groups based on their thematic similarities. Latent Dirichlet Allocation (LDA) is a popular topic modeling technique that uses unsupervised learning to automatically identify topics in the text data.

Text Classification: Text classification, also known as text categorization, is the process of assigning predefined categories or labels to a given text document. It is widely used in applications such as spam detection, sentiment analysis, and document classification. Machine learning algorithms such as Naive Bayes, support vector machines, and deep learning models like convolutional neural networks can be used for text classification.

Real-World Applications

Text mining has found numerous applications across various industries and domains. Here are a few real-world examples:

Customer Feedback Analysis: Text mining techniques can be used to analyze customer feedback data from social media, reviews, or surveys. Companies can gain valuable insights into customer sentiments, preferences, and pain points, enabling them to make data-driven decisions for product improvements, marketing strategies, and customer satisfaction.

News Analysis: Text mining can help news organizations or media companies analyze large volumes of news articles, tweets, or other textual sources to identify important trends, topics, or events. This analysis can be useful in understanding public opinion, identifying fake news, or generating personalized news recommendations.

Healthcare and Medical Research: Text mining techniques enable the analysis of medical literature, clinical notes, and patient records to extract valuable information for medical research, disease diagnosis, and drug discovery. It can help medical professionals stay up-to-date with the latest research findings, identify potential drug interactions, or predict disease outcomes.

Challenges and Ethical Considerations

While text mining offers exciting opportunities, it also presents several challenges and ethical considerations:

Data Quality and Bias: Text data can be noisy, unstructured, and biased. It is important to address data quality issues during the preprocessing stage to ensure accurate analysis. Moreover, biases present in the data, such as gender or racial biases, can propagate and affect the outcomes of text mining algorithms. It is essential to carefully consider and mitigate biases in the analysis.

Privacy and Data Protection: Text mining involves processing and analyzing large volumes of textual data. Privacy concerns and data protection regulations need to be carefully adhered to. Anonymization techniques should be employed to protect sensitive information while still allowing meaningful analysis.

Transparency and Explainability: Text mining models and algorithms can be complex and difficult to interpret. Ensuring transparency and explainability of these models is crucial, especially in sensitive domains like healthcare or finance. Researchers and practitioners should strive to develop and deploy text mining systems that are understandable by humans and can provide clear justifications for their decisions.

Exercises

1. Explain how tokenization is performed in text mining. Give an example.

2. What are the advantages and disadvantages of stemming and lemmatization in text mining? Provide examples.

3. Discuss the importance of data quality and bias in text mining. How can these challenges be addressed?

4. Compare and contrast document similarity measures such as cosine similarity and Jaccard similarity. When would you use each measure?

5. Design a sentiment analysis system using machine learning techniques for analyzing customer reviews of a product.

Resources

1. Christopher D. Manning, Prabhakar Raghavan, and Hinrich Schütze. *Introduction to Information Retrieval*. Cambridge University Press, 2008.

2. Nitin Indurkhya and Fred J. Damerau. *Handbook of Natural Language Processing*. Chapman and Hall/CRC, 2010.

3. Jacob Eisenstein, Regina Barzilay, and David M. Blei (eds.). *Natural Language Processing and Text Mining*. Cambridge University Press, 2019.

4. Ignazio Gallo. *Text Mining for Qualitative Data Analysis in the Social Sciences: A Study on Democratic Discourse in Germany*. Springer, 2017.

5. Radim Řehůřek and Petr Sojka. *Software Framework for Topic Modelling with Large Corpora*. In *Proceedings of the LREC 2010 Workshop on New ChallenJaccard similarityges for NLP Frameworks*, 2010.

Trick: Word Embeddings

Word embeddings are a powerful tool in text mining that represent words as dense vectors in a high-dimensional space. They capture semantic and syntactic relationships between words, allowing for more robust analysis and modeling. Popular word embedding techniques include Word2Vec, GloVe, and FastText. These pre-trained embeddings can be directly used or further trained on domain-specific text data to enhance their performance.

Time Series Analysis

Time series analysis is a fundamental concept in the field of data analysis and plays a crucial role in understanding and predicting patterns in sequential data. In this section, we will explore the principles and techniques used in time series analysis, including data preparation, modeling, forecasting, and evaluation.

Understanding Time Series Data

Time series data consists of a sequence of data points collected over time at regular intervals. This data can be used to analyze historical patterns, detect trends, and make predictions about future values. Time series data is commonly encountered in various domains, such as finance, economics, meteorology, and social sciences.

Before diving into the analysis, it is essential to understand the characteristics of time series data. Here are some key aspects:

- **Trend:** Trend refers to the long-term upward or downward movement of the data. Trends can be linear, nonlinear, or even seasonal.

- **Seasonality:** Seasonality represents the predictable pattern that repeats itself over a fixed period, such as daily, weekly, or annually. For example, sales of ice cream tend to increase during summer months.

- **Cyclicality:** Cyclicality refers to the recurrent and irregular patterns that are not of a fixed period. These irregular cycles can last for several years and are often associated with economic fluctuations.

- **Irregularity:** Irregularity represents the random and unpredictable fluctuations in the data that cannot be explained solely by the trend, seasonality, or cyclicality.

Exploratory Analysis of Time Series Data

Before applying any modeling techniques to time series data, it is crucial to explore and understand the underlying patterns and relationships. Exploratory analysis helps us identify trends, seasonality, and other significant characteristics.

- **Time Plot:** A time plot, also known as a line plot or a run sequence plot, is a simple graphical representation of time series data. It displays the data points against their corresponding time periods, helping us visualize trends, seasonality, and irregularities.

- **Seasonal Plot:** A seasonal plot displays the data, focusing on seasonal patterns. It involves dividing the data into seasons or subintervals and plotting their averages or totals. This visualization technique allows us to analyze variations across different seasons.

- **Autocorrelation Analysis:** Autocorrelation analysis measures the correlation between a time series and its lagged values. It helps identify the presence of recurring patterns at specific time lags, indicating seasonality or other temporal dependencies.

Time Series Modeling and Forecasting

Time series modeling aims to capture and represent the underlying patterns and relationships in the data. Several modeling techniques have been developed to analyze and forecast time series data. Here are some commonly used methods:

- **Moving Average (MA) Model:** The MA model assumes that the current value of a time series depends on the average of the previous observed values and a stochastic term. It is particularly useful for capturing short-term patterns and irregularities.

- **Autoregressive (AR) Model:** The AR model assumes that the current value of a time series depends on its previous values, weighted by coefficients. It is useful for capturing long-term trends and dependencies.

- **Autoregressive Moving Average (ARMA) Model:** The ARMA model combines the AR and MA models, taking into account both the short-term and long-term dependencies in the data.

- **Autoregressive Integrated Moving Average (ARIMA) Model:** The ARIMA model extends the ARMA model to handle non-stationary time series. It includes differencing to make the series stationary, allowing for the modeling of trends.

- **Exponential Smoothing Methods:** Exponential smoothing methods, such as Simple Exponential Smoothing (SES) and Holt-Winters' Method, are used to capture trends and seasonality in time series data. These methods assign weights to previous observations to forecast future values.

- **Vector Autoregression (VAR) Model:** The VAR model is used to model and forecast multiple interrelated time series simultaneously. It captures the dependencies and interactions between different variables in the system.

Evaluating Time Series Models

To ensure the reliability and accuracy of time series models, it is essential to evaluate their performance. Here are some evaluation metrics commonly used for time series forecasting:

- **Mean Absolute Error (MAE):** MAE measures the average absolute difference between the predicted and actual values. It provides a straightforward interpretation of the model's forecasting error.

- **Mean Squared Error (MSE):** MSE measures the average squared difference between the predicted and actual values. It gives more weight to large errors and is useful for penalizing outliers.

- **Root Mean Squared Error (RMSE):** RMSE is the square root of MSE and provides a more interpretable measure of error. It is in the same unit as the original data, making it easier to understand.

- **Mean Absolute Percentage Error (MAPE):** MAPE measures the percentage difference between the predicted and actual values. It helps assess the accuracy of the model relative to the scale of the data.

- **Theil's U Statistic:** Theil's U statistic compares the performance of the forecasting model with that of a naive forecast. It measures the improvement achieved by the model over the naive approach.

In addition to these metrics, visual inspection of the forecasted values compared to the actual values is also essential to assess the model's performance.

Practical Applications of Time Series Analysis

Time series analysis finds applications in various fields, including finance, economics, meteorology, and social sciences. Here are a few examples of its practical applications:

- **Stock Market Prediction:** Time series analysis techniques can be used to forecast stock prices based on historical market data. By identifying patterns and trends, investors can make informed decisions about buying, selling, or holding stocks.

- **Demand Forecasting:** Time series analysis helps businesses predict customer demand for products and services. By analyzing historical sales data, companies can optimize their inventory management, production, and supply chain operations.

- **Energy Consumption Forecasting:** Utility companies can use time series analysis to forecast energy demand and optimize their energy generation, transmission, and distribution systems. This helps in efficient utilization of resources and planning for future energy needs.

- **Climate Modeling:** Time series analysis is fundamental to climate modeling and weather forecasting. By analyzing historical weather data, scientists can make predictions about future climate patterns, enabling policymakers to develop effective strategies for climate change mitigation and adaptation.

Conclusion

Time series analysis is a powerful tool for understanding, modeling, and forecasting sequential data. Through exploratory analysis, modeling techniques, and evaluation metrics, we can uncover hidden patterns and make informed predictions about future values. With its wide range of applications, time series analysis is a crucial discipline for data scientists, economists, and researchers in various fields. By mastering the principles and techniques of time series analysis, we can turn data into actionable insights and make better decisions in an ever-evolving world.

Anomaly Detection

In the world of Artificial Intelligence, anomaly detection plays a vital role in identifying patterns that deviate from the norm. It enables us to identify unusual behaviors, outliers, or deviations from expected patterns in data. Anomaly detection is widely used in various fields, including cybersecurity, finance, manufacturing, and healthcare, to detect fraudulent activities, equipment failures, or abnormal patient conditions.

Understanding Anomalies

Before we dive into the intricacies of anomaly detection, let's take a moment to understand what anomalies are. An anomaly, also known as an outlier, is an observation that significantly deviates from the expected standard or behavior. It can be caused by errors, faults, or unusual patterns in data.

Anomalies can be broadly categorized into two types: point anomalies and contextual anomalies. Point anomalies are individual data points that are considered anomalous, while contextual anomalies are a collection of data points that are collectively anomalous when observed together but might not be considered anomalous individually.

Approaches to Anomaly Detection

There are several approaches to detecting anomalies in data. Let's explore a few commonly used methods:

Statistical Methods: Statistical methods rely on the assumption that normal data points follow a specific statistical distribution. Any data point that falls outside a specified range or deviates significantly from the expected distribution is considered an anomaly. Popular statistical approaches include z-score analysis, Gaussian distribution, and the use of box plots.

Machine Learning Methods: Machine learning techniques can be used to train models on existing data and then use these models to classify new observations as normal or anomalous. These models can be categorized into supervised, unsupervised, and semi-supervised learning methods.

Supervised Learning: In supervised learning, a model is trained on labeled data, where anomalies are already identified and labeled. The model learns the patterns and characteristics of normal data, enabling it to identify anomalies in new, unlabeled data.

Unsupervised Learning: Unsupervised learning methods aim to identify anomalies in unlabeled data, without any prior knowledge of anomalous instances. These methods typically involve clustering algorithms or density-based methods that detect deviations from the expected patterns.

Semi-Supervised Learning: As the name suggests, semi-supervised learning combines elements of both supervised and unsupervised learning. A small portion of labeled training data is used to train the model, along with a larger unlabeled dataset, allowing the model to detect anomalies using both labeled and unlabeled information.

Evaluation and Challenges

Evaluating the performance of an anomaly detection model is critical to ensure its effectiveness. Common evaluation metrics include precision, recall, F1-score, and area under the receiver operating characteristic curve (AUC-ROC).

However, anomaly detection can be a challenging task due to its inherent nature. Here are some common challenges in anomaly detection:

Imbalanced Data: Anomalies are typically rare events compared to normal data points, resulting in imbalanced datasets. This can lead to biased models that prioritize accuracy with normal instances, but fail to detect anomalies effectively.

Data Quality: Anomaly detection heavily relies on the quality and accuracy of data. Noisy or incomplete data can introduce false positives or negatives, making it challenging to distinguish between anomalies and normal instances.

Interpretability: Interpreting the results of anomaly detection algorithms can be challenging. Understanding the reasons behind an identified anomaly and the factors contributing to it can be crucial for decision-making.

Real-World Applications

Anomaly detection has a wide range of applications across various industries. Here are a few examples:

Cybersecurity: Anomaly detection is used to detect and prevent cyber threats and attacks. It can identify unusual network traffic, unauthorized access attempts, or abnormal user behavior, helping organizations protect their systems and data.

Manufacturing: Anomaly detection in manufacturing can help identify faulty components, deviations in production processes, or abnormalities in sensor readings, minimizing defects and improving product quality.

Finance: In the finance sector, anomaly detection is used to detect fraudulent activities, such as credit card fraud or insider trading. Unusual patterns in transactions or account activities can be identified, enabling prompt action to prevent financial loss.

Healthcare: Anomaly detection plays a crucial role in healthcare, where it can aid in the early detection of diseases or anomalies in patient monitoring. It can identify irregularities in vital signs, abnormal test results, or unusual patient behavior, facilitating timely intervention.

Example: Anomaly Detection in Credit Card Fraud

Let's consider the example of anomaly detection in credit card fraud. Credit card companies face the constant challenge of detecting fraudulent transactions amidst a large number of legitimate transactions. Anomaly detection algorithms can play a vital role in flagging suspicious transactions for investigation.

In this case, a supervised learning approach can be used, where historical data containing labeled instances of fraud and legitimate transactions is available. Models such as decision trees or support vector machines (SVM) can be trained on this data to learn the patterns and characteristics of both types of transactions.

During real-time processing of transactions, the trained model can classify each new transaction as either normal or potentially fraudulent. If a transaction is classified as anomalous, additional verification steps can be triggered, such as requesting cardholder confirmation or conducting further investigation.

It is important to continually update and refine the anomaly detection model to adapt to evolving fraud patterns and techniques. Regular monitoring and evaluation of the model's performance ensure its effectiveness in combating credit card fraud.

Conclusion

Anomaly detection is a crucial component of Artificial Intelligence, enabling the identification of unusual patterns or behaviors in data. With the advent of advanced machine learning techniques and the availability of big data, anomaly detection is becoming increasingly powerful and effective.

By understanding the principles and approaches of anomaly detection, we can leverage its capabilities to safeguard against cyber threats, improve manufacturing processes, detect fraudulent activities, and enhance healthcare outcomes. However, challenges such as imbalanced data and the interpretability of results must be addressed to ensure the reliability and usefulness of anomaly detection algorithms.

An intelligent and thoughtful approach to anomaly detection allows us to harness the power of Artificial Intelligence to turn data into actionable insights, ultimately driving outcomes and ensuring success in the modern world.

Predictive Modeling

In the age of artificial intelligence, predictive modeling has become a powerful tool for making accurate forecasts and informed decisions. This section will introduce the concept of predictive modeling, its applications, and the techniques used to build predictive models.

What is Predictive Modeling?

Predictive modeling is a process of using historical data to build a model that can predict future outcomes or behaviors. It involves analyzing patterns and relationships in the data and using this information to make predictions about unknown or future events. Predictive modeling has wide-ranging applications in various industries, such as finance, healthcare, marketing, and manufacturing. It enables organizations to anticipate trends, optimize resources, and make data-driven decisions.

Principles of Predictive Modeling

To understand predictive modeling, it is important to grasp the underlying principles and concepts. The key elements of predictive modeling include:

1. **Training Data:** Predictive models are trained using historical data that captures the relationship between input variables (also known as predictors or features) and the target variable (the variable to be predicted). The training data should be representative and diverse enough to capture different scenarios and patterns.

2. **Feature Selection:** Selecting relevant features is crucial for predictive modeling. By choosing the right set of features, the model can capture the most important information from the data. Feature selection techniques, such as correlation analysis and step-wise regression, help identify the most influential features.

3. **Model Building:** Predictive models can take various forms, including linear regression, decision trees, support vector machines, and neural networks. The choice of the model depends on the complexity and nature of the problem at hand. Each model has its own strengths and weaknesses, and it is important to select an appropriate model to achieve accurate predictions.

4. **Training and Evaluation:** The training process involves fitting the model to the training data. The model learns the patterns and relationships in the data and adjusts its parameters to minimize the prediction error. Once the model is trained, it needs to be evaluated using validation data or cross-validation techniques to assess its performance and generalization ability.

5. **Prediction and Decision-Making:** The trained predictive model can be used to make predictions on new, unseen data. These predictions can guide decision-making processes, such as identifying potential risks, optimizing business strategies, or improving customer targeting. It is essential to interpret the predictions and consider their limitations when making decisions.

Techniques for Predictive Modeling

There are several techniques and algorithms available for predictive modeling. Here are some commonly used approaches:

1. **Linear Regression:** Linear regression is a simple yet powerful technique that models the relationship between a dependent variable and one or more independent

variables. It assumes a linear relationship and estimates the coefficients that best fit the data. Linear regression is widely used for predicting continuous numerical variables.

2. **Decision Trees:** Decision trees are tree-like structures that represent decisions and their possible consequences. Each internal node represents a decision based on a specific feature, and each leaf node represents an outcome. Decision trees are intuitive and can handle both numerical and categorical data. They are especially useful for classification and can be easily visualized.

3. **Random Forest:** Random forest is an ensemble learning technique that combines multiple decision trees to improve prediction accuracy. It creates a forest of decision trees by introducing randomness in the training process. Random forest is robust against overfitting and can handle high-dimensional data.

4. **Support Vector Machines:** Support vector machines (SVM) are powerful supervised learning models used for both classification and regression. SVMs find the best hyperplane that separates different classes or predicts continuous values. They work well with complex datasets and can handle both linear and nonlinear relationships.

5. **Deep Learning and Neural Networks:** Deep learning and neural networks have gained tremendous popularity in recent years due to their ability to learn complex patterns. Neural networks are inspired by the human brain and consist of interconnected nodes (neurons) organized in layers. Deep learning models, such as convolutional neural networks (CNNs) and recurrent neural networks (RNNs), can handle large-scale, unstructured data like images and text.

Real-World Examples

Predictive modeling is applied in various domains to solve real-world problems. Here are a few examples:

1. **Predictive Maintenance:** In manufacturing, predictive modeling can be used to anticipate equipment failure and schedule maintenance operations accordingly. By analyzing sensor data and historical maintenance records, organizations can build models that predict when a machine is likely to fail, allowing proactive maintenance to prevent costly downtime.

2. **Credit Scoring:** Financial institutions use predictive modeling to assess the creditworthiness of individuals or businesses applying for loans or credit cards. By analyzing a range of factors, such as income, credit history, and employment status, predictive models can provide insights into the likelihood of loan defaults and guide lending decisions.

3. Demand Forecasting: Retailers use predictive modeling to forecast demand for products, enabling optimal inventory management and supply chain planning. By analyzing historical sales data, seasonal patterns, and external factors like promotions or economic conditions, organizations can make accurate predictions about future demand and adjust their operations accordingly.

Resources and Further Reading

If you're interested in learning more about predictive modeling, here are some useful resources:

- Books:
    - Hastie, T., Tibshirani, R., & Friedman, J. (2009). *The Elements of Statistical Learning: Data Mining, Inference, and Prediction*. Springer.
    - James, G., Witten, D., Hastie, T., & Tibshirani, R. (2013). *An Introduction to Statistical Learning: With Applications in R*. Springer.
- Online Courses:
    - Coursera - Machine Learning by Andrew Ng
    - edX - Data Science and Machine Learning Bootcamp with R
- Websites and Blogs:
    - Kaggle - kaggle.com
    - Towards Data Science - towardsdatascience.com
    - DataCamp - datacamp.com

Exercise

To practice predictive modeling, here is an exercise for you:

Problem: You work for a ridesharing company and are tasked with predicting the estimated fare for a ride. You are provided with a dataset that contains information about the distance traveled, duration of the ride, pickup location, and other relevant variables. Build a predictive model to estimate the fare based on these factors.

Solution: Start by exploring the dataset and performing data cleaning and validation. Identify any missing values or outliers and preprocess the data accordingly. Then, split the dataset into training and validation sets.

Next, select appropriate features that are likely to influence the fare, such as distance, duration, and surge pricing. Perform feature engineering if needed (e.g., creating new variables based on existing ones).

Choose a suitable predictive modeling technique based on the nature of the problem and the available data. For example, you can try using a linear regression model to predict the fare based on the selected features.

Train the predictive model using the training dataset and evaluate its performance using appropriate evaluation metrics, such as mean squared error or mean absolute error. Fine-tune the model as necessary to achieve better performance.

Once the model is trained and evaluated, use it to predict the fare for new rides. Validate the predictions by comparing them with the actual fare and analyze any discrepancies for further improvements.

Remember to consider the limitations and assumptions of your predictive model and interpret the results with caution.

Conclusion

Predictive modeling is a powerful technique that utilizes historical data to make accurate predictions about future outcomes. By understanding the principles and techniques behind predictive modeling, you can develop models that guide decision-making processes and uncover valuable insights from data. Keep exploring and experimenting with different algorithms and datasets to enhance your predictive modeling skills.

Natural Language Processing

Introduction to Natural Language Processing

Language Modeling

In the exciting field of Natural Language Processing (NLP), one fundamental concept that forms the backbone of many language-related tasks is language modeling. Language modeling refers to the process of predicting the probability of a sequence of words occurring in a given context. It allows us to generate coherent and meaningful sentences, as well as understand the structure and semantics of text data.

The Importance of Language Modeling

Language modeling plays a crucial role in various NLP applications, including machine translation, speech recognition, text generation, and sentiment analysis. By capturing the underlying patterns and relationships between words, language models enhance the accuracy and fluency of these tasks.

For example, in machine translation, a language model enables us to generate accurate and contextually appropriate translations based on the source language. Similarly, in speech recognition, language modeling helps to convert spoken words into written text by predicting the most likely sequence of words given the audio input.

In addition to these practical applications, language modeling is also vital for advancing our understanding of human language. By training models on large corpora of text, researchers can gain insights into the structure, complexity, and evolution of languages.

Traditional Language Models

Before delving into modern approaches to language modeling, let's explore some traditional methods used to build language models.

N-gram Models   One popular approach is the N-gram model, which makes predictions based on the previous N-1 words in a sequence. For example, in a trigram model (N=3), the next word is predicted using the context of the two previous words.

To estimate the probability of a word given its context, N-gram models rely on counting the occurrences of different word sequences in a training corpus. However, as the value of N increases, the number of possible word sequences grows exponentially, making it challenging to estimate probabilities accurately and efficiently.

Backoff and Smoothing Techniques   To overcome the limitations of N-gram models, backoff and smoothing techniques are often employed. These methods aim to assign non-zero probabilities to unseen or infrequent word sequences.

One commonly used technique is Katz backoff, which allows the model to "back off" to an N-1 gram model if the higher-order N-gram is not observed in the training data. This approach provides a more robust estimate of word probabilities, especially for rare or unseen sequences.

Smoothing techniques, such as add-one (Laplace) smoothing or Good-Turing smoothing, are also employed to redistribute probability mass from observed to unseen events. These techniques prevent the model from assigning zero probabilities to unseen word sequences, leading to better generalization.

Neural Language Models

While traditional methods have their merits, recent advancements in deep learning have revolutionized language modeling. Neural language models, particularly those based on recurrent neural networks (RNNs), have gained popularity and achieved state-of-the-art performance in various NLP tasks.

Recurrent Neural Networks   RNNs are a class of neural networks specifically designed for sequential data modeling. In language modeling, RNNs capture the contextual relationships between words by maintaining an internal memory or hidden state that passes information from one word to the next.

The most commonly used RNN-based language model is the Long Short-Term Memory (LSTM) model. LSTMs address the vanishing gradient problem, which occurs when training deep networks on long sequences, by introducing gating mechanisms that regulate information flow in the network.

Transformer Models In recent years, transformer models have emerged as a hugely successful architecture for language modeling. Unlike RNNs, transformers rely on self-attention mechanisms to capture dependencies between words in a sequence.

By attending to all words simultaneously, transformers can more efficiently capture long-range dependencies, leading to better contextual understanding. The breakthrough Transformer model, introduced by Vaswani et al. (2017), has since become the go-to architecture for various NLP tasks.

Evaluation Metrics for Language Models

To assess the performance of language models, several evaluation metrics are commonly used.

Perplexity Perplexity is a widely used metric that measures how well a language model predicts a given dataset. It provides an estimate of the average uncertainty or confusion the model has when making predictions.

Formally, perplexity is defined as the inverse probability of the test set normalized by the number of words:

$$\text{Perplexity}(W) = P(w_1, w_2, \ldots, w_N)^{-\frac{1}{N}}$$

where $w_1, w_2, \ldots, w_N$ are the words in the test set.

A lower perplexity score indicates better performance, as it reflects higher confidence and accuracy in the model's predictions.

Bits per Character (BPC) Bits per Character is an alternative evaluation metric that measures the average number of bits needed to encode each character in a text sequence. It is derived from the entropy of the language model over the test set.

Lower BPC scores indicate better compression of the input data and a more efficient use of model capacity.

Challenges and Future Directions

While modern language models have achieved remarkable success, several challenges still persist.

Long-range Dependencies   Current models, including transformers, struggle to capture very long-range dependencies in text sequences. As a result, they may struggle to generate meaningful context or predict words that depend heavily on distant context.

Contextual Ambiguity   Language often contains inherent ambiguity, with words having multiple possible interpretations depending on the context. Resolving this ambiguity remains a significant challenge for language models.

Ethical Considerations   With the increasing use of language models in various applications, ethical considerations, such as bias, fairness, and privacy, require careful attention. Bias in training data can lead to biased predictions, while fairness ensures equitable treatment across different groups. Additionally, privacy concerns arise when models are trained on sensitive or personal data.

Addressing these challenges and ensuring the responsible development and deployment of language models will be crucial for the future of NLP.

Conclusion

Language modeling is a cornerstone of NLP and plays a vital role in various applications, from machine translation to sentiment analysis. Traditional methods, such as N-gram models with backoff and smoothing techniques, paved the way for modern neural approaches, including RNNs and transformer models.

Evaluation metrics like perplexity and BPC help measure the performance of language models. However, challenges related to long-range dependencies, contextual ambiguity, and ethical considerations remain areas of active research.

As the field of NLP continues to evolve, advancements in language modeling hold the key to unlocking the full potential of AI-driven language understanding and generation.

Further Reading

If you want to dive deeper into language modeling, here are some recommended resources:

- Bengio, Y., Ducharme, R., Vincent, P., & Jauvin, C. (2003). A Neural Probabilistic Language Model. *Journal of Machine Learning Research*, 3, 1137–1155.

- Vaswani, A., et al. (2017). Attention is All You Need. In *Advances in Neural Information Processing Systems*, Vol. 30.

- Jurafsky, D., & Martin, J. H. (2020). *Speech and Language Processing* (3rd ed.). Pearson.

- Goldberg, Y. (2017). *Neural Network Methods for Natural Language Processing*. Morgan & Claypool Publishers.

These resources provide a comprehensive understanding of language modeling, covering both traditional and modern approaches, along with the latest research in the field.

Exercises

1. Compare and contrast N-gram models with neural language models, discussing their strengths and limitations.

2. Explain the concept of perplexity and how it is used to evaluate language models. Calculate the perplexity of a language model given a test set.

3. Discuss the ethical considerations involved in the development and deployment of language models. Provide examples of potential bias, fairness, and privacy issues.

4. Research and describe an application of language modeling in a specific NLP task (e.g., text generation, sentiment analysis) and the challenges involved. Offer potential solutions or improvements.

5. Implement a simple N-gram language model in Python using a text corpus of your choice. Use the model to generate a random sentence and evaluate its fluency.

Text Classification

In the world of artificial intelligence, text classification plays a crucial role in understanding, categorizing, and making sense of vast amounts of textual data. Whether it's sorting emails into spam and non-spam folders, classifying news articles into different topics, or analyzing sentiment in customer reviews, text classification enables machines to process and interpret written language with remarkable accuracy. In this section, we will dive into the principles, techniques, and challenges of text classification, and explore how it is used in real-world applications.

Principles of Text Classification

Text classification, also known as text categorization, is the process of automatically assigning predefined categories or labels to a piece of text based on its content. The goal is to teach a machine learning model to recognize and generalize patterns in text data, enabling it to classify new, unseen text accurately. Text classification can be framed as a supervised learning problem, where we provide the algorithm with a labeled training dataset, consisting of text samples and their corresponding categories, to learn from.

The key principle behind text classification is the extraction of relevant features from the text data that can serve as input to a machine learning algorithm. The choice of features heavily influences the accuracy and effectiveness of the classifier. Commonly used features include:

- **Bag-of-Words (BoW):** This representation disregards the order of words in the text and treats them as a collection or "bag" of individual words. Each word becomes a feature, and its presence or absence in a document determines the value of the feature. BoW is simple and computationally efficient but fails to capture the semantic meaning and context of words.

- **Term Frequency-Inverse Document Frequency (TF-IDF):** TF-IDF considers both the occurrence of a word in a document (term frequency) and its rarity across the entire corpus (inverse document frequency). It assigns higher weight to words that are more relevant to a document while penalizing frequently occurring words across the corpus.

- **Word Embeddings:** Word embeddings are dense, low-dimensional vector representations that capture the semantic relationships between words. Techniques like Word2Vec and GloVe learn these embeddings by predicting the context or proximity of words in large text corpora. Word embeddings capture the meaning and context of words, enabling models to understand semantic similarities and differences.

- **N-grams:** N-grams are contiguous sequences of n words in a document. By considering adjacent words as features, N-grams capture local word order and provide a more contextual representation of the text. For example, a bigram approach would analyze pairs of consecutive words like "artificial intelligence," capturing the inherent relationship between them.

These features serve as inputs to various machine learning algorithms, such as Naive Bayes, Support Vector Machines (SVM), and deep neural networks, to build effective text classifiers.

Techniques for Text Classification

Several machine learning algorithms and techniques have proven successful in text classification tasks. Let's explore some of the commonly used approaches.

1. Naive Bayes: Naive Bayes is a simple probabilistic classifier based on Bayes' theorem, assuming strong independence of features. Despite its naive assumption, Naive Bayes often performs well in text classification tasks, particularly when dealing with high-dimensional data such as text. It computes the conditional probability of a document belonging to a particular class based on the observed features.

2. Support Vector Machines (SVM): SVM is a powerful and widely used algorithm for text classification. It maps the input features into a high-dimensional feature space and finds an optimal hyperplane that separates different classes with maximum margin. SVMs are effective when the data is not linearly separable.

3. Deep Learning: Deep learning, particularly neural networks, has revolutionized many areas of artificial intelligence, including text classification. Convolutional Neural Networks (CNNs) and Recurrent Neural Networks (RNNs) with Long Short-Term Memory (LSTM) units have proven to be highly effective in capturing intricate patterns and dependencies in text data. These models are capable of learning hierarchical representations of text, leveraging both local and global information.

4. Ensemble Methods: Ensemble methods combine the predictions of multiple, diverse classifiers to improve classification accuracy. Techniques like Random Forests and Gradient Boosting have shown excellent performance in text classification, aligning with the idea that collaboration among different models can yield better results.

Challenges and Considerations

While text classification has been remarkably successful, it does come with challenges that require careful consideration. Let's explore a few of these challenges:

1. Imbalanced Datasets: Often, text classification datasets suffer from class imbalance, where the number of samples in one class significantly outweighs others. This can lead to biased models that tend to predict the majority class more frequently. Addressing class imbalance requires techniques like oversampling, undersampling, or algorithmic modifications like cost-sensitive learning.

2. **Handling Out-of-Vocabulary Words:** Language is diverse and constantly evolving, leading to the introduction of new words, slang, or technical terms that may not exist in pre-trained language models. Handling out-of-vocabulary words requires techniques like word normalization, stemming, or leveraging external resources like domain-specific dictionaries or word embeddings.

3. **Interpretability:** As the field of AI progresses, interpretability becomes increasingly important. Understanding why a model makes a particular classification decision is crucial, especially in applications where human-in-the-loop decision-making is essential. Techniques like attention mechanisms and saliency maps can shed light on which parts of the text were most important for classification.

Real-World Applications

Text classification has found extensive use in various real-world applications. Some notable examples include:

1. **Sentiment Analysis:** Text classification is widely employed in sentiment analysis, where the goal is to determine the sentiment or emotional tone expressed in a piece of text. Companies use sentiment analysis to gauge customer opinions, monitor public sentiment on social media, and make data-driven decisions.

2. **Spam Filtering:** Email providers rely on text classification to accurately detect and filter spam emails, preventing them from reaching users' inboxes. By classifying emails as spam or non-spam, users can enjoy a cleaner and more manageable email experience.

3. **News Categorization:** Text classification is used to categorize news articles into topics like sports, politics, entertainment, or finance. This enables news aggregators to provide personalized news recommendations to users based on their preferences.

4. **Customer Support:** Many companies employ text classification to automatically categorize and route customer support tickets. By routing tickets to the appropriate department or team, companies can provide faster and more efficient customer support services.

Further Resources and Exercises

To further explore the world of text classification, here are some resources and exercises:

Books:

- "Natural Language Processing with Python" by Steven Bird, Ewan Klein, and Edward Loper.

- "Text Mining and Analysis: Practical Methods, Examples, and Case Studies Using SAS" by Goutam Chakraborty and Murali Pagolu.

- "Applied Text Analysis with Python: Enabling Language-Aware Data Products with Machine Learning" by Benjamin Bengfort, Rebecca Bilbro, and Tony Ojeda.

Online Courses:

- Coursera: "Natural Language Processing" by Nitin Madnani.

- edX: "Text Mining and Analytics" by Rafael A. Irizarry.

- DataCamp: "Text Mining with Python" by Charles Tapley Hoyt.

Exercises:

1. Collect a dataset of customer reviews for a product or service. Perform text classification to classify these reviews into positive or negative sentiments using a machine learning algorithm of your choice. Evaluate the performance of your model using appropriate evaluation metrics such as accuracy, precision, recall, and F1-score.

2. Build a spam classifier using a dataset of email messages labeled as spam or non-spam. Experiment with different feature extraction techniques such as BoW, TF-IDF, or word embeddings. Compare the performance of different algorithms like Naive Bayes, SVM, and deep neural networks.

3. Explore a large corpus of news articles and create a topic classification model that can assign categories like politics, sports, science, or entertainment to new articles. Experiment with different feature representations (e.g., BoW, TF-IDF) and model architectures (e.g., traditional classifiers, deep learning models) to achieve the best accuracy.

By actively engaging with these exercises and resources, you will deepen your understanding of text classification and its applications, ultimately becoming a proficient practitioner in this field.

Remember, text classification is like teaching a machine to read and comprehend language. It's a powerful tool that allows us to extract insights, automate processes, and make sense of the vast amount of textual data we encounter every day. So, unleash the power of text classification and let it add value to your AI endeavors!

Introduction

In the world of natural language processing (NLP), named entity recognition (NER) is a crucial task that involves identifying and classifying named entities in text. Named entities are specific words or phrases that represent real-world objects, such as people, organizations, locations, dates, and more. NER plays a vital role in a wide range of applications, including information extraction, question answering, machine translation, and sentiment analysis.

Named Entity Recognition, also known as entity identification or entity extraction, is the process of automatically identifying and classifying named entities in unstructured text into predefined categories such as person names, organizations, locations, medical codes, time expressions, quantities, monetary values, percentages, etc. Named entities are an essential piece of information in text that provide context and meaning to the content.

For instance, consider a sentence: "Barack Obama, the former president of the United States, gave a speech at Harvard University." A named entity recognition system would be able to identify "Barack Obama" as a person and "the United States" and "Harvard University" as geopolitical entities and locations, respectively.

In this section, we will explore the principles, techniques, and applications of named entity recognition, and discuss the challenges and advancements in this field.

Challenges in Named Entity Recognition

Named entity recognition is not a trivial task as it requires understanding the context, syntax, and semantics of the text. Several challenges make it a complex problem to solve:

Ambiguity and Polysemy

One of the major challenges in NER is dealing with the ambiguity and polysemy of named entities. Words like "Apple" can refer to both the technology company and the fruit. Resolving such ambiguities and accurately classifying entities based on the context is a non-trivial task.

For example, in the sentence "I bought apples from the Apple store," it is crucial to correctly identify "Apple" as an organization and "apples" as a generic noun.

Nested Entities

Another challenge in NER is handling the presence of nested entities. In many cases, named entities can be present within other named entities. For example, in

INTRODUCTION

the sentence "I visited New York City," both "New York" and "New York City" refer to the same location. Identifying and correctly classifying such nested entities is a complex task.

Ambiguous Boundaries

Determining the boundaries of named entities is another challenge. Sometimes, it is not clear where one entity starts and another ends. For example, in the sentence "I live in San Francisco Bay Area," it is difficult to determine whether "San Francisco," "San Francisco Bay," or "San Francisco Bay Area" should be considered as separate entities.

Limited Training Data

Training a robust named entity recognition system requires a significant amount of annotated data. However, creating large-scale and diverse annotated datasets can be expensive and time-consuming. Limited training data can affect the performance and generalizability of NER models.

Approaches to Named Entity Recognition

To tackle the challenges of named entity recognition, various approaches and techniques have been developed. In this section, we will explore two popular approaches: rule-based and machine learning-based.

Rule-Based Approach

Rule-based approaches rely on predefined patterns and rules to identify and classify named entities. These rules are typically designed by linguists or domain experts and capture common patterns associated with various types of named entities.

For example, a rule-based approach might use language patterns like "President [PERSON]" to identify and tag a person's name preceding the word "President" in the text. Similarly, certain patterns can be defined to identify locations, organizations, and other named entities.

While rule-based approaches can be effective in certain scenarios, they often struggle with the flexibility to handle new or unseen patterns. Additionally, they may require substantial manual effort to design and maintain the rules.

Machine Learning-Based Approach

Machine learning-based approaches have gained popularity in recent years due to their ability to learn patterns from data and generalize to unseen examples. These approaches utilize annotated datasets to train models that can automatically learn to recognize and classify named entities.

The most common machine learning algorithms used for NER include Conditional Random Fields (CRF), Support Vector Machines (SVM), and Recurrent Neural Networks (RNNs). These models are typically trained on large datasets with annotated named entities to learn the patterns and features associated with different entity types.

Machine learning-based approaches offer the advantage of adaptability to new patterns and the ability to generalize well beyond the training data. However, they also require substantial labeled data for training and can be computationally expensive.

Evaluation Metrics

To evaluate the performance of a named entity recognition system, several metrics are commonly used:

Precision

Precision measures the proportion of correctly identified named entities out of all entities identified by the NER system. It is calculated as the ratio of true positive entities to the sum of true positive and false positive entities.

$$\text{Precision} = \frac{\text{True Positives}}{\text{True Positives} + \text{False Positives}}$$

Recall

Recall, also known as sensitivity or true positive rate, measures the proportion of correctly identified named entities out of all true named entities in the text. It is calculated as the ratio of true positive entities to the sum of true positive and false negative entities.

$$\text{Recall} = \frac{\text{True Positives}}{\text{True Positives} + \text{False Negatives}}$$

F1-Score

The F1-score is the harmonic mean of precision and recall. It provides a single metric that balances both precision and recall. The F1-score is often used as a comprehensive evaluation measure for named entity recognition systems.

$$F1 = 2 \times \frac{\text{Precision} \times \text{Recall}}{\text{Precision} + \text{Recall}}$$

Applications of Named Entity Recognition

Named entity recognition has a wide range of applications across various domains. Here are some examples:

Information Extraction

NER plays a vital role in information extraction tasks, where extracting specific information from unstructured text is required. For example, in the medical domain, NER can be used to extract information such as disease names, medications, dosages, and patient names from medical records.

Question Answering

In question answering systems, NER can assist in extracting relevant named entities from the questions and finding the corresponding answers. For example, in a question like "Who wrote Harry Potter?", NER can identify "Harry Potter" as a named entity representing a book series.

Sentiment Analysis

In sentiment analysis, identifying named entities can help determine the sentiments associated with specific entities. For example, in a movie review, NER can identify and classify the named entities like the movie title, director, or actors mentioned, and associate sentiment labels accordingly.

Resources and Tools

Several open-source libraries and tools are available for named entity recognition. Some popular ones include:

NLTK (Natural Language Toolkit)

NLTK is a widely used Python library for natural language processing tasks. It provides several modules and functions for performing named entity recognition, including pre-trained models for different entity types.

SpaCy

SpaCy is another popular Python library for NLP that includes named entity recognition capabilities. It offers high-performance pre-trained models for various languages and also allows fine-tuning for specific domains.

Stanford NER

Stanford NER is a Java-based library developed by Stanford University. It provides robust named entity recognition models and supports both rule-based and machine learning-based approaches.

Conclusion

Named entity recognition is a fundamental task in natural language processing that involves identifying and classifying named entities in text. It plays a crucial role in numerous applications, ranging from information extraction to sentiment analysis. While challenges such as ambiguity and limited training data persist, advances in rule-based and machine learning approaches have significantly improved the accuracy and performance of NER systems. As NLP continues to evolve, named entity recognition will remain a critical component in unlocking the full potential of artificial intelligence in understanding human language.

Sentiment Analysis

Sentiment analysis, also known as opinion mining, is a fascinating field within natural language processing (NLP) that focuses on understanding and extracting emotions, opinions, and sentiments expressed in text. In this section, we will explore the principles and techniques behind sentiment analysis, and how it has become an essential tool for understanding public perception and sentiment towards products, services, and various social issues.

INTRODUCTION

Introduction to Sentiment Analysis

In today's digital age, where vast amounts of user-generated text data are generated daily through social media, customer reviews, and online discussions, sentiment analysis plays a crucial role in helping organizations make sense of this huge volume of information. By automatically classifying and analyzing the sentiment present in textual data, sentiment analysis enables businesses and researchers to gain valuable insights into customer feedback, market trends, and public opinion.

At its core, sentiment analysis involves determining the polarity of a given piece of text, i.e., whether it expresses positive, negative, or neutral sentiment. The challenge lies in accurately identifying and interpreting the sentiment expressed in the text, given the nuances of language and the context in which the sentiments are expressed.

Approaches to Sentiment Analysis

There are different approaches to sentiment analysis, ranging from rule-based methods to machine learning techniques. Let's explore some of the commonly used approaches:

1. **Lexicon-based Approaches:** These approaches rely on sentiment lexicons, which contain pre-defined lists of words and phrases associated with positive or negative sentiment. By counting the occurrences of positive and negative words in a given text, the sentiment polarity can be determined. However, lexicon-based approaches often struggle with nuanced sentiment and sarcasm, as they don't capture context or word co-occurrences.

2. **Machine Learning Approaches:** Machine learning techniques have revolutionized sentiment analysis by enabling the development of more robust models that can learn from data. These approaches involve training a classifier using labeled examples of sentiment data, where the sentiment of each example is manually annotated. The classifier learns patterns and features that help it distinguish between positive and negative sentiment. Popular machine learning algorithms for sentiment analysis include Support Vector Machines (SVM), Naive Bayes, and Recurrent Neural Networks (RNNs).

3. **Hybrid Approaches:** Hybrid approaches combine the strengths of both rule-based and machine learning techniques. These approaches typically use machine learning models but incorporate domain-specific rules or features

to enhance the performance of sentiment classification. For example, sentiment scores from lexicons might be used as additional features in a machine learning model to capture sentiment nuances.

Challenges in Sentiment Analysis

Sentiment analysis, despite its potential, faces several challenges that must be addressed for accurate and reliable results. Some of the main challenges include:

- **Contextual Understanding:** Sentiment analysis often requires an understanding of context, as the same words can have different sentiment orientations depending on the context. For example, the word "sick" can refer to an illness or describe something that is excellent or impressive. Overcoming this challenge requires models that can capture the semantic meaning and context of words and phrases.

- **Negation and Irony:** Negation and irony are common linguistic phenomena that pose challenges in sentiment analysis. Negation occurs when the sentiment of a statement is reversed by the presence of negating words such as "not." Irony occurs when the intended meaning is opposite to the literal meaning of the words used. Both negation and irony require models that can detect and handle these linguistic nuances effectively.

- **Subjectivity and Tone:** Sentiments expressed in text can vary based on the subjectivity and tone of the author. For example, a user might express an opinion about a product using strong language, but their true sentiment might still be positive. Handling subjectivity and tone in sentiment analysis requires models that can understand the intensity of sentiment and detect modifications made to sentiment-bearing words.

- **Data Bias and Labeling:** Training data for sentiment analysis often suffers from bias, as subjective labeling can vary among annotators. The presence of biased training data can lead to biased sentiment analysis models, impacting downstream applications. Addressing data bias requires careful data collection strategies, diverse annotators, and techniques such as data augmentation.

Applications of Sentiment Analysis

Sentiment analysis has a wide range of applications across various industries and domains. Let's explore some of the common applications:

1. **Brand Monitoring and Reputation Management:** By analyzing customer feedback, social media posts, and online reviews, sentiment analysis helps businesses gauge public sentiment towards their brand. This information can be invaluable for managing reputation and implementing strategies to address customer concerns.

2. **Market Research and Competitive Analysis:** Sentiment analysis allows organizations to assess market trends and gather insights on customer preferences. By analyzing sentiment towards different products or services, companies can identify strengths and weaknesses in their offerings and stay ahead of their competitors.

3. **Customer Feedback Analysis:** Sentiment analysis helps businesses understand customer satisfaction levels by analyzing feedback received through surveys, call center logs, and social media interactions. This information can be used to improve products, make informed business decisions, and enhance customer experience.

4. **Political and Social Sentiment Analysis:** Sentiment analysis can be applied to analyze public opinion on political topics, social issues, and public figures. By understanding sentiment patterns, policymakers and organizations can make data-driven decisions and respond effectively to public sentiment.

Ethical Considerations in Sentiment Analysis

While sentiment analysis has immense potential, it also raises ethical considerations that must be addressed. These include:

- **Privacy and Data Protection:** Sentiment analysis often involves analyzing personal data, such as social media posts or customer reviews. It is crucial to handle this data with discretion, ensuring compliance with privacy regulations and protecting individuals' personal information.

- **Bias and Fairness:** Sentiment analysis models can inadvertently inherit biases present in the training data, leading to unfair or discriminatory results. It is important to regularly evaluate and mitigate bias, ensuring that sentiment analysis systems are fair and unbiased across different demographic groups.

- **Transparency and Explainability:** Sentiment analysis models should be transparent and explainable, enabling users to understand how the sentiment classification is performed. This fosters trust in the technology and helps detect and rectify any biases or errors in the system.

Summary

In this section, we explored the fascinating field of sentiment analysis, which allows us to understand and analyze public sentiment within textual data. We discussed various approaches to sentiment analysis, such as lexicon-based, machine learning, and hybrid approaches. We also explored some of the challenges faced in sentiment analysis, including contextual understanding, negation and irony, subjectivity and tone, and data bias. Furthermore, we examined the wide range of applications of sentiment analysis across industries and discussed the ethical considerations in its implementation.

Sentiment analysis continues to evolve with advancements in natural language processing and machine learning techniques. As we delve deeper into the realm of sentiment analysis, it is important to embrace responsible practices to ensure fair and unbiased sentiment analysis results that respect user privacy and foster trust in AI-powered systems.

Speech Recognition and Generation

Automatic Speech Recognition

In this section, we will dive into the fascinating world of Automatic Speech Recognition (ASR), a technology that allows computers to convert spoken language into written text. ASR plays a crucial role in various applications, including virtual assistants, transcription services, and language translation. We will explore the principles behind ASR, the challenges it faces, and the techniques used to achieve accurate and reliable speech recognition.

Principles of Automatic Speech Recognition

ASR is based on the principles of signal processing, pattern recognition, and statistical modeling. It involves several steps, starting from capturing the speech signal and ending with the transcription of spoken words into text.

The first step in ASR is **pre-processing**, where the raw speech signal is transformed to remove noise, enhance speech components, and normalize the signal. This helps in improving the quality and clarity of the input.

Next, the pre-processed speech signal is **segmented** into smaller units, such as phonemes or sub-phonetic units. These units represent the basic building blocks of speech sounds and are used to model the acoustic properties of spoken words.

SPEECH RECOGNITION AND GENERATION

In the **acoustic modeling** stage, statistical models are built to capture the relationship between the acoustic features of speech and the corresponding phonemes or sub-phonetic units. This involves training a large dataset of labeled speech data, where the acoustic features are extracted and mapped to the corresponding phonetic units.

The next step is **language modeling**, which involves capturing the grammatical and semantic structures of the spoken language. Language models are trained using large text corpora and help in constraining the search space during the transcription process.

Finally, in the **transcription** stage, the ASR system uses the trained acoustic and language models to generate the most likely sequence of words that match the input speech signal. This is achieved using a search algorithm, such as the Viterbi algorithm, which finds the best path through the sequence of possible word hypotheses.

Challenges in Automatic Speech Recognition

ASR systems face several challenges due to the variability and complexity of human speech. Here are some of the key challenges:

- **Variability in speech patterns:** Different individuals have unique speech patterns, accents, and dialects, making it challenging to build universal ASR models that work accurately for all speakers. Variations in speech due to emotions, background noise, and speaking styles also add to the complexity.

- **Limited training data:** Training ASR models requires a large amount of labeled speech data. However, collecting and transcribing such data for every possible speaker and language is a time-consuming and costly process. Limited training data can affect the performance of ASR systems, especially for underrepresented languages or specific domains.

- **Out-of-vocabulary words:** ASR systems usually perform well for words present in their training data. However, they struggle with recognizing words that are not part of the training vocabulary or are rare. This poses a challenge for handling domain-specific terminology or proper nouns.

- **Ambiguities and homophones:** Homophones are words that sound the same but have different meanings, such as "write" and "right." ASR systems need to disambiguate such words based on the context in which they are spoken. Ambiguities arising from coarticulation (overlapping sounds) and speech errors further complicate the transcription process.

- **Real-time processing**: In some applications, ASR systems need to process speech input in real-time, such as voice command recognition in virtual assistants or speech-to-text services during live events. Achieving low-latency processing while maintaining accuracy is a challenge.

Techniques in Automatic Speech Recognition

To address the challenges mentioned above, ASR researchers and engineers have developed several techniques and approaches. Here are some commonly used ones:

- **Deep Learning**: Deep Neural Networks (DNNs) have revolutionized ASR by providing better modeling of complex relationships between acoustic features and phonemes. Recurrent Neural Networks (RNNs) and Convolutional Neural Networks (CNNs) are often used for language modeling, acoustic modeling, and joint modeling.

- **Data Augmentation**: To mitigate the limited training data problem, techniques like data augmentation are employed. This involves artificially creating variations of existing speech data by applying audio effects, changing speaking styles, or simulating background noise. Augmentation helps in training more robust ASR models.

- **Adaptation**: ASR models can be adapted to specific speakers or domains by fine-tuning them using additional data from the target speaker or domain. This helps in improving recognition accuracy for individual users or specialized applications.

- **Combining Multiple Models**: Hybrid ASR systems combine the outputs of different ASR models, such as acoustic models trained using DNNs and traditional Hidden Markov Models (HMMs). This ensemble approach reduces errors and improves overall performance.

- **Noise Reduction and Enhancement**: Advanced signal processing techniques, such as beamforming, spectral subtraction, and Wiener filtering, are used to reduce background noise and enhance speech components. These techniques improve the quality of the input signal and enhance recognition accuracy.

Example Application: Voice Assistants

Voice assistants, like Siri, Alexa, and Google Assistant, have gained immense popularity in recent years. They rely heavily on ASR technology to transcribe users' spoken queries into text and provide accurate responses.

For example, when a user says, "Hey Alexa, what's the weather like today?" the speech signal is captured and processed by the ASR system. The acoustic features are extracted, and the language model helps narrow down the search space for the most likely words.

The ASR system then transcribes the speech into text, which is further analyzed to understand the user's intention (weather query) and provide the appropriate response.

In this application, challenges such as speaker variability, background noise, and real-time processing need to be considered. To ensure a seamless user experience, voice assistants rely on sophisticated ASR models trained on large and diverse datasets, as well as continuous improvement through user feedback and adaptation techniques.

Further Resources and Challenges

If you want to dive deeper into the field of Automatic Speech Recognition, there are several resources available:

- **Books:**
    - "Spoken Language Processing: A Guide to Theory, Algorithm, and System Development" by Xuedong Huang, Alex Acero, and Hsiao-Wuen Hon.
    - "Automatic Speech Recognition: A Deep Learning Approach" by Dong Yu and Li Deng.
- **Research Papers:** Many research papers are published in conferences like Interspeech and journals like IEEE Transactions on Audio, Speech, and Language Processing. They cover the latest advancements and challenges in ASR.
- **Online Courses:** Platforms like Coursera and edX offer courses on speech recognition and natural language processing, which include modules on ASR.

One of the ongoing challenges in the field of ASR is achieving better accuracy for low-resource languages and diverse speech patterns. Building ASR systems that understand emotions and speaker intentions in real-time is also an active area of research.

Moreover, improving the robustness of ASR systems in noisy environments and reducing the errors caused by out-of-vocabulary words remain key objectives. As the field of AI continues to evolve, Automatic Speech Recognition will play a vital role in enabling seamless human-computer interaction and transforming the way we interact with technology.

Exercises

1. Explain the concept of data augmentation in the context of automatic speech recognition. How can it help improve the performance of ASR models?

2. Discuss the challenges and considerations involved in developing automatic speech recognition systems for low-resource languages. What techniques can be employed to address these challenges?

3. Imagine you are designing an ASR system for a virtual assistant. How would you handle the issue of speaker variability, considering that the assistant needs to recognize and adapt to the voices of different users?

4. Research and compare the performance of different ASR systems for a specific language, such as Mandarin or Arabic. What factors contribute to the variations in performance, and how can these systems be further improved?

Conclusion

Automatic Speech Recognition is a complex and dynamic field that has made significant advancements in recent years. From voice assistants to transcription services, ASR technology has revolutionized the way we interact with speech-based applications.

In this section, we explored the principles behind ASR, the challenges it faces, and the techniques used to address these challenges. We discussed the role of deep learning, data augmentation, adaptation, and noise reduction in improving the performance of ASR systems.

Furthermore, we examined the application of ASR in voice assistants and the importance of real-time processing, speaker variability, and user adaptation.

As the field of AI continues to advance, automatic speech recognition will continue to evolve and shape the future of human-computer interaction. In the next section, we will delve into the exciting world of language translation and the role of AI in bridging the language barrier.

Text-to-Speech Synthesis

Text-to-speech (TTS) synthesis is a fascinating field of artificial intelligence that focuses on converting written text into spoken words. With the advancement of deep learning and natural language processing techniques, TTS has seen significant progress in recent years. In this section, we will explore the fundamental concepts, techniques, and applications of text-to-speech synthesis.

Introduction to TTS

Text-to-speech synthesis involves the generation of human-like speech from written text. The goal is to create a system that can convert any given text into understandable and natural-sounding speech. TTS systems have various applications, ranging from accessibility for visually impaired individuals to voice assistants and audiobook production.

TTS synthesis can be divided into two main components: text processing and speech synthesis. In the text processing stage, the system analyzes the input text, identifies linguistic and phonetic features, and generates a phonetic representation of the text. The speech synthesis stage then converts the phonetic representation into audible speech.

Phonetics and Prosody

To generate realistic speech, TTS systems must understand the linguistic properties and pronunciation rules of the input text. This involves analyzing the phonetic content, prosody (intonation, stress, and rhythm), and other linguistic features.

Phonetics is the study of the physical sounds of human speech. It focuses on speech sounds, including vowels, consonants, and their articulatory properties. TTS systems utilize phonetic knowledge to accurately pronounce words and sentences.

Prosody refers to the melodic and rhythmic aspects of speech. It includes intonation, stress, and duration patterns used to convey meaning and emotion. Incorporating prosody in TTS synthesis is crucial for generating natural-sounding speech.

Traditional TTS Approaches

Traditional TTS systems relied on concatenative synthesis and formant synthesis methods. Concatenative synthesis involves assembling pre-recorded speech units (phonemes, diphones, or syllables) to generate speech. Although this approach can produce high-quality speech, it requires a large database of recorded speech, making it less flexible and harder to maintain.

Formant synthesis, on the other hand, generates speech by modeling the vocal tract properties involved in speech production. It uses mathematical models to recreate the resonance frequencies and articulatory movements of the vocal tract. While formant synthesis can generate speech with a small memory footprint, the resulting speech often lacks naturalness.

Deep Learning in TTS

Advances in deep learning techniques, particularly recurrent neural networks (RNNs) and transformer models, have revolutionized text-to-speech synthesis. These models can learn the complex relationships between input text, linguistic features, and corresponding speech waveform.

RNN-based TTS models utilize sequence-to-sequence architectures, where an encoder-decoder framework is used to map input text to acoustic features, such as phonemes and durations. These acoustic features are then converted into speech waveforms using vocoders, which are neural networks designed to produce high-quality speech.

Transformer-based TTS models have also gained prominence in recent years. Transformers use self-attention mechanisms to capture long-range dependencies in the input text, improving the naturalness of the synthesized speech. They have shown excellent results in generating accurate phonetic representations and prosody, making them increasingly popular in TTS research.

Training and Evaluation

Training TTS models requires a large dataset of annotated speech recordings aligned with their corresponding text. These datasets, often referred to as parallel corpora, are used to train the models to associate text with the corresponding phonetic representations and speech waveforms.

During training, models learn to predict the acoustic features or the parameters of the vocoder that generate speech. These models are optimized using various loss functions, such as mean squared error or mean absolute error, to minimize the difference between the predicted and target acoustic features.

Evaluating TTS systems involves assessing the naturalness, intelligibility, and overall quality of the synthesized speech. Common evaluation metrics include mean opinion score (MOS) ratings, where human listeners rate the synthesized speech on a scale from 1 to 5. Listeners' preferences and subjective opinions play a crucial role in refining and improving TTS models.

Applications of TTS

Text-to-speech synthesis has diverse applications in various fields. Voice assistants, like Siri and Alexa, utilize TTS to interact with users through spoken language. TTS is also used to create audiobooks, allowing visually impaired individuals to access written content. In the entertainment industry, TTS technology enables the creation of virtual characters and voice dubbing for movies and TV shows.

Additionally, TTS can be utilized in language learning applications to improve pronunciation skills by providing accurate speech feedback. In the accessibility domain, TTS assists individuals with reading difficulties or those who require auditory assistance, such as in navigation systems or public announcements.

Ethics and Challenges

As with any AI technology, text-to-speech synthesis comes with ethical considerations and challenges. Ensuring fairness and inclusivity in synthesized speech is crucial, as biases in training data or model design can lead to unequal representation or misrepresentation of certain linguistic groups. Consequently, efforts are being made to address bias and improve the diversity and accuracy of TTS systems.

Privacy concerns also arise regarding the use of personal data for voice synthesis. Protecting user privacy and data security is essential to maintain public trust in TTS applications.

Conclusion

Text-to-speech synthesis has come a long way, thanks to advances in deep learning and natural language processing. TTS systems can now generate intelligible and natural-sounding speech, enabling a wide range of applications in accessibility, entertainment, education, and more. As technology continues to evolve, text-to-speech synthesis holds exciting possibilities for creating even more realistic and expressive speech.

Language Translation

Machine Translation Techniques

Machine translation (MT) is a subfield of natural language processing (NLP) that focuses on the automatic translation of text or speech from one language to another. With the increasing need for multilingual communication in a globalized

LANGUAGE TRANSLATION

world, machine translation has become a crucial tool in bridging language barriers and enabling effective communication across different cultures.

In this section, we will explore the fundamental techniques used in machine translation, ranging from rule-based approaches to state-of-the-art neural machine translation (NMT) models. We will discuss the strengths and limitations of each approach, along with real-world examples and applications.

Rule-based Machine Translation

The earliest approaches to machine translation were rule-based systems, which relied on a set of linguistic rules and dictionaries to perform translation. These rules were designed by linguists and language experts, and they encoded grammar, vocabulary, and syntactic structures of both the source and target languages.

Rule-based machine translation (RBMT) systems operated on the principle of analyzing the input sentence, breaking it down into its grammatical constituents, and then generating the corresponding sentence in the target language. These systems often utilized hand-crafted syntactic and semantic rules to ensure accurate translation.

One of the notable rule-based machine translation systems is SYSTRAN, which emerged in the early 1970s. SYSTRAN was created by Peter Toma and used linguistic rules and dictionaries to translate text between English and Russian. However, rule-based approaches had several limitations, including difficulty in accommodating the complexity and idiosyncrasies of natural languages. Building and maintaining the rule sets was a labor-intensive task, often resulting in translations that lacked fluency and naturalness.

Statistical Machine Translation

The rise of computational power and the availability of large-scale bilingual corpora paved the way for statistical machine translation (SMT) systems. Unlike rule-based methods, SMT does not rely on explicit linguistic rules. Instead, it utilizes statistical models to learn translation patterns from vast amounts of parallel or aligned corpora.

The core idea behind statistical machine translation is to estimate the probability of a target sentence given a source sentence. This is done using various components, including language models and translation models. Language models capture the probability distribution of words or phrases in the target language, while translation models learn the probability of translating a word or a phrase from the source language to the target language.

One popular SMT framework is the phrase-based model. In this approach, source sentences are divided into phrases, and each phrase is assigned a translation probability. These phrases are then recombined to generate the translated sentence. The translation probabilities are estimated from the parallel corpus using statistical techniques such as n-gram models and word alignments.

The Moses toolkit, developed in the early 2000s, is widely used for implementing statistical machine translation systems. It provides a framework for training and decoding models, along with tools for pre-processing and post-processing of the text.

Despite the success of statistical machine translation, it still suffers from some limitations. These include difficulties in handling morphologically rich languages, lack of context-awareness, and the presence of sparse data. To address these challenges, researchers have shifted their focus to neural machine translation.

Neural Machine Translation

Neural machine translation (NMT) represents a paradigm shift in machine translation, leveraging deep learning techniques to create end-to-end models that directly map a source sentence to its target translation. NMT models are based on neural networks, which are capable of learning complex patterns and capturing the semantic and syntactic structures of natural languages.

The key component of an NMT model is the sequence-to-sequence (seq2seq) model, which consists of an encoder and a decoder. The encoder processes the input sentence and generates a fixed-length representation called the "context vector" or the "thought vector." The decoder then takes this representation and generates the corresponding translated sentence in the target language.

Recurrent neural networks (RNNs), especially long short-term memory (LSTM) networks, were initially used in NMT models. However, the introduction of attention mechanisms revolutionized the field. Attention mechanisms allow the model to focus on different parts of the input sentence while generating the translation, enabling better handling of long sentences and improving translation quality.

One of the pioneering NMT models is the Google Neural Machine Translation (GNMT) system, which was introduced in 2016. GNMT achieved significant improvements over existing approaches and set new benchmarks in machine translation quality.

Since then, many variants and improvements to NMT models have been proposed. Transformer models, introduced in the seminal paper "Attention is All You Need" by Vaswani et al. in 2017, have gained immense popularity.

Transformer models utilize self-attention mechanisms to capture long-range dependencies and enable parallelization during training, resulting in faster and more accurate translations.

Challenges and Future Directions

While neural machine translation has shown remarkable progress, there are still several challenges that researchers are actively working on. Some of these challenges include:

- **Low-resource languages:** Many languages lack sufficient parallel corpora for training NMT models. Developing effective translation systems for low-resource languages remains a major research area.

- **Domain adaptation:** NMT models trained on general domain data may not perform well in specialized domains. Adapting models to specific domains, such as medical or legal, is an ongoing challenge.

- **Rarity and ambiguity:** Translating rare or ambiguous words or phrases accurately is a challenge for NMT models. Techniques such as subword tokenization and enhanced training data creation are being explored to address this issue.

- **Multimodal translation:** Integrating image or video information into translation is an emerging area of research. Multimodal translation aims to generate translations that incorporate both textual and visual cues.

Looking ahead, the field of machine translation holds great promise. Advancements in deep learning, coupled with the availability of large-scale multilingual datasets, are driving the development of more powerful and accurate translation systems. As the demand for seamless cross-lingual communication continues to grow, machine translation techniques will play a pivotal role in breaking down language barriers and fostering global understanding.

Neural Machine Translation

In the field of Natural Language Processing (NLP), one of the most challenging and fascinating tasks is language translation. The ability to automatically translate text from one language to another has countless applications, from creating multilingual chatbots to enabling global communication. However, traditional statistical machine translation (SMT) models have their limitations and often produce translations that are not as fluent or accurate as human-generated translations.

Enter neural machine translation (NMT), a revolution in language translation that leverages the power of artificial neural networks to achieve remarkable translation accuracy and fluency. NMT models have transformed the way we approach translation tasks and have become the go-to method for many translation applications.

The Basics of Neural Machine Translation

At its core, NMT is a sequence-to-sequence (Seq2Seq) model that takes a source language sentence as input and generates the corresponding target language sentence as output. The Seq2Seq architecture consists of two components: an encoder and a decoder.

The encoder processes the source sentence and converts it into a fixed-length vector representation called the *context vector*. This vector contains the semantic and contextual information of the source sentence, which is crucial for generating an accurate translation. The encoder typically consists of recurrent neural network (RNN) layers, such as Long Short-Term Memory (LSTM) or Gated Recurrent Unit (GRU), which can capture the sequential dependencies in the input.

The decoder, on the other hand, takes the context vector as input and generates the target sentence word by word. Similar to the encoder, the decoder is also an RNN-based model that uses a softmax layer to predict the probability distribution over the target vocabulary at each time step. The decoder generates the target sentence by sampling words from this probability distribution.

Training Neural Machine Translation Models

Training an NMT model involves two essential steps: data preparation and model optimization.

Data preparation begins with collecting a parallel corpus, a large dataset that contains pairs of source sentences and their corresponding translations. This corpus serves as the training data for the NMT model. The quality and size of the parallel corpus play a crucial role in the performance of the NMT model, as models trained on larger datasets generally yield better translations.

Once the dataset is prepared, the NMT model is trained using a technique called *teacher forcing*. Teacher forcing involves feeding the model with the correct target sequence during training, enabling it to learn the correct translation for each input sentence. The model's parameters are optimized using gradient descent and backpropagation, reducing the difference between the predicted translation and the actual target translation.

Challenges and Advances in Neural Machine Translation

While NMT has shown tremendous success in various translation tasks, it still faces challenges that impact its performance. One primary challenge is handling rare or unknown words in the target language. As NMT models learn from the training data, they may struggle to generate accurate translations for words they have never encountered before. This is especially problematic in low-resource languages where training data is limited.

To address this challenge, researchers have proposed various techniques, including using subword units instead of individual words and incorporating external knowledge sources such as bilingual dictionaries or monolingual data.

Another challenge in NMT is mitigating the problem of *exposure bias*. Exposure bias refers to the discrepancy between training and inference, where the model is trained with access to the correct target sequence but during inference, it relies on its own generated output. This discrepancy can lead to errors accumulating and affecting the quality of the translation.

To overcome exposure bias, techniques such as scheduled sampling and reinforcement learning have been introduced. Scheduled sampling gradually transitions the model from teacher forcing to its own predictions during training, better aligning the training and inference processes. Reinforcement learning, on the other hand, introduces a reward mechanism to guide the model towards generating more accurate translations.

Real-World Applications of Neural Machine Translation

The advancements in NMT have opened up exciting possibilities for numerous real-world applications. Here are a few examples:

- **Multilingual Communication Platforms:** NMT can power multilingual chatbots and communication platforms, enabling real-time translation between users speaking different languages.

- **Global E-Commerce:** NMT can facilitate seamless cross-border e-commerce by automatically translating product descriptions, reviews, and customer support inquiries.

- **International News and Media:** News agencies can leverage NMT to provide instant translations of news articles, making their content accessible to a global audience in multiple languages.

- **Language Learning and Education:** NMT can enhance language learning platforms by providing instant translation and feedback to learners, helping them understand and communicate in foreign languages.

Conclusion

Neural Machine Translation has revolutionized the field of language translation, leading to more accurate and fluent translations than ever before. By leveraging the power of artificial neural networks, NMT models have overcome many of the limitations of traditional machine translation approaches. And as NMT continues to advance, we can expect even more exciting developments and applications in the fields of multilingual communication, global commerce, media, and education.

Now, let's dive deeper into the fascinating world of computer vision in the next section.

Challenges in Language Translation

Language translation is a complex task that involves converting text or speech from one language into another. While advancements in artificial intelligence have greatly improved the accuracy and efficiency of translation systems, there are still several challenges that need to be addressed. In this section, we will explore some of these challenges and discuss possible solutions.

Ambiguity and Context

One of the major challenges in language translation is dealing with ambiguity. Many words and phrases have multiple meanings depending on the context in which they are used. For example, the word "bank" can refer to a financial institution or the edge of a river.

To tackle this challenge, translators employ various techniques. One approach is to use statistical models that analyze the surrounding words to determine the most probable meaning. Another method is to leverage contextual information and incorporate it into the translation process. This can be done by using larger segments of text instead of individual words to capture the overall context.

LANGUAGE TRANSLATION

Idiomatic Expressions and Cultural Nuances

Idiomatic expressions, proverbs, and cultural nuances pose significant challenges in language translation. These are phrases that have a figurative or specialized meaning that may not be directly translatable. For example, the English phrase "kick the bucket" means to die, but a literal translation in another language would not convey the intended meaning.

Translators often face the dilemma of choosing between a literal translation that preserves the exact words but sacrifices the meaning, or an adaptive translation that captures the intended meaning but may not be a word-for-word representation.

To overcome this challenge, translators rely on their cultural knowledge and expertise to find equivalent expressions in the target language. Additionally, machine learning models can be trained on large corpora of translated texts to learn common idiomatic expressions and their translations.

Lack of Parallel Data

Language translation models typically rely on large amounts of parallel data, which are pairs of sentences in the source and target languages. These data are used to train machine learning models by learning the correspondence between the source and target languages.

However, obtaining high-quality parallel data for many language pairs is challenging. Some languages have limited resources available, making it difficult to train accurate translation models. This lack of parallel data can lead to poor performance in translation systems.

To address this challenge, researchers are exploring unsupervised learning techniques that do not require parallel data. These methods aim to learn the underlying structure of languages based on monolingual data and use it to generate translations. While still in its early stages, unsupervised learning holds promise for improving translation performance for language pairs with limited resources.

Domain-Specific Translations

Different domains have their own unique terminologies and conventions. Translating specialized texts such as medical or legal documents requires domain-specific knowledge and expertise. Without this expertise, machine translation systems may produce inaccurate or nonsensical translations.

One solution to this challenge is the development of domain-specific translation models. These models are trained on data from specific domains, allowing them to capture the domain-specific terminologies and conventions. Additionally, human post-editing can be used to refine the translations produced by machine translation systems for domain-specific texts.

Evaluation of Translation Quality

Evaluating the quality of machine translations is a challenging task. While metrics such as BLEU (Bilingual Evaluation Understudy) have been widely used to assess translation quality, they have limitations and may not always align with human judgments.

To overcome this challenge, researchers are exploring alternative evaluation approaches, such as using human evaluators or crowdsourcing platforms to collect feedback on translation quality. Additionally, the development of new metrics that take into account factors such as fluency, fidelity to the source text, and cultural appropriateness is an active area of research.

In conclusion, language translation presents several challenges that require innovative approaches and ongoing research. From dealing with ambiguity and idiomatic expressions to addressing the lack of parallel data and evaluating translation quality, the field of language translation is continually evolving. By combining the power of artificial intelligence with human expertise, we can overcome these challenges and achieve more accurate and nuanced translations.

Exercises

1. Give an example of an idiomatic expression in your native language and explain its meaning. How would you translate this expression into English, and what challenges would you encounter?

2. Research and compare different evaluation metrics used in machine translation. Discuss their strengths and weaknesses.

3. Describe a domain-specific translation task (e.g., medical, legal, technical) and explain the challenges it presents for machine translation. How would you approach translating texts in this domain?

Resources

- Koehn, P. (2010). *Statistical Machine Translation*. Cambridge University Press.

- Jurafsky, D., & Martin, J. H. (2020). *Speech and Language Processing*. Pearson.

- Liu, Y., & Zhang, Q. (2020). *Neural Machine Translation and Sequence-to-Sequence Models: A Tutorial.* arXiv preprint arXiv:1904.09077.

- Papineni, K., Roukos, S., Ward, T., & Zhu, W. J. (2002). BLEU: a method for automatic evaluation of machine translation. In *Proceedings of the 40th Annual Meeting of the Association for Computational Linguistics* (pp. 311-318).

Additional Reading

- Halevy, A., Norvig, P., & Pereira, F. (2009). The Unreasonable Effectiveness of Data. *IEEE Intelligent Systems*, 24(1), 8-12.

- Luong, M. T., Pham, H., & Manning, C. D. (2015). Effective Approaches to Attention-based Neural Machine Translation. In *Proceedings of the Conference on Empirical Methods in Natural Language Processing* (pp. 1412-1421).

- Vaswani, A., Shazeer, N., Parmar, N., Uszkoreit, J., Jones, L., Gomez, A. N., ... & Polosukhin, I. (2017). Attention is All You Need. In *Proceedings of the Conference on Neural Information Processing Systems* (pp. 5998-6008).

Conclusion

In this section, we explored the challenges faced in language translation. From ambiguity and idiomatic expressions to the lack of parallel data and domain-specific translations, these challenges require innovative techniques and ongoing research. Through the combined efforts of artificial intelligence and human expertise, we can continue to improve the accuracy and effectiveness of language translation systems. The field of language translation is an exciting and dynamic area, offering immense potential for bridging linguistic and cultural barriers in our increasingly interconnected world.

Computer Vision

Introduction to Computer Vision

Image Processing

Image processing is a fundamental aspect of computer vision and plays a crucial role in analyzing and understanding visual data. In this section, we will explore the principles, techniques, and applications of image processing.

Introduction to Image Processing

Images are visual representations of the real world, composed of pixels that contain information about color and intensity. Image processing involves manipulating and analyzing these pixels to enhance or extract useful information from the images.

The goal of image processing is to improve the visual quality of images, correct distortions, remove noise, perform transformations, and extract relevant features. This is achieved through a series of operations applied to the pixels of the image.

Image Representation

Before diving into image processing techniques, let's first understand how images are represented. In digital image processing, images are represented as a two-dimensional grid of pixels.

Each pixel in the image represents a specific location and contains information about the color and intensity at that location. The most common color models used in image processing are grayscale and RGB.

In a grayscale image, each pixel represents a different shade of gray, ranging from black (0 intensity) to white (maximum intensity). The intensity value is usually represented by an 8-bit value (0-255).

In an RGB image, each pixel contains three color channels: red, green, and blue. The intensity of each channel determines the contribution of that color to the overall appearance of the pixel. Each color channel is usually represented by an 8-bit value (0-255).

Image Enhancement

Image enhancement techniques aim to improve the visual quality of images by reducing noise, increasing contrast, and sharpening edges. These techniques are widely used in various applications, such as medical imaging, surveillance, and photography.

One commonly used technique for image enhancement is histogram equalization. The histogram of an image represents the distribution of pixel intensities. Histogram equalization redistributes the intensities in such a way that the histogram becomes more balanced, resulting in improved contrast and detail in the image.

Another technique is image denoising, which removes unwanted noise from the image. Noise can be caused by various factors such as sensor limitations, transmission errors, or environmental conditions. Denoising algorithms aim to preserve important image details while reducing the noise components.

Image Filtering

Image filtering involves applying a filter or a mask to an image to perform operations such as blurring, sharpening, and edge detection. Filters can be applied using various techniques, including convolution and frequency domain analysis.

Convolution is a widely used technique in image processing that involves sliding a filter across the image and performing element-wise multiplication and summation operations. The resulting output represents the filtered image. Common filter types include Gaussian filters, which blur the image, and Laplacian filters, which enhance edges.

Frequency domain analysis, on the other hand, transforms the image into its frequency components using techniques like the Fast Fourier Transform (FFT). By manipulating the frequency components, it is possible to perform operations such as sharpening or removing periodic noise.

Image Segmentation

Image segmentation is the process of partitioning an image into multiple regions or objects. It is a crucial step in many computer vision applications, including object

INTRODUCTION TO COMPUTER VISION

recognition, image understanding, and medical imaging.

Segmentation techniques aim to group pixels into meaningful regions based on their characteristics, such as color, intensity, texture, or motion. One commonly used technique is thresholding, where pixels with intensity values above or below a certain threshold are assigned to different regions.

Other segmentation techniques include region-based approaches, where regions are grown based on similarity criteria, and edge-based approaches, which use image gradients to detect boundaries between regions.

Image Compression

Image compression techniques aim to reduce the size of digital images to facilitate storage and transmission. These techniques exploit redundancies in the image data to achieve compression.

There are two main types of image compression: lossless and lossy. Lossless compression techniques ensure that the original image can be perfectly reconstructed from the compressed data. Lossy compression techniques, on the other hand, sacrifice some image quality to achieve higher compression ratios.

One widely used image compression technique is the JPEG (Joint Photographic Experts Group) compression algorithm. It uses a combination of lossy compression techniques, including discrete cosine transform (DCT) and quantization, to achieve high compression ratios while preserving acceptable image quality.

Applications of Image Processing

Image processing has numerous applications in various fields. Some examples include:

- Medical Imaging: Image processing techniques are used in medical diagnostics, such as X-ray analysis, MRI, and CT scans. They help in detecting abnormalities, segmenting organs, and enhancing image quality.

- Surveillance: Image processing plays a crucial role in video surveillance systems. It is used for object detection and tracking, facial recognition, and behavior analysis.

- Robotics: Image processing is an integral part of robotics, enabling robots to perceive and understand their environment. It is used for tasks like object recognition, navigation, and grasping.

- Augmented Reality: Image processing techniques are used in augmented reality applications to overlay digital information onto the real-world view, enhancing the user experience.

- Remote Sensing: Image processing is used to analyze satellite imagery, aerial photography, and other remote sensing data. It helps in mapping, land cover classification, and environmental monitoring.

Conclusion

Image processing is a fascinating field that plays a vital role in computer vision and has a wide range of applications. Through techniques such as enhancement, filtering, segmentation, and compression, images can be manipulated and analyzed to extract valuable information.

Understanding the principles and techniques of image processing is essential for anyone working in the field of artificial intelligence and computer vision. By harnessing the power of image processing, we can transform raw visual data into meaningful insights and drive innovation in various domains.

So, sharpen your pixels, blur your edges, and let the algorithms work their magic - it's time to dive deep into the captivating world of image processing!

Object Detection and Recognition

Object detection and recognition is a fundamental task in computer vision and plays a crucial role in many AI applications. It involves identifying and locating objects of interest within an image or video stream. Object detection enables machines to perceive their surroundings, understand the content, and make intelligent decisions based on the visual information.

Introduction to Object Detection

Object detection is the process of locating and classifying multiple objects within an image. The goal is to accurately identify the presence and locations of different objects in a given scene. This task is challenging due to variations in object appearance, scale, orientation, occlusions, and cluttered backgrounds.

The traditional approach to object detection involved using handcrafted features and classifiers to identify objects based on the properties such as edges, texture, color, or shape. However, these methods had limited success due to the complexity and variability of real-world scenes.

Convolutional Neural Networks (CNNs) for Object Detection

In recent years, Convolutional Neural Networks (CNNs) have revolutionized the field of object detection. CNNs are deep learning models specifically designed to process visual data like images and video. They excel at extracting high-level features from raw pixel values, enabling them to learn complex patterns and representations.

The two most popular approaches for object detection using CNNs are region-based methods and single-shot methods.

Region-based methods: These methods divide the image into a grid of potential object regions, known as region proposals. Each region proposal is then classified to determine if it contains an object of interest. The famous region-based method is the Region-based Convolutional Neural Network (R-CNN), which performs region proposals using techniques like Selective Search and then uses a CNN to classify these regions.

Single-shot methods: These methods perform object detection in a single pass through the network, without requiring region proposals. They simultaneously predict the object class labels and the bounding box coordinates of the objects. Examples of single-shot methods include You Only Look Once (YOLO) and Single Shot MultiBox Detector (SSD).

Both region-based and single-shot methods have their advantages and trade-offs. Region-based methods generally have higher detection accuracy but are slower due to the two-stage process. On the other hand, single-shot methods are faster but may sacrifice some accuracy.

Training Object Detection Models

Training an object detection model involves two main components: generating a labeled dataset and optimizing the model parameters.

Dataset creation: Creating a labeled dataset for object detection requires annotating images with bounding boxes around the objects of interest and associating class labels with each bounding box. This process can be time-consuming and requires expertise in object labeling. However, there are pre-existing datasets such as COCO (Common Objects in Context) and Pascal VOC (Visual Object Classes) available that contain labeled images for various object categories.

Model optimization: Once the dataset is prepared, the model is trained using a process called backpropagation, where the model learns to adjust its parameters to minimize the difference between predicted and ground truth bounding boxes and class labels. The optimization process typically involves minimizing a loss function such as the mean squared error (MSE) or the smooth L1 loss.

Challenges and Solutions

Object detection faces several challenges that can impact the accuracy and reliability of the models. Some of the main challenges include:

Scale variations: Objects can appear at different scales in images, making it difficult to detect them accurately. One solution to this challenge is using multi-scale object detection techniques, where the image is processed at multiple resolutions to capture objects of different sizes.

Occlusions: Objects are often occluded by other objects or the scene itself, making their detection more challenging. Advanced object detection algorithms use contextual information and spatial reasoning to handle partial occlusions.

Cluttered backgrounds: Objects can blend with cluttered backgrounds, making them harder to detect. Techniques like non-maximum suppression (NMS) are used to discard overlapping bounding box proposals and output only the most confident detection results.

Real-time processing: Many applications require real-time object detection, such as autonomous driving or surveillance systems. To achieve real-time performance, optimizations like model pruning, network compression, and hardware acceleration are employed.

Applications of Object Detection and Recognition

Object detection and recognition have a wide range of applications in various domains. Here are a few examples:

Autonomous driving: Object detection enables self-driving cars to detect and track pedestrians, vehicles, and other objects on the road to make informed decisions and avoid collisions.

Surveillance and security: Object detection is used to monitor public spaces, identify suspicious activities, and track individuals of interest in surveillance systems.

Retail and inventory management: Object detection can be used for automated checkout systems, shelf monitoring, and inventory management in retail stores.

Medical imaging: Object detection helps in detecting and localizing abnormalities in medical images, assisting in the diagnosis of diseases like cancer.

Augmented reality: Object detection is essential in augmenting virtual objects onto the real-world scene in applications like mobile gaming or virtual try-on experiences.

Conclusion

Object detection and recognition are essential components of computer vision and artificial intelligence. With the advancements in deep learning and CNNs, we have witnessed significant progress in accurate and efficient object detection algorithms. These technologies have enabled a wide range of applications in various domains, from autonomous driving to healthcare. Understanding the principles and techniques of object detection allows us to build intelligent systems that can visually perceive and interpret the world around us.

Further Reading

If you're interested in diving deeper into the world of object detection and recognition, here are some recommended resources:

- "Deep Learning for Object Detection: A Comprehensive Review" by Xudong Wang and Qiang Liu.
- "Object Detection and Recognition in Digital Images: Theory and Practice" by Bogdan Raducanu and Dhanendra Singh.
- "Deep Learning for Computer Vision" by Rajalingappaa Shanmugamani.
- "Computer Vision: Algorithms and Applications" by Richard Szeliski.

Image Segmentation

Image segmentation is a fundamental task in computer vision that involves partitioning an image into multiple regions or segments. Each segment represents a distinct object or region of interest within the image. The goal of image segmentation is to accurately assign pixels to their corresponding segments, enabling higher-level analysis and interpretation of images.

Principles of Image Segmentation

The principles of image segmentation can be understood through two main approaches: *thresholding* and *region-based segmentation*.

Thresholding: Thresholding is a simple and commonly used technique for image segmentation. It is based on the idea of dividing the image into distinct regions based on pixel intensity values. A threshold value is selected, and each pixel is classified as belonging to a specific segment based on whether its intensity is above or below the threshold. This method is particularly suitable for images with well-defined intensity differences between regions of interest.

Region-based Segmentation: Region-based segmentation approaches consider both local and global image properties to divide it into meaningful regions. These methods take into account various image features such as intensity, color, texture, and shape to determine segment boundaries. One popular approach is the *watershed algorithm*, which mimics the process of water filling up valleys to separate distinct regions based on intensity values. Another common method is *graph-based segmentation*, where pixels are represented as nodes in a graph and segment boundaries are defined by the edges connecting these nodes.

Challenges in Image Segmentation

Image segmentation is a challenging task due to several factors:

Ambiguity: Some images may have areas where the boundaries between objects or regions are unclear or ambiguous. This ambiguity makes it difficult to accurately segment the image, as the boundaries may not be well-defined or easily distinguishable.

Complexity: Images can contain complex structures such as overlapping objects, occlusions, or varying lighting conditions. These factors can make it challenging to separate objects or regions accurately, requiring more advanced segmentation techniques.

Noise and Variability: Images are often affected by noise or variations in image acquisition, such as sensor noise, blurriness, or changes in lighting. These factors can introduce inconsistencies and irregularities that affect segmentation accuracy.

Computational Complexity: Image segmentation can be a computationally intensive task, especially for large images or real-time applications. Efficient algorithms and optimizations are necessary to achieve fast and accurate segmentation results.

State-of-the-Art Techniques

Several state-of-the-art techniques have been developed to address the challenges in image segmentation. Here are a few notable ones:

Convolutional Neural Networks (CNNs): CNNs have revolutionized image segmentation by learning feature representations directly from the data. Fully Convolutional Networks (FCNs) have been widely used for pixel-level segmentation tasks. FCNs take an input image and produce a pixel-wise segmentation map, assigning each pixel to a specific class or segment.

U-Net Architecture: U-Net is a popular CNN architecture specifically designed for medical image segmentation. It consists of an encoder network to capture context and a decoder network to recover the spatial information. U-Net has achieved state-of-the-art results in various medical image segmentation tasks.

Graph Cuts: Graph cuts-based algorithms use graph theory to model image segmentation. By representing an image as a graph, with each pixel as a node and pairwise relationships between pixels as graph edges, graph cuts optimize an energy function to find the optimal segmentation. This technique is particularly useful for segmenting images with clear object boundaries.

Applications of Image Segmentation

Image segmentation has wide-ranging applications in various domains. Some notable applications include:

Medical Imaging: Image segmentation plays a crucial role in medical imaging for diagnosing and analyzing various diseases and conditions. It helps in segmenting organs, tumors, and other pathological structures from medical images like CT scans, MRI scans, and ultrasound images.

Object Recognition and Tracking: Image segmentation is used to identify and track objects in computer vision tasks such as autonomous driving, surveillance, and robotics. It helps in distinguishing objects of interest from the background and enables higher-level perception algorithms.

Image Editing and Augmentation: Image segmentation is utilized in image editing software to provide more precise editing capabilities. It enables selective editing of specific regions or objects within an image, allowing for tasks such as background removal, object manipulation, and image synthesis.

Conclusion

Image segmentation is a fundamental task in computer vision that allows us to divide images into meaningful regions or objects. It is a challenging problem due to factors like ambiguity, complexity, and noise. However, with the advancements in deep learning and other state-of-the-art techniques, accurate and efficient image segmentation is now achievable. The applications of image segmentation are vast and impact various domains, including medicine, object recognition, and image editing. As computer vision continues to advance, image segmentation will play a crucial role in unlocking the full potential of artificial intelligence.

Face Recognition

Face recognition is a fascinating application of computer vision and artificial intelligence that has gained significant attention in recent years. It involves the identification or verification of individuals based on their facial features. With the advent of deep learning and advanced algorithms, face recognition has become highly accurate and widely used in various domains, including surveillance systems, biometric authentication, and social media applications.

The Basics of Face Recognition

The first step in face recognition is face detection, where the system identifies and localizes faces in an image or video stream. This is often achieved using Haar cascades or convolutional neural networks (CNNs) trained specifically to recognize faces. Once the faces are detected, the next step is feature extraction, where the unique characteristics of each face are encoded into a numerical representation known as a feature vector.

One of the most popular algorithms for face feature extraction is the *Eigenfaces* method. It uses Principal Component Analysis (PCA) to reduce the dimensionality of a face image and extract the most discriminative features. Another commonly used technique is *Local Binary Patterns* (LBP), which encodes the texture and appearance of different regions of the face.

Face Recognition Techniques

Once the feature vectors are generated, the face recognition algorithm compares them with the feature vectors of enrolled individuals to make a match. There are two main techniques used for this purpose: *Traditional Methods* and *Deep Learning*.

1. **Traditional Methods:** Traditional face recognition methods rely on statistical and mathematical algorithms to compare and match feature vectors. The most widely used approach is the *Euclidean Distance* or *Cosine Similarity* method, where the similarity between two feature vectors is calculated using these measures. If the similarity exceeds a certain threshold, the faces are considered a match.

2. **Deep Learning:** Deep learning has revolutionized the field of face recognition, achieving state-of-the-art performance. Convolutional Neural Networks (CNNs) are commonly used for this task. A widely known CNN architecture for face recognition is *FaceNet*, which maps faces into a high-dimensional feature space, making the similarity calculation easier. Similar to traditional methods, a threshold is used to determine if the faces match.

Challenges and Limitations

Although face recognition has made significant progress, it still faces challenges and limitations that need to be addressed:

1. **Variability in Facial Appearance:** Faces can exhibit variations in illumination, pose, expression, and occlusions. These factors can affect the accuracy of face recognition algorithms and lead to false rejections or false acceptances.

2. **Privacy Concerns:** Face recognition systems raise privacy concerns, as the technology can be used for unauthorized surveillance or invasive identification.

3. **Demographic Bias:** Some face recognition algorithms exhibit bias towards certain demographic groups, particularly those with darker skin tones or female individuals. This can lead to unfair outcomes and implications.

4. **Adversarial Attacks:** Face recognition systems are vulnerable to adversarial attacks, where subtle modifications to faces can fool the algorithm into misclassification.

Addressing these challenges requires ongoing research and development in the field of face recognition.

Real-World Applications

Face recognition technology is used in various real-world applications, some of which include:

1. **Biometric Authentication:** Face recognition is widely used for biometric authentication, providing secure access to devices, online accounts, or physical spaces without the need for passwords or identification cards.

2. **Surveillance Systems:** Face recognition plays a crucial role in surveillance systems, assisting in identifying and tracking individuals of interest for law enforcement or security purposes.

3. **Social Media and Photo Tagging:** Social media platforms utilize face recognition to automatically tag individuals in photos, making it easier to share and organize memories.

4. **Emotion Detection:** Facial expressions can be analyzed using face recognition to detect and interpret human emotions, which is useful in areas such as market research and mental health.

Exercises

1. Research and evaluate the ethical implications of using face recognition technology in surveillance systems. Discuss potential concerns and benefits.

2. Experiment with OpenCV, a popular computer vision library, to implement a simple face recognition system that can recognize faces from images or video streams.

3. Investigate and compare different face recognition algorithms, such as Eigenfaces, Fisherfaces, and Local Binary Patterns, in terms of accuracy and computational complexity.

4. Explore the concept of adversarial attacks in face recognition systems. Implement an attack to fool a face recognition algorithm using subtle facial modifications.

Recommended Resources

- Microsoft Research "Face Recognition" - An overview of face recognition technology, including its applications and challenges. Available at: https://www.microsoft.com/en-us/research/theme/face-recognition/

- OpenFace - An open-source deep learning facial recognition toolkit that provides models and tools for face detection, alignment, and recognition. Available at: https://cmusatyalab.github.io/openface/

- Khan Academy "Face recognition" - A video tutorial series on the basics of face recognition and the mathematics behind it. Available at: https://www.khanacademy.org/math/multivariable-calculus/applications-of-multivariable-derivatives/

In conclusion, face recognition is a powerful technology that has tremendous potential in various applications. While it comes with its own set of challenges and limitations, continuous advancements in algorithms and techniques are enabling face recognition systems to become more accurate and reliable. With proper ethical considerations and further research, face recognition can continue to evolve and contribute to the development of intelligent systems.

Convolutional Neural Networks

Basics of CNNs

Convolutional Neural Networks (CNNs) are a powerful class of neural networks that have revolutionized the field of computer vision. They have enabled significant advancements in tasks such as image classification, object detection, and image generation. In this section, we will explore the fundamentals of CNNs, their architecture, and how they operate.

Introduction to Convolutional Neural Networks

Convolutional Neural Networks are specifically designed to process data with a known grid-like structure, such as images. They are inspired by the visual cortex of animals, which contains cells that are sensitive to small regions of the visual field, known as receptive fields. Similarly, CNNs employ a hierarchical architecture that consists of convolutional layers, pooling layers, and fully connected layers.

Convolutional Layers

The main building block of a CNN is the convolutional layer. Each layer is composed of a set of learnable filters, also known as kernels or feature detectors. These filters slide across the input data and perform convolutions to extract local features. The key idea is that each filter focuses on a specific pattern or feature present in the input data.

Let's consider a color image as an example. The image consists of three channels: red, green, and blue (RGB). Each channel can be represented as a 2D grid of pixel values. A filter in the first convolutional layer, also called a kernel, is a smaller 2D grid of learnable weights.

During the convolution operation, the kernel slides over the input image, performing element-wise multiplication between the kernel weights and the corresponding pixel values in the receptive field. The resulting values are summed up to produce a single value, which forms a new pixel in the output feature map. This process of sliding and summing is repeated for every possible receptive field in the input image.

The choice of filter size, stride, and padding can greatly influence the output feature map's dimensions. Common choices for filter size include 3x3, 5x5, and 7x7. The stride value represents the number of pixels the filter moves at each step, determining the downsampling factor. Padding can be added to preserve the spatial dimensions of the input image, which is crucial in avoiding information loss.

Pooling Layers

Pooling layers are often used in CNNs to reduce the spatial dimensions of the feature maps while retaining the most important information. The most common pooling operation is max-pooling, where the input feature map is divided into non-overlapping regions, and the maximum value within each region is selected to form the output feature map.

Max-pooling helps in making the representation more robust to variations, reducing the amount of computation needed, and controlling overfitting. By performing downsampling using max-pooling, the CNN becomes invariant to small translations in the input data, which is desirable for tasks such as object recognition.

Fully Connected Layers

After several convolutional and pooling layers, the output features are connected to fully connected layers. These layers are responsible for making the final predictions based on the learned representations. Each neuron in a fully connected layer receives input from all neurons in the previous layer. These layers can be thought of as traditional feedforward neural networks, where each neuron applies a weight to its inputs, passes the result through an activation function, and produces an output.

The fully connected layers typically have a large number of parameters, and their purpose is to learn complex relationships between the extracted features and the target variable. This makes the CNN capable of capturing high-level abstract representations of the input data.

Training and Optimization

Training a CNN involves initializing the network's parameters and updating them iteratively to minimize a loss function. The loss function quantifies the dissimilarity between the predicted output and the true output. The most common loss function for classification problems is the categorical cross-entropy, while mean squared error is commonly used for regression problems.

CONVOLUTIONAL NEURAL NETWORKS

The optimization process in CNNs is typically done using gradient-based optimization algorithms, such as stochastic gradient descent (SGD) or its variants. The gradients are computed through a technique called backpropagation, which efficiently calculates the gradients of the loss with respect to all the parameters in the network.

Applications and Examples

CNNs have demonstrated remarkable performance in a wide range of computer vision tasks. For instance, in image classification tasks, CNNs can accurately classify images into different categories, such as identifying whether an image contains a cat or a dog. In object detection tasks, CNNs can localize and classify objects within an image, enabling applications such as self-driving cars and surveillance systems.

Another fascinating application of CNNs is in image generation and style transfer. Generative Adversarial Networks (GANs), a type of CNN architecture, can generate realistic synthetic images that resemble real-world data. Neural Style Transfer, on the other hand, can merge the content of one image with the artistic style of another, resulting in visually appealing images.

Resource and Further Reading

Learning about CNNs is an exciting journey, and there are numerous resources available to deepen your understanding. Some recommended resources for further reading and exploration include:

- "Deep Learning" by Ian Goodfellow, Yoshua Bengio, and Aaron Courville.
- "Convolutional Neural Networks for Visual Recognition" course by Stanford University, available online.
- "Deep Learning Specialization" on Coursera, offered by deeplearning.ai.
- Blogs, tutorials, and code repositories related to CNNs on platforms like Medium, Towards Data Science, and GitHub.

These resources provide a comprehensive overview of CNNs, their architecture, training techniques, and their applications in various domains. Additionally, exploring research papers and staying up to date with the latest advancements in computer vision can foster a deeper understanding of this exciting field.

Exercise

To reinforce your understanding of CNNs, consider the following exercise:

Suppose you are given a dataset of images representing different fruits, such as apples, bananas, and oranges. Design a CNN architecture that can classify these fruits with high accuracy. Describe the structure of your network, including the number of convolutional layers, pooling layers, and fully connected layers. Explain why you chose this architecture and how you would train and evaluate it.

Remember, correctness and accuracy are crucial when designing CNN architectures. Consider the number of parameters, overfitting, and generalization ability while designing your network.

Training CNNs

Training Convolutional Neural Networks (CNNs) is a crucial step in building powerful computer vision models. In this section, we will explore the fundamentals of CNN training, including data preprocessing, optimization, and regularization techniques. We will also discuss common challenges and best practices to improve the performance of CNNs.

Data Preprocessing

Before training a CNN, it is essential to preprocess the data to ensure optimal performance. The following preprocessing steps are commonly applied:

- **Data normalization**: CNNs work best when the input data has zero mean and equal variance. Normalizing the data to a standard range, such as [0, 1] or [-1, 1], helps prevent extreme gradients during training. This can be achieved by scaling the pixel values of images or using techniques like feature scaling for other types of data.

- **Data augmentation**: Increasing the amount of training data can help prevent overfitting and improve generalization. Data augmentation techniques, such as random cropping, rotation, flipping, and zooming, are commonly used to artificially expand the dataset. This introduces variations in the input data, making the model more robust.

- **Label encoding**: For classification tasks, it is necessary to encode categorical labels into numerical values. This can be done using techniques like one-hot encoding or label encoding, depending on the nature of the problem.

Proper data preprocessing ensures that the CNN learns meaningful features from the input data and reduces the chances of it being biased towards any specific properties.

Optimization

Training a CNN involves optimizing its parameters to minimize a loss function. This is typically done using gradient-based optimization algorithms, such as stochastic gradient descent (SGD) and its variants. The key components of optimization are discussed below:

- **Loss function:** The loss function quantifies the difference between the predicted output and the actual output. For classification tasks, cross-entropy loss is commonly used, while mean squared error (MSE) loss is often utilized for regression problems. Choosing an appropriate loss function depends on the nature of the task.

- **Backpropagation:** Backpropagation is a technique used to compute the gradients of the loss function with respect to the weights and biases of the CNN. It allows for efficient computation of these gradients by propagating them backwards through the network. This step is crucial for updating the model's parameters during optimization.

- **Learning rate:** The learning rate determines the step size taken during parameter updates. A high learning rate may lead to unstable training, while a low learning rate can result in slow convergence. Finding an optimal learning rate is crucial for efficient training. Techniques like learning rate scheduling and adaptive learning rate methods, such as Adam and RMSprop, can be employed to improve optimization.

- **Batch size:** During training, the data is divided into batches, and the weights are updated based on the gradients computed on these batches. The batch size determines the trade-off between computational efficiency and the accuracy of the gradient estimate. Smaller batch sizes may result in noisy gradients but faster training, while larger batch sizes provide more accurate gradients at the cost of increased memory usage.

- **Regularization:** Regularization techniques are used to prevent overfitting, where the model performs well on the training data but poorly on unseen data. Common regularization techniques for CNNs include L1 and L2 regularization, dropout, and batch normalization. These techniques introduce additional constraints or modify the network's architecture to improve its generalization capabilities.

Improving CNN Performance

Training CNNs can be challenging due to various factors like vanishing gradients, overfitting, and convergence issues. To enhance the performance of CNNs, consider the following strategies:

- **Transfer learning**: Transfer learning allows leveraging pre-trained CNN models on large datasets to solve similar tasks with limited data. By utilizing features learned from a different but related task, the model can generalize better. Fine-tuning the pre-trained model by adjusting its weights can further enhance performance.

- **Early stopping**: Monitoring the model's performance during training can prevent overfitting. Using a validation set, one can stop training when the model's performance on the validation set starts to degrade. This prevents the model from learning noise in the training data and improves generalization.

- **Ensemble learning**: Combining predictions from multiple CNN models can often lead to better results. Ensemble methods, such as averaging or stacking the outputs of different models, can reduce model variance and improve overall accuracy.

- **Regularization techniques**: As mentioned earlier, regularization techniques like dropout, batch normalization, and weight regularization can help improve the generalization capabilities of CNNs. Experimenting with different regularization techniques can be beneficial in achieving better performance.

- **Hyperparameter tuning**: CNNs have various hyperparameters, such as the number of layers, filter sizes, and learning rate. Finding the optimal combination of these hyperparameters can significantly impact the model's performance. Techniques like grid search, random search, or Bayesian optimization can be employed to search for the best hyperparameters.

Real-World Example: Image Classification

Let's consider a real-world example of training a CNN for image classification. Suppose we want to classify images of cats and dogs. We have a dataset with 10,000 labeled images, evenly distributed between cats and dogs.

To train the CNN, we divide the dataset into training and validation sets, with 80% of the data used for training and 20% for validation. We preprocess the images by resizing them to a fixed size, normalizing the pixel values between 0 and 1, and applying data augmentation techniques like random flipping and rotation.

Next, we construct a CNN architecture using Convolutional, MaxPooling, and Dense layers. We initialize the weights randomly and use the cross-entropy loss function for classification. During optimization, we employ stochastic gradient descent with a learning rate of 0.001 and a batch size of 32. We monitor the model's performance on the validation set to decide when to stop training using early stopping.

After training for several epochs, we evaluate the model on a test set consisting of unseen images. We calculate metrics like accuracy, precision, recall, and F1 score to assess the model's performance. If the performance is not satisfactory, we can experiment with different regularization techniques, adjust hyperparameters, or try transfer learning with pre-trained models to improve accuracy.

By following a systematic approach to data preprocessing, optimization, and model evaluation, we can train CNNs to achieve high accuracy in real-world image classification tasks.

Additional Resources

To further enhance your understanding of training CNNs, here are some additional resources:

- **Books:**
    - "Deep Learning" by Ian Goodfellow, Yoshua Bengio, and Aaron Courville
    - "Hands-On Machine Learning with Scikit-Learn, Keras, and TensorFlow" by Aurélien Géron
- **Online Courses:**
    - Coursera: "Deep Learning Specialization" by deeplearning.ai
    - Udacity: "Deep Learning Nanodegree Program" by Udacity

- **Online Platforms:**

    - TensorFlow Tutorials: Official TensorFlow website provides tutorials and examples on CNN training using TensorFlow framework.
    - Keras Documentation: Keras documentation provides detailed explanations and examples of training CNNs using the Keras library.

Remember, training CNNs requires practice and experimentation. So, dive in, get your hands dirty, and enjoy the process of transforming data into dominance with the power of artificial intelligence!

Exercises

Now that we have covered the training of CNNs, let's test your understanding with some exercises:

1. Explain the concept of data normalization and its importance in training CNNs. How does it prevent extreme gradients?

2. Suppose you are training a CNN for image classification, and you notice that the model is starting to overfit the training data. Suggest at least two regularization techniques that you can apply to overcome this problem.

3. What is the role of the learning rate in CNN optimization? How does a high learning rate and a low learning rate impact the training process?

4. Explain transfer learning and how it can be used to improve the performance of CNNs in a classification task. Provide an example where transfer learning would be useful.

5. Why is it essential to monitor the model's performance on a validation set during training? How does early stopping help prevent overfitting?

Take your time to answer these questions thoroughly, and feel free to refer back to the concepts and examples discussed in this section. Remember, practice and understanding are the keys to mastering the training of CNNs.

CONVOLUTIONAL NEURAL NETWORKS

Object Localization and Detection

In the vast realm of computer vision, object localization and detection play a crucial role in enabling machines to perceive and understand the visual world. This section dives into the fundamentals of object localization and detection, exploring the techniques and algorithms that allow machines to identify and locate objects in images and videos.

Introduction to Object Localization

Object localization involves pinpointing the location of specific objects within an image or video. It is an essential task in computer vision, enabling applications such as autonomous driving, augmented reality, and object recognition. The primary objective of object localization is to draw bounding boxes around objects of interest accurately.

To achieve this, several techniques have been developed, each catering to different scenarios and requirements. However, before delving into the specifics of object localization techniques, it is crucial to understand the underlying concept of object detection.

Introduction to Object Detection

Object detection goes hand in hand with localization, as it not only involves identifying objects but also determining their precise boundaries within an image or video. The goal is to detect multiple objects simultaneously and accurately assign appropriate class labels to each object.

Object detection algorithms fall into two broad categories: two-stage detectors and one-stage detectors. Two-stage detectors, such as the R-CNN (Region-based Convolutional Neural Network) family, first generate candidate regions likely to contain objects and then classify those regions. One-stage detectors, such as YOLO (You Only Look Once) and SSD (Single Shot MultiBox Detector), directly predict bounding boxes and class labels in a single pass.

Object Localization Techniques

Object localization techniques can be classified into two main categories: handcrafted feature-based and deep learning-based approaches.

1. **Handcrafted Feature-based Approaches:** These techniques rely on manually designed features that capture relevant information about objects. One popular approach is the Histogram of Oriented Gradients (HOG), which

computes local gradients and orientations to create feature representations. Another method is the Scale-Invariant Feature Transform (SIFT), which extracts scale-invariant keypoints and descriptors.

2. **Deep Learning-based Approaches:** With the advent of deep learning, object localization has witnessed remarkable advancements. Convolutional Neural Networks (CNNs) have revolutionized the field, allowing machines to learn discriminative and hierarchical representations automatically. CNN-based approaches, such as Faster R-CNN and RetinaNet, have become state-of-the-art methods for object detection and localization.

Faster R-CNN: Combining Accuracy and Speed

Faster R-CNN (Region Convolutional Neural Network) is a widely used object detection model that achieved a significant breakthrough in accuracy and speed. It consists of two main components: region proposal network (RPN) and region classification network.

The RPN generates potential bounding box proposals by sliding a small network, called an anchor, over the convolutional feature maps. The anchors are pre-defined boxes with various sizes and aspect ratios, enabling the model to handle objects of different scales and shapes. The RPN predicts two outputs for each anchor: objectness score (probability of containing an object) and bounding box regression offsets.

The region classification network takes the proposed regions from the RPN and classifies each region into different object classes. It extracts features from each region using RoI (Region of Interest) pooling and passes them through fully connected layers for classification.

Faster R-CNN combines the accuracy of region-based methods with the efficiency of single-stage detectors. By sharing convolutional feature maps between the RPN and region classification network, it reduces redundant computation and achieves impressive detection performance.

RetinaNet: Addressing the Imbalance Problem

One of the challenges in object detection is the class imbalance problem, where background regions vastly outnumber the regions containing objects. This imbalance can lead to biased learning and poor performance.

RetinaNet, an influential object detection model, addresses this problem by introducing a novel loss function called the Focal Loss. The Focal Loss assigns higher weights to hard examples (i.e., rare and misclassified samples), focusing the model's attention on challenging regions. This effectively reduces the dominance of easy negative samples, thereby improving detection accuracy.

Moreover, RetinaNet adopts a feature pyramid network (FPN) architecture, which aggregates features from multiple scales to enhance the model's ability to detect objects at various sizes. FPN enables better handling of objects with large variations in scale and aspect ratio.

Applications and Challenges

Object localization and detection have numerous real-world applications across various domains. For instance, in autonomous driving, accurate detection and localization of pedestrians, vehicles, and traffic signs are critical for ensuring safety. In the retail industry, object detection is used for inventory management, shelf analysis, and theft prevention. These are just a few examples of how object localization and detection have transformed different sectors.

However, the field also faces some challenges. First, occlusions, cluttered backgrounds, and variations in lighting conditions can make object localization and detection more challenging. Second, accurately detecting small objects or objects with low resolution remains a challenge, particularly in surveillance scenarios. Finally, there is a need to address privacy concerns when deploying object detection systems, ensuring that they respect ethical and legal boundaries.

Summary

Object localization and detection are fundamental tasks in computer vision that enable machines to perceive and understand the visual world. Through handcrafted feature-based approaches and deep learning-based methods, machines can accurately localize and detect objects in images and videos.

We explored two influential models in object detection, Faster R-CNN and RetinaNet, which have pushed the boundaries of detection accuracy and efficiency. Both models leverage convolutional neural networks, but Faster R-CNN focuses on improving speed, while RetinaNet addresses the class imbalance problem.

Object localization and detection have vast applications, ranging from autonomous driving and augmented reality to inventory management and surveillance. However, challenges such as occlusions, small object detection, and privacy concerns pose ongoing research areas within the field.

Now that we have a solid understanding of object localization and detection, let's explore the exciting world of computer vision further and discover its applications in other domains.

Image Generation and Style Transfer

Generative Adversarial Networks (GANs)

In the world of artificial intelligence, one of the most fascinating and powerful concepts is that of Generative Adversarial Networks (GANs). These remarkable systems have the ability to generate new and original content, such as images, music, and even text. GANs have revolutionized the field of computer vision and have opened up new possibilities for creativity and innovation.

Understanding GANs

At the heart of a GAN is a dual network structure consisting of a generator and a discriminator. The generator network is responsible for creating new samples, while the discriminator network acts as a critic, trying to distinguish the generated samples from real ones. The two networks are engaged in a continuous adversarial game, where the generator learns to produce more realistic samples in response to feedback from the discriminator.

The process begins with the generator creating a random output, often referred to as "noise." This noise is fed into the generator network, which transforms it into a sample that resembles real data. The discriminator then receives both real and generated samples and attempts to classify them correctly. As the two networks compete against each other, the generator becomes increasingly skilled at producing realistic samples that can fool the discriminator.

Training GANs

Training a GAN is a delicate process that requires careful optimization. The loss function, which quantifies the performance of the two networks, plays a critical role in training. The discriminator's loss function aims to correctly classify real and generated samples, while the generator's loss function aims to generate samples that fool the discriminator.

The training process involves multiple iterations, where the generator and discriminator networks are updated in an alternating manner. This back-and-forth process helps both networks improve their performance over time. However, achieving convergence between the two networks can be challenging, as one may outperform the other at different stages of training. Finding the right balance between the generator and discriminator is a crucial aspect of GAN training.

Applications of GANs

GANs have found remarkable success in various domains, leading to exciting applications. One of the most well-known applications is in computer vision, where GANs can generate realistic images that resemble photographs. For instance, GANs have been used to create highly realistic images of celebrities who don't actually exist.

Another application of GANs is in the field of natural language processing, where they have been used to generate coherent and contextually appropriate text. GANs have also been employed in music generation, allowing composers to explore new possibilities and create original pieces that mimic the style of famous musicians.

Beyond the creative realm, GANs have been invaluable in data augmentation. By generating synthetic data, GANs can increase the diversity of training datasets and improve the performance of machine learning models. This has proven particularly useful in medical imaging, where large and diverse datasets are often hard to come by.

Challenges and Limitations

While GANs have achieved remarkable success, they are not without their challenges and limitations. One of the primary challenges is mode collapse, where the generator produces a limited variety of samples, failing to explore the entire space of possible outputs. Another challenge is training instability, where the generator and discriminator networks struggle to reach convergence, making the training process difficult to control.

Ethical considerations also arise with the use of GANs. For instance, GAN-generated deepfakes, which are incredibly realistic manipulated images and videos, have raised concerns about the potential for misinformation and manipulation. It is important to develop safeguards and ethical guidelines to mitigate the misuse of this powerful technology.

Conclusion

Generative Adversarial Networks (GANs) have significantly advanced the field of artificial intelligence by enabling the creation of realistic and original content. From generating lifelike images to composing music, GANs have demonstrated their potential for creativity and innovation. However, challenges in training stability and ethical concerns require ongoing research and responsible development. As technology continues to evolve, GANs hold the promise of pushing the boundaries of what machines can create and inspire.

Neural Style Transfer

Neural Style Transfer is a fascinating application of deep learning that allows us to combine the content of one image with the style of another image, creating a unique and visually appealing artwork. It is a technique that has gained tremendous popularity in the field of computer vision and has produced stunning results in various creative domains.

Understanding Style Transfer

The concept of Neural Style Transfer is inspired by the idea of separating and recombining the content and style of two different images. The content of an image refers to the underlying objects and their spatial relationships, while the style encompasses the visual patterns, textures, and colors that define the artistic characteristic of an image.

In Neural Style Transfer, a pre-trained convolutional neural network (CNN) is used as a feature extractor. The network is typically trained on a large dataset, such as ImageNet, to learn hierarchical representations of visual features. By utilizing the network's internal representations, we can extract both the content and style information from an image.

The Content Loss

The content loss is a key component in Neural Style Transfer. It measures the difference between the feature representations of the content image and the generated image. By minimizing this difference, we ensure that the generated image captures the content information of the content image.

Mathematically, let C represent the content image, and G represent the generated image. We first pass both images through the CNN and extract the feature maps at a certain layer. Let F_C and F_G denote the feature maps obtained from the content image and generated image, respectively. The content loss is then defined as the mean squared error (MSE) between F_C and F_G:

$$L_{\text{content}}(C, G) = \frac{1}{2} \sum_{i,j}(F_{C_{ij}} - F_{G_{ij}})^2$$

IMAGE GENERATION AND STYLE TRANSFER 217

By optimizing the generated image with respect to the content loss, we encourage the network to focus on capturing the content of the content image.

The Style Loss

The style loss is responsible for transferring the artistic style from the style image to the generated image. It compares the correlations of different features across multiple layers of the CNN and ensures that the generated image replicates the style patterns of the style image.

To calculate the style loss, we introduce a Gram matrix, which captures the correlations between the feature maps. Let F_l be the reshaped feature map at layer l of the CNN. The Gram matrix G_l is computed by multiplying the reshaped matrix with its transpose:

$$G_{l_{ij}} = \sum_k F_{l_{ik}} F_{l_{jk}}$$

The style loss is then defined as the mean squared error (MSE) between the Gram matrices of the style image and the generated image:

$$L_{\text{style}}(S, G) = \sum_l w_l \frac{1}{4N_l^2 M_l^2} \sum_{i,j} (G_{S_{l_{ij}}} - G_{G_{l_{ij}}})^2$$

Here, S represents the style image, w_l is a weighting factor, and N_l and M_l represent the dimensions of the feature map at layer l. By minimizing the style loss, we encourage the network to capture the style patterns and textures of the style image.

Total Variation Regularization

Total Variation (TV) regularization is often employed in Neural Style Transfer to ensure spatial smoothness in the generated image. It prevents the output from having high-frequency noise and results in visually pleasing and coherent stylized images.

The TV regularizer is computed by taking the sum of the absolute differences between neighboring pixels:

$$L_{\text{TV}}(G) = \sum_{i,j} (|G_{i+1,j} - G_{i,j}| + |G_{i,j+1} - G_{i,j}|)$$

By incorporating the TV regularization term into the loss function, we encourage smooth transitions between neighboring pixels in the generated image.

Optimization Process

To generate stylized images using Neural Style Transfer, we optimize an objective function that combines the content loss, style loss, and TV regularization term. The objective function is formulated as follows:

$$L_{\text{total}}(C, S, G) = \alpha L_{\text{content}}(C, G) + \beta L_{\text{style}}(S, G) + \gamma L_{\text{TV}}(G)$$

Here, α, β, and γ are hyperparameters that control the influence of each loss term on the final output.

To optimize the objective function, we initialize the generated image randomly, and then use gradient descent to update it iteratively. The gradients are computed with respect to the generated image, while keeping the content and style images fixed. By iteratively updating the generated image, we gradually minimize the loss function and generate images that exhibit the content of the content image and the style of the style image.

Applying Neural Style Transfer

Neural Style Transfer has found practical applications in various creative domains, such as creating unique artworks, generating stylized photos, and even transferring the style of a famous artist to a given photo. It provides a powerful tool for artists, designers, and photographers to explore new possibilities and unleash their creativity.

Potential Challenges and Limitations

While Neural Style Transfer produces impressive results, it also faces certain challenges and limitations. One particular challenge is the speed of the optimization process, which can be time-consuming, especially for high-resolution images. Various techniques, such as fast style transfer algorithms and parallel computing, have been developed to address this issue.

Another challenge is the sensitivity to hyperparameters, such as the weights assigned to the content loss, style loss, and TV regularization. Finding the right balance between content preservation and style transfer is an ongoing research area.

Furthermore, Neural Style Transfer heavily relies on pre-trained CNN models, which may not capture all style details accurately. Incorporating user feedback or incorporating additional style images can help improve the quality of stylized outputs.

Summary

Neural Style Transfer is an exciting application of deep learning that allows us to combine the content of one image with the style of another image. By leveraging pre-trained CNN models and optimizing an objective function that considers content loss, style loss, and TV regularization, we can generate visually appealing and unique stylized images. While challenging, Neural Style Transfer holds great potential in various creative domains and continues to inspire researchers and artists alike.

Further Reading

If you're interested in exploring Neural Style Transfer further, I recommend the following resources:

- Gatys, Leon A., Alexander S. Ecker, and Matthias Bethge. "A neural algorithm of artistic style." arXiv preprint arXiv:1508.06576 (2015).

- Li, Yijun, et al. "A closed-form solution to photorealistic image stylization." European Conference on Computer Vision. Springer, Cham, 2018.

- Johnson, Justin, Alexandre Alahi, and Li Fei-Fei. "Perceptual losses for real-time style transfer and super-resolution." European conference on computer vision. Springer, Cham, 2016.

These papers will provide you with a deeper understanding of the underlying principles and techniques involved in Neural Style Transfer. So, grab your favorite style image and start exploring the world of creative AI!

AI and Robotics

Robotics in the Age of AI

Robot Perception

In the age of artificial intelligence (AI) and robotics, one of the key challenges is enabling robots to perceive and understand the world around them. Robot perception refers to the ability of robots to gather information from their environment using various sensing modalities, such as vision, touch, and hearing. By perceiving and interpreting sensory data, robots can make informed decisions and interact with their surroundings effectively.

The Role of Sensors

Sensors play a vital role in robot perception by capturing data about the robot's environment. There are several types of sensors commonly used in robotics, including cameras, depth sensors, LIDAR sensors, and tactile sensors. Each sensor provides different types of information, allowing the robot to perceive its surroundings from multiple perspectives.

Cameras: Visual perception is often achieved using cameras that capture images or video footage of the robot's surroundings. These images can then be processed using computer vision techniques to identify objects, determine their locations, and extract meaningful information.

Depth Sensors: Depth sensors, such as time-of-flight cameras and structured light sensors, capture depth information along with visual data. This additional depth information enables robots to perceive the 3D structure of their environment, which is crucial for tasks such as obstacle avoidance and object manipulation.

LIDAR Sensors: LIDAR (Light Detection and Ranging) sensors use laser beams to measure distances and create detailed 3D maps of the robot's surroundings. By scanning the environment, LIDAR sensors provide precise measurements of distances, allowing robots to navigate complex environments and detect objects with high accuracy.

Tactile Sensors: Tactile sensors, such as pressure sensors or force-sensitive resistors, enable robots to interact with their environment and perceive physical contact. By detecting changes in pressure or touch, robots can grasp objects securely, detect texture, and even perform delicate tasks that require a sense of touch.

Perception Techniques

Once sensory data is captured, it needs to be processed and interpreted to extract meaningful information. Several perception techniques are commonly employed in robotics to make sense of sensory data and enable robots to understand their environment.

Image Processing: Image processing techniques are used to enhance, analyze, and extract valuable information from images captured by cameras. This includes tasks such as image filtering, edge detection, object recognition, and tracking. By applying these techniques, robots can identify objects, track their movements, and even estimate their poses.

Point Cloud Processing: Point cloud processing is a technique commonly used with 3D sensors, such as LIDAR or depth cameras. It involves analyzing the dense collection of 3D points that represent the robot's environment. Point cloud processing is critical for tasks such as mapping, localization, and 3D object recognition.

Feature Extraction: Feature extraction involves identifying salient characteristics or patterns in sensory data that are relevant to the task at hand. For example, in computer vision, features such as corners, edges, or textures can be extracted from images to represent objects or regions of interest. These features are then used for further processing, classification, or tracking.

ROBOTICS IN THE AGE OF AI

Challenges in Robot Perception

Despite significant advancements in robot perception, several challenges still persist. These challenges arise from the complexity of real-world environments and the limited capabilities of current perception systems. Some of the key challenges include:

Variability and Uncertainty: Real-world environments are diverse and often exhibit variability and uncertainty. Lighting conditions, object appearances, and background clutter can vary significantly, making it challenging for robots to perceive and recognize objects consistently.

Perception in 3D Space: Perceiving the 3D structure of the environment accurately is crucial for many robotic tasks. However, accurately estimating depth and understanding the spatial relationships between objects remains a complex problem, especially in dynamic and cluttered environments.

Real-time Processing: Perception systems in robots often need to operate in real-time to enable fast decision-making and quick responses. Real-time processing requires efficient algorithms and hardware to handle the computational demands of perception tasks within strict time constraints.

Example: Object Recognition

Object recognition is a fundamental task in robot perception, enabling robots to identify and classify objects in their environment. For example, a robot in a warehouse can use object recognition to identify and locate specific items on a shelf, improving its efficiency in handling and picking tasks.

Object Detection: Object detection refers to the process of locating and identifying objects in an image or a scene. By analyzing the visual features extracted from sensory data, object detection algorithms can determine the location, size, and shape of objects within the robot's field of view.

Classification and Recognition: Object classification involves assigning labels or categories to the detected objects. This can be done by training machine learning models on labeled datasets, enabling robots to recognize various objects based on their visual features. Common techniques for object classification include deep learning models such as convolutional neural networks (CNNs).

Applications: Object recognition has numerous applications in robotics, ranging from industrial automation to autonomous vehicles. In manufacturing, robots equipped with object recognition capabilities can identify and sort different products, improving production efficiency. In autonomous vehicles, object recognition plays a vital role in detecting and tracking pedestrians, vehicles, and traffic signs for safe navigation.

Resources and Further Reading

For those interested in delving deeper into robot perception and related topics, the following resources are highly recommended:

- Book: "Robotics, Vision and Control" by Peter Corke provides a comprehensive introduction to robot perception and computer vision in the context of robotics.

- Online Course: "Perception for Autonomous Robots" on Coursera, offered by the University of Zurich, covers various aspects of robot perception, including image processing, 3D perception, and object recognition.

- Research Papers: The Proceedings of the International Conference on Robotics and Automation (ICRA) and the IEEE International Conference on Computer Vision (ICCV) are excellent resources for the latest advancements in robot perception and computer vision.

Summary

Robot perception plays a crucial role in enabling robots to understand and interact with their environment effectively. By leveraging sensors and applying perception techniques, robots can gather information and make informed decisions in real-time. Object recognition is one of the fundamental tasks in robot perception, allowing robots to identify and classify objects accurately. However, challenges such as variability, uncertainty, and real-time processing still exist, pushing researchers and engineers to develop innovative solutions in the field of robot perception.

Remember, perception is the key to achieving dominance in the world of artificial intelligence and robotics. As we continue to advance in technology, new breakthroughs in robot perception will pave the way for intelligent and autonomous systems that can truly understand and navigate the world around us.

So, stay curious, keep learning, and let's turn data into dominance with the power of AI!

Exercise: Imagine you are developing a mobile robot capable of object recognition in a household environment. Describe a real-world scenario where object recognition would be useful in improving the robot's functionality and efficiency.

Challenge: Implement a simple object recognition system using an image dataset of various objects. Train a deep learning model (e.g., a CNN) and evaluate its performance in accurately classifying unseen objects from the dataset.

Robot Navigation

Robot navigation is a crucial aspect of artificial intelligence in robotics. It involves the ability of a robot to move from one location to another in a given environment. The navigation process requires the robot to perceive its surroundings, plan a path, and execute that path while avoiding obstacles and achieving its goal. In this section, we will explore the foundations of robot navigation and the various techniques and algorithms used in practice.

Perception in Robot Navigation

In order for a robot to navigate effectively, it needs to have a comprehensive understanding of its environment. This is achieved through perception, which involves gathering sensory information from the surroundings. For robot navigation, the primary sources of perception are vision and distance sensing.

Visual perception allows the robot to identify objects, landmarks, and obstacles in its environment. It involves the use of cameras and image processing techniques to extract meaningful information from the captured images. For example, a robot equipped with a camera can detect the presence of walls, doors, and other objects in its surroundings, which will help it plan an appropriate path.

Distance sensing is another critical aspect of robot navigation. Robots often use sensors such as sonar, lidar, or infrared sensors to measure the distance between the robot and its surroundings. This information is crucial for detecting obstacles or determining the proximity of walls and other objects. By combining visual perception with distance sensing, a robot can build a reliable map of its environment and make informed navigation decisions.

Path Planning

Once the robot has a good understanding of its environment, it needs to generate a path that will take it from its current location to its desired destination. Path planning algorithms aim to find an optimal or near-optimal trajectory that avoids obstacles and minimizes travel time.

One fundamental approach to path planning is grid-based methods. The environment is divided into a grid, and each cell is labeled as either occupied or free. The robot then searches for a path by traversing the grid from its starting position to the goal position. This can be achieved using popular algorithms such as Dijkstra's algorithm or A* search algorithm.

Another commonly used approach is potential fields, which model the robot's trajectory as a series of attractive and repulsive forces. The attractive forces pull the robot towards the goal position, while the repulsive forces push it away from obstacles. By balancing these forces, the robot can navigate through narrow passages and avoid collisions.

Motion Control

Once a path has been planned, the robot needs to execute the planned trajectory. This involves motion control, which refers to the algorithms and techniques used to control the robot's movements.

In simple cases, motion control can be achieved by using basic techniques such as proportional-integral-derivative (PID) control. PID control adjusts the robot's velocity based on the difference between its desired pose and its current pose. By continuously monitoring the pose and adjusting the control parameters, the robot can accurately follow the planned path.

For more complex scenarios, such as navigating in dynamic environments or dealing with non-holonomic constraints, more advanced techniques like model predictive control (MPC) may be required. MPC employs a predictive model of the robot's dynamics to optimize its control actions over a finite time horizon. This allows the robot to account for uncertainties and react adaptively to changes in its environment.

Simultaneous Localization And Mapping (SLAM)

Simultaneous Localization And Mapping (SLAM) is a fundamental problem in robot navigation that involves building a map of an unknown environment while simultaneously estimating the robot's pose within the map. SLAM is crucial for autonomous robots, as it enables them to navigate in previously unexplored or dynamic environments.

SLAM algorithms utilize sensor measurements, such as odometry, vision, and range data, to create a map of the environment and estimate the robot's location in real-time. These algorithms combine probabilistic filtering techniques, such as extended Kalman filters or particle filters, with sensor fusion to accurately estimate both the map and the robot's pose.

SLAM has numerous applications in robotics, including autonomous navigation, exploration, and virtual reality. It has proven to be a challenging problem due to the inherent uncertainties in robot localization and the complexity of building consistent and accurate maps. However, with advancements in sensor technology and computational power, SLAM has become an active research area and a crucial component of modern robot navigation systems.

Challenges and Future Directions

While significant progress has been made in robot navigation, several challenges still remain. One major challenge is robustness in dynamic environments. Robots need to constantly adapt their navigation strategies to handle moving obstacles, varying lighting conditions, and changing terrains.

Another challenge is the integration of multiple perception modalities. Combining data from visual sensors, distance sensors, and other sources introduces complexity and requires sophisticated fusion algorithms to handle the heterogeneity of sensory data.

Furthermore, ethical considerations in robot navigation also need to be taken into account. Robots operating in human-populated environments must exhibit safe and socially acceptable behavior. This involves adhering to laws and regulations, respecting personal privacy, and ensuring the safety of both the robot and the humans around it.

Looking ahead, the future of robot navigation lies in leveraging advancements in artificial intelligence and machine learning. Deep learning techniques, such as convolutional neural networks, have shown promising results in object recognition and scene understanding. Integrating these techniques with traditional navigation algorithms could lead to more intelligent and efficient robot navigation systems.

In conclusion, robot navigation is a complex and exciting field within artificial intelligence and robotics. It requires a combination of perception, path planning, motion control, and mapping techniques to enable robots to navigate autonomously in their environments. As technology continues to advance, we can expect significant progress in robot navigation, leading to safer, more efficient, and more capable robotic systems.

Human-Robot Interaction

In the field of artificial intelligence, human-robot interaction (HRI) is a multidisciplinary area of study that focuses on understanding and improving the ways in which humans and robots interact with each other. HRI plays a vital role in the development of robotic systems that are not only intelligent but also socially aware and capable of engaging with humans in a natural and meaningful way.

Importance of Human-Robot Interaction

Robots are becoming increasingly integrated into our daily lives, from healthcare settings to manufacturing plants and even our own homes. As robots take on more complex and interactive roles, it becomes crucial to design and develop systems that can effectively communicate and collaborate with human users. Human-robot interaction serves as the foundation for achieving this goal.

One of the main goals of HRI is to create robots that are intuitive to interact with, capable of understanding human intentions, and capable of adapting to the needs and preferences of different users. By enabling effective communication and collaboration between humans and robots, HRI enhances user satisfaction, usability, and overall system performance.

Challenges in Human-Robot Interaction

Designing robots that are capable of seamless and natural interaction with humans poses several challenges. Here are some of the key challenges in HRI:

1. **Perception:** Robots must be able to perceive and interpret human cues and signals, such as facial expressions, gestures, and speech, in order to understand human intentions and respond appropriately.

2. **Natural Language Processing:** The ability to understand and generate natural language is crucial for effective communication between humans and robots. Natural language processing techniques enable robots to process and interpret spoken or written instructions, engage in meaningful conversations, and provide informative responses.

3. **Emotion Recognition:** Emotions play a significant role in human communication, and robots need to be able to recognize and respond to

human emotions appropriately. Emotion recognition techniques, such as facial expression analysis and voice tone analysis, enable robots to understand and adapt to the emotional states of their human counterparts.

4. **Action and Intent Recognition:** Robots need to be able to recognize human actions and intentions to engage in cooperative tasks effectively. Action and intent recognition techniques, such as motion analysis and activity recognition, allow robots to understand and follow human actions and anticipate their needs.

5. **Social and Ethical Considerations:** As robots become more integrated into society, it is essential to address social and ethical considerations in HRI. This includes ensuring privacy and data protection, promoting fairness and transparency in decisions made by AI systems, and considering the impact of AI-driven automation on employment and societal dynamics.

Solutions and Approaches

To address the challenges in HRI, researchers and engineers have developed various solutions and approaches that enhance the interaction between humans and robots. Here are a few notable ones:

1. **Human-Centered Design:** Designing robots with a human-centered approach involves taking into account the capabilities, needs, and preferences of the human users throughout the development process. This approach ensures that the robot's capabilities and behaviors align with human expectations, making the interaction more intuitive and user-friendly.

2. **Socially Assistive Robotics:** Socially assistive robots are designed to provide assistance and support to individuals during everyday tasks while also promoting social interaction. These robots can assist in therapy sessions for individuals with special needs, provide cognitive support for elderly individuals, or even act as companions for people living alone.

3. **Explainable AI:** In complex HRI scenarios, it is crucial for robots to explain their decisions and actions to humans in a transparent and understandable manner. Explainable AI techniques provide insights into the robot's decision-making processes, increasing human trust and acceptance of the robot's behavior.

4. **Shared Autonomy**: Shared autonomy refers to a collaboration between humans and robots in which both parties contribute to the decision-making process. This approach leverages the strengths of both humans and robots, allowing them to work together on tasks that require a combination of human judgment and robot precision.

5. **Robot Ethics**: Considering the ethical implications of the interaction between humans and robots is essential to ensuring responsible and respectful HRI. This involves addressing issues such as robot autonomy, privacy, data security, and the potential impact of robots on human psychology and social dynamics.

Real-World Examples

HRI is already making significant contributions across various domains. Here are a few real-world examples:

1. **Healthcare**: Robots are being used in healthcare settings to support medical professionals and assist patients. For instance, robotic surgical assistants help surgeons perform minimally invasive procedures with greater precision, while socially assistive robots provide companionship and cognitive support to elderly individuals in nursing homes.

2. **Manufacturing**: Human-robot collaboration is transforming the manufacturing industry. Robots have been integrated into assembly lines to work alongside human workers, performing repetitive and physically demanding tasks, thereby enhancing productivity and reducing the risk of injuries.

3. **Education**: Robots are being used in educational settings to support and enhance learning experiences. They can serve as interactive teachers' aids, providing personalized tutoring and engaging students in interactive activities that promote learning in a fun and engaging way.

4. **Domestic and Personal Assistance**: Home robots are being developed to assist with household chores, childcare, and personal tasks, aiming to improve the quality of life for individuals with disabilities or those in need of assistance with daily activities.

Conclusion

Human-robot interaction is a fascinating and rapidly evolving field that aims to create intelligent and socially aware robots capable of effective communication and collaboration with humans. By understanding the challenges, developing appropriate solutions, and addressing ethical considerations, we can shape a future in which humans and robots interact seamlessly and work together to enhance various aspects of our lives. As the field continues to progress, it will undoubtedly open up new horizons and possibilities for human-robot collaboration in diverse domains.

Reinforcement Learning for Robotics

Policy Gradient Methods

In the exciting world of reinforcement learning, policy gradient methods have emerged as a powerful approach to train agents to make intelligent decisions. These methods utilize the concept of optimizing a policy, which is essentially a strategy or set of actions that an agent takes in different situations. In this section, we will dive into the principles, algorithms, and applications of policy gradient methods and explore how they contribute to the advancements in AI and robotics.

The Reinforcement Learning Framework

Before we delve into policy gradient methods, let's quickly recap the basics of reinforcement learning (RL). RL is a type of machine learning where an agent learns to make sequential decisions in an environment to maximize a cumulative reward. The agent interacts with the environment by observing its current state and taking actions. The environment then transitions to a new state, and the agent receives a reward based on the transition. The goal of RL is to find an optimal policy that maximizes the long-term reward.

Optimizing Policies with Gradients

Policy gradient methods take a different approach compared to traditional value-based methods in RL. Instead of estimating the value function and deriving policies from it, policy gradient methods directly optimize the policy itself. They use gradient-based optimization to search for policies that maximize the expected cumulative reward.

The key idea behind policy gradient methods is to formulate the problem as an optimization one, where the objective is to find the policy parameters that maximize the expected return. The policy is typically represented by a parametric function, such as a neural network, which maps states to actions. By adjusting the parameters of this function, the policy can be improved over time through an iterative learning process.

The Policy Gradient Theorem

To understand policy gradient methods more deeply, we need to introduce the policy gradient theorem. This fundamental theorem provides the foundation for computing gradients of policy objectives. Let's denote the policy as π_θ, where θ represents the parameters of the policy function. The policy gradient theorem states that the gradient of an expected return objective function, denoted as $J(\theta)$, with respect to the policy parameters is given by:

$$\nabla J(\theta) = \mathbb{E}_{\pi_\theta}\left[\nabla \log \pi_\theta(s,a) Q^{\pi_\theta}(s,a)\right]$$

Here, $\nabla \log \pi_\theta(s,a)$ represents the gradient of the policy log-probability for taking action a in state s, and $Q^{\pi_\theta}(s,a)$ is the state-action value function, also known as the Q-value, under the policy π_θ.

Policy Gradient Algorithms

Several policy gradient algorithms have been developed to optimize policies based on the policy gradient theorem. Let's explore a few popular ones:

REINFORCE: REINFORCE is one of the simplest policy gradient algorithms. It estimates the policy gradient from sampled trajectories and updates the policy parameters accordingly. The process involves sampling trajectories, computing the policy gradients, and updating the policy parameters using stochastic gradient ascent.

Proximal Policy Optimization (PPO): PPO is a state-of-the-art policy gradient algorithm that aims to strike a balance between sample efficiency and policy stability. It employs a surrogate objective function and implements a trust region policy optimization approach to update policy parameters.

Actor-Critic Methods: Actor-critic methods combine ideas from both value-based and policy-based RL. The actor part is responsible for defining the policy, while the critic estimates the state-value function or the Q-value function. This combination helps stabilize the learning process. Examples of actor-critic methods include Advantage Actor-Critic (A2C) and Advantage Actor-Critic with Generalized Advantage Estimation (A2C-GAE).

Applications of Policy Gradient Methods

Policy gradient methods have found numerous applications across various domains. Here are a few notable examples:

Game Playing: Policy gradient methods have been successfully applied to game playing scenarios, such as training agents to play video games or even complex board games like Go. These methods enable agents to learn effective strategies through trial and error, ultimately achieving superhuman performance.

Robotics: Policy gradient methods have revolutionized the field of robotics by enabling robots to learn complex tasks and movements. By training policies through trial and error, robots can acquire skills and adapt to different environments, making them more versatile and capable.

Autonomous Vehicles: Policy gradient methods play a crucial role in training autonomous vehicles to navigate complex road scenarios. By optimizing policies based on real-world driving data, these methods enable vehicles to make safe and efficient driving decisions.

Natural Language Processing: Policy gradient methods are also applicable to natural language processing tasks. They can be used to train models to generate coherent and contextually relevant text, facilitate dialogue systems, and perform sentiment analysis, among other tasks involving textual data.

Policy Gradient Methods in Practice

While policy gradient methods have shown great promise in various applications, there are a few challenges to consider. One challenge is the high variance in policy gradient estimates, which can make learning unstable and slow. To address this, variance reduction techniques such as baselines and advantage functions are often employed.

Another challenge is the exploration-exploitation dilemma. In RL, it is crucial to explore new actions and states to gather data, but also exploit the current policy to maximize rewards. Striking the right balance between exploration and exploitation remains an active area of research in policy gradient methods.

Conclusion

Policy gradient methods have emerged as a powerful approach in reinforcement learning, allowing agents to learn intelligent decision-making in complex environments. By directly optimizing policies using the policy gradient theorem, these methods provide a versatile framework for training agents. With applications ranging from game playing to robotics and autonomous vehicles, policy gradient methods continue to push the boundaries of AI and drive advancements in various fields. So, buckle up and get ready to dive deeper into the world of policy gradient methods!

Inverse Reinforcement Learning

Inverse Reinforcement Learning (IRL) is a subfield of machine learning that focuses on uncovering the hidden underlying rewards or goals of an agent by observing its behavior. In traditional reinforcement learning, agents learn a policy to maximize their expected rewards based on a predefined reward function. However, in many real-world scenarios, the reward function is unknown or difficult to specify, making it challenging to design an optimal policy. This is where IRL comes into play.

Principle of Inverse Reinforcement Learning

The principle behind IRL is to infer the underlying reward function that the agent is optimizing by observing its behavior in a given environment. By understanding the rewards that the agent values, we can replicate its behavior or learn a policy that performs similarly to the expert.

The key idea in IRL is that an expert agent's behavior implicitly encodes its preferences or goals. The expert's behavior is assumed to be optimal with respect to an unknown reward function, and the goal of IRL is to recover this hidden reward function. Once we have the reward function, we can use traditional reinforcement learning techniques to find an optimal policy.

Solving Inverse Reinforcement Learning

To solve the IRL problem, we need a set of experts' demonstrations consisting of state-action trajectories. These trajectories are used to identify patterns and learn the underlying reward function that explains the expert's behavior. There are several approaches to solving IRL, each with its own strengths and weaknesses. Let's discuss two popular methods: Maximum Entropy IRL and Bayesian IRL.

Maximum Entropy IRL (MaxEnt IRL) MaxEnt IRL seeks to find the reward function that maximizes the entropy of the expert's behavior while remaining consistent with observed demonstrations. It assumes that the expert's behavior is not only optimal but also maximally random among all possible optimal policies. By maximizing entropy, MaxEnt IRL avoids the problem of bias towards a specific behavior.

The basic idea behind MaxEnt IRL is to use inverse reinforcement learning as a maximum likelihood estimation problem. The algorithm iteratively updates the reward function until it matches the expert's behavior. This process involves estimating the state visitation distribution and computing the expected feature counts.

Bayesian Inverse Reinforcement Learning (Bayesian IRL) Bayesian IRL treats the reward function as a random variable and makes Bayesian inference to estimate its distribution. It assumes a prior distribution over reward functions and updates it based on observed behavior. Bayesian IRL provides a more probabilistic framework for IRL, allowing for uncertainty in the inferred reward function.

The process of Bayesian IRL involves sampling reward functions from the posterior distribution and then using these reward functions to compute the expected feature counts. The reward function is updated based on the log-likelihood of the observed behavior. This process is repeated iteratively until convergence.

Applications of Inverse Reinforcement Learning

IRL has found applications in various domains, including autonomous driving, human-robot interaction, and healthcare. Here are a few examples:

Autonomous Driving IRL can be used to understand driver behavior and preferences, allowing autonomous vehicles to mimic human driving patterns. By learning the underlying reward function, autonomous vehicles can make decisions that align with human expectations and norms.

Human-Robot Interaction In collaborative settings, robots need to understand and adapt to human behavior. IRL can help robots infer human preferences and goals, enabling them to assist humans more effectively and efficiently.

Healthcare In healthcare, IRL can be used to analyze patient data and infer personalized treatment plans. By understanding patient preferences and goals, healthcare professionals can tailor treatments to individual needs and improve patient outcomes.

Challenges and Future Directions

While IRL has shown promising results in various applications, it faces several challenges. One significant challenge is the need for expert demonstrations, which can be expensive or impractical to obtain in some cases. Additionally, IRL algorithms can be computationally expensive and sensitive to noise in the demonstrations.

Future research in IRL aims to tackle these challenges and develop more robust and scalable algorithms. This includes exploring new techniques for learning from demonstrations, addressing the issue of sample efficiency, and incorporating uncertainty into the IRL framework.

Conclusion

Inverse Reinforcement Learning is a powerful tool for understanding the hidden rewards or goals behind an agent's behavior. By leveraging expert demonstrations, IRL allows us to uncover the underlying reward function and learn optimal policies. With applications in various domains, IRL has the potential to revolutionize decision-making and assist in the development of AI systems that align with human preferences and values.

Exercises

1. In autonomous driving, explain how Inverse Reinforcement Learning can be used to model human driver behavior and improve the decision-making of autonomous vehicles.

2. Discuss the limitations and challenges of using Inverse Reinforcement Learning in healthcare applications.

3. Research and explain an alternative approach to Inverse Reinforcement Learning that addresses the problem of expensive or impractical expert demonstrations.

Resources

- Ng, A. Y., & Russell, S. (2000). Algorithms for inverse reinforcement learning. In Proceedings of the Seventeenth International Conference on Machine Learning (pp. 663-670).

- Ziebart, B. D., Maas, A. L., Bagnell, J. A., & Dey, A. K. (2008). Maximum entropy inverse reinforcement learning. In Proceedings of the 23rd national conference on Artificial intelligence (pp. 1433-1438).

- Ramachandran, D., & Amir, E. (2007). Bayesian inverse reinforcement learning. In Proceedings of the 20th International Joint Conference on Artificial Intelligence (pp. 2586-2591).

Future Directions of AI and Robotics

AI-Driven Autonomous Systems

In this section, we will explore the exciting intersection of artificial intelligence (AI) and autonomous systems. We will discuss how AI is revolutionizing various industries by enabling machines to make intelligent decisions and take autonomous actions. From self-driving cars to drones and robotic systems, AI-driven autonomous systems are transforming our world.

The Evolution of Autonomous Systems

Autonomous systems have come a long way since their inception. Initially, they were designed to perform repetitive tasks in controlled environments, such as assembly lines in manufacturing. However, with advancements in AI, these systems have become more intelligent and capable of making decisions in real-time, even in complex and uncertain environments.

The main driver behind the evolution of autonomous systems is the integration of AI algorithms, which allow machines to perceive and understand the world around them, reason about possible actions, and act autonomously based on learned or pre-determined strategies. This ability to learn and adapt is a key characteristic of AI-driven autonomous systems.

Perception and Sensing

One of the crucial aspects of autonomous systems is their ability to perceive and sense the environment. AI algorithms enable machines to process vast amounts of sensor data and extract meaningful information. This information can include visual data from cameras, depth information from LIDAR sensors, or even audio data from microphones.

For example, in the case of self-driving cars, AI algorithms analyze the data from various sensors to detect and track objects, such as other vehicles, pedestrians, and traffic signs. These algorithms can also estimate the speed and trajectory of objects in real-time, allowing the autonomous system to make informed decisions about its own actions, such as changing lanes or stopping at an intersection.

Decision-Making and Planning

Once an autonomous system has sensed and perceived the environment, it needs to make decisions on how to act. This is where AI algorithms come into play. Machine learning techniques, such as reinforcement learning, allow the system to learn from experience and optimize its decision-making process.

For example, in autonomous drones, AI algorithms can learn to navigate complex environments, avoiding obstacles and reaching a target location. These algorithms take into account the drone's dynamics, the surroundings, and any mission-specific constraints to plan the optimal path.

Furthermore, AI-driven autonomous systems can make decisions in real-time, adapting to changing conditions and unforeseen events. This flexibility is critical in ensuring safe and efficient operation in dynamic environments.

Safety and Reliability

Safety is of paramount importance in the development and deployment of AI-driven autonomous systems. As these systems autonomously interact with the physical world, it is crucial to ensure their reliability and robustness.

To achieve this, several techniques are employed. First, redundancy is built into the system, with multiple sensors and actuators providing backup and fault-tolerance. Second, AI algorithms are trained on diverse datasets, encompassing a wide range of scenarios and edge cases. This helps ensure that the system can handle unexpected situations with minimal errors.

Additionally, rigorous testing and validation processes are conducted to assess the reliability and safety of autonomous systems. This includes simulated testing in virtual environments as well as real-world testing in controlled settings before deployment in the field.

Real-World Applications

AI-driven autonomous systems have a wide range of applications across industries. Let's explore a few examples:

1. **Transportation:** Self-driving cars are a prime example of AI-driven autonomous systems. They aim to improve road safety, reduce traffic congestion, and enhance the overall efficiency of transportation.

2. **Logistics and Delivery:** Autonomous drones and robots are being developed for delivery services. These systems can navigate through complex environments to deliver packages, reducing the need for human intervention.

3. **Healthcare:** Autonomous robotic systems are being used for various healthcare tasks, such as surgical procedures and patient care. These systems can assist doctors, enhance precision, and improve patient outcomes.

4. **Agriculture:** AI-driven autonomous systems are being deployed in agriculture for tasks such as crop monitoring, weed detection, and autonomous harvesting. This improves yield, reduces costs, and promotes sustainable farming practices.

Ethical and Social Considerations

As AI-driven autonomous systems become more prevalent, it raises important ethical and social considerations. These include:

1. **Safety and Liability:** Determining liability in case of accidents involving autonomous systems is a complex issue. Clear guidelines and regulations must be established to ensure accountability and protect human lives.

2. **Job Displacement:** The widespread adoption of autonomous systems may lead to job displacement in certain industries. Efforts should be made to provide retraining and upskilling opportunities to affected workers to minimize the social impact.

3. **Privacy and Security:** Autonomous systems generate and process vast amounts of data. Ensuring the privacy and security of this data is crucial to maintain public trust and protect against potential misuse.

4. **Equity and Access:** There is a concern that the benefits of AI-driven autonomous systems may not be equally distributed. Efforts should be made to ensure equitable access to these technologies to avoid exacerbating existing inequalities.

Conclusion

AI-driven autonomous systems have the potential to revolutionize various industries and improve our lives in numerous ways. They rely on the integration of AI algorithms with sophisticated perception, decision-making, and planning capabilities. However, ethical and social considerations must be taken into account to ensure their responsible development and deployment. As we move towards a future where autonomous systems are an everyday reality, it is crucial to strike a balance between innovation and addressing these important concerns.

Ethics and Safety in AI-Enabled Robotics

In the rapidly evolving field of AI-enabled robotics, ethics and safety considerations play a crucial role. As robots become more capable and intelligent, it is essential to address the ethical implications of their actions and ensure their safety in human-centric environments. This section explores the ethical challenges and safety measures associated with AI-enabled robotics and provides insights into the future of ethical robotics.

Ethical Challenges in AI-Enabled Robotics

AI-enabled robotics raise a host of ethical challenges that need careful consideration. One significant concern is the potential for robots to cause harm to humans or other living beings. As robots become more autonomous and capable of making decisions, ensuring that they prioritize human safety is paramount. This raises questions about the responsibility of robot designers, manufacturers, and users in ensuring the ethical conduct of robots.

Another ethical challenge is the issue of transparency and accountability. As AI-enabled robots make decisions based on complex algorithms, it becomes challenging to understand the rationale behind their actions. This lack of transparency can lead to ethical dilemmas, especially in critical situations where human lives are at stake. It is crucial to develop mechanisms that allow humans to understand and interpret the decision-making process of AI-enabled robots.

AI-enabled robotics also raises concerns about job displacement and socioeconomic inequalities. As robots take on more tasks traditionally performed by humans, there is a need to address the potential impact on employment and job opportunities. Ensuring a just transition and creating new avenues for human work in the age of robotics is a significant ethical challenge.

Safety Measures in AI-Enabled Robotics

To ensure the safe operation of AI-enabled robots, several measures need to be implemented. One crucial aspect is designing robots with built-in safety features, such as collision avoidance systems, emergency stop buttons, and fail-safe mechanisms. These features are essential to prevent accidents and minimize the risk of harm to humans.

Another safety measure is the development of robust and reliable control algorithms. AI-enabled robots must be able to detect and respond to unexpected situations effectively. This requires advanced sensing technologies, real-time monitoring systems, and sophisticated control algorithms to ensure safe and reliable behavior.

In addition to technical measures, it is essential to establish regulatory frameworks and standards for the ethical conduct and safety of AI-enabled robots. These frameworks should address issues such as privacy, data security, and liability in the context of robotics. They should also account for the unique challenges posed by AI-enabled robotics, such as algorithmic transparency and accountability.

Case Study: Autonomous Vehicles

One prominent example of AI-enabled robotics that raises ethical and safety concerns is autonomous vehicles. Autonomous cars rely on AI algorithms to make complex decisions, such as lane changes, speed adjustments, and avoiding obstacles. Ensuring the ethical behavior and safety of autonomous vehicles is of utmost importance.

Ethical challenges arise when programming autonomous vehicles to make decisions in situations where harm is unavoidable, such as choosing between hitting a pedestrian or swerving into oncoming traffic. These ethical dilemmas highlight the need for clear guidelines and ethical frameworks for decision-making in autonomous systems.

Safety measures in autonomous vehicles include the use of advanced sensors, such as radar and lidar, to detect and respond to the surrounding environment. Redundant systems and fail-safe mechanisms are also crucial to prevent accidents caused by technical failures.

Future Directions in Ethics and Safety

As AI-enabled robotics continues to advance, addressing ethical challenges and ensuring safety will become even more critical. Future directions in this field include:

- Developing explainable AI models: Efforts should be made to create AI models that can provide transparent explanations for their decisions. This will enhance trust and facilitate the interpretation of AI-enabled robotic behaviors.

- Incorporating ethical guidelines into AI algorithms: Embedding ethical principles directly into the decision-making process of AI-enabled robots can help ensure that they prioritize human safety and adhere to ethical standards.

- Collaborative approach to ethical decision-making: In complex scenarios, designing AI-enabled systems that incorporate input from a broad range of stakeholders, including ethicists, policymakers, and the public, can lead to more socially acceptable and ethical outcomes.

In conclusion, ethics and safety in AI-enabled robotics are essential considerations in the development and deployment of AI systems. Addressing ethical challenges and implementing robust safety measures are crucial for the responsible advancement of AI-enabled robotics. By prioritizing human well-being and societal impact, we can shape a future where AI-enabled robots coexist safely and ethically with humans.

AI in Business

AI Applications in Marketing and Sales

Personalized Marketing

In today's digital age, marketing strategies have evolved significantly. No longer can businesses rely on generic advertisements and mass promotions to attract customers. Instead, they must adopt personalized marketing techniques that cater to individual preferences and needs. The advent of artificial intelligence (AI) has revolutionized the way marketers connect with their target audience.

Understanding Personalized Marketing

Personalized marketing is an approach that tailors marketing messages and offers to individual consumers based on their characteristics, behaviors, and preferences. Rather than treating all customers as a homogeneous group, personalized marketing aims to create unique and engaging experiences for each individual. This approach recognizes that consumers have diverse needs and motivations, and aims to deliver relevant content that resonates with them.

Benefits of Personalized Marketing

Personalized marketing offers several benefits for businesses, including:

- Enhanced customer experience: By delivering personalized content, businesses can provide a more engaging and relevant experience for customers. This can lead to increased customer satisfaction and loyalty.

- Improved conversion rates: Personalized marketing allows businesses to target customers with tailored offers and messages that are more likely to resonate with them. This can result in higher conversion rates and improved sales.

- Increased customer lifetime value: By building stronger relationships with customers through personalized marketing, businesses can increase customer loyalty and lifetime value. Satisfied customers are more likely to become repeat buyers and advocates for the brand.

- Competitive advantage: In today's crowded marketplace, personalized marketing can provide a significant competitive advantage. By delivering personalized experiences, businesses can differentiate themselves from competitors and attract more customers.

Methods and Techniques

To implement personalized marketing strategies, businesses rely on AI technologies such as machine learning and natural language processing. These technologies enable the collection, analysis, and interpretation of vast amounts of data to understand consumer preferences and behaviors.

Data Collection and Analysis: Personalized marketing begins with the collection of customer data. Businesses gather data from various sources, both online and offline, including purchase history, website interactions, social media activity, and demographic information. AI algorithms then analyze this data to identify patterns, preferences, and other relevant insights.

Segmentation and Targeting: Once the data is analyzed, businesses can segment their customer base into distinct groups based on shared characteristics and behaviors. These segments allow for more targeted marketing campaigns, ensuring that the right message reaches the right audience. AI algorithms can automate this segmentation process, making it more efficient and accurate.

Content Personalization: Personalized marketing involves creating customized content for different customer segments. This can range from personalized product recommendations and tailored email offers to dynamic website content that adapts to the individual user. AI-powered algorithms can analyze customer data in real-time and generate personalized content that is most likely to resonate with each individual.

Predictive Analytics: Personalized marketing also uses predictive analytics to anticipate customer behaviors and preferences. By leveraging historical data and machine learning algorithms, businesses can predict future actions, such as purchases or product interests. This allows for proactive marketing strategies that can influence customer decisions and improve targeting.

Challenges and Considerations

While personalized marketing offers numerous benefits, there are also challenges and considerations that businesses must address:

Privacy Concerns: Personalized marketing relies on collecting and analyzing customer data, which raises privacy concerns. Businesses must ensure that they are transparent about data collection practices and comply with relevant privacy regulations. Providing options for customers to control their data preferences is crucial in building trust and maintaining ethical practices.

Data Accuracy and Quality: Personalized marketing heavily depends on the accuracy and quality of customer data. Inaccurate or incomplete data can lead to ineffective targeting and irrelevant messages. Implementing data validation and cleaning processes is essential to ensure the reliability of the collected data.

Balancing Personalization and Intrusiveness: There is a fine line between personalized marketing and intrusiveness. Businesses should be mindful of not crossing this line and avoid overwhelming customers with excessive personalization. Striking the right balance between customization and privacy is key to successful personalized marketing.

Ethical Considerations: Personalized marketing raises ethical considerations regarding the responsible use of customer data. Businesses should be transparent about their data practices, obtain appropriate consent for data collection, and use data in ways that benefit and respect the customer. Ethical considerations should guide the development and implementation of personalized marketing strategies.

Case Study: Netflix

One notable example of successful personalized marketing is Netflix. The streaming giant leverages AI algorithms to analyze vast amounts of user data, including viewing history, ratings, and interactio

Customer Segmentation

Customer segmentation is a key strategy for businesses to better understand and cater to the unique needs and preferences of different groups of customers. By dividing customers into distinct segments based on key characteristics, businesses can personalize their marketing efforts, improve customer satisfaction, and ultimately increase their profitability.

Why is Customer Segmentation Important?

In today's competitive market, businesses cannot afford to treat all customers the same. Each customer has specific needs, preferences, and behaviors that should be recognized and addressed. By segmenting customers into meaningful groups, businesses can tailor their products, services, and marketing campaigns to better meet the specific needs of each segment. This leads to improved customer satisfaction, increased customer loyalty, and ultimately higher revenue and profits.

Types of Customer Segmentation

There are various approaches to segmenting customers, depending on the specific goals and characteristics of the business. Here are some common types of customer segmentation:

1. Demographic Segmentation: Dividing customers based on demographic factors such as age, gender, income, education, and occupation. This type of segmentation is useful for businesses targeting specific age groups, genders, or income levels.

2. Psychographic Segmentation: Classifying customers based on their lifestyles, personality traits, attitudes, and values. This type of segmentation helps businesses understand customers' motivations and emotions, allowing for more targeted marketing messages.

3. Behavioral Segmentation: Segmenting customers based on their behaviors, such as purchase history, frequency of purchases, brand loyalty, and usage patterns. This type of segmentation is valuable for businesses looking to target customers based on their specific buying behaviors.

4. Geographic Segmentation: Dividing customers based on their geographic location, such as country, region, city, or zip code. This type of segmentation is essential for businesses operating in different regions or countries with distinct customer preferences and needs.

Segmentation Techniques and Tools

Segmenting customers is more than simply dividing them into groups; it involves analyzing and understanding the characteristics of each segment. Here are some common techniques and tools used in customer segmentation:

AI APPLICATIONS IN MARKETING AND SALES

1. Data Analysis: Businesses collect vast amounts of data, including customer demographics, purchase history, and online behavior. By analyzing this data, businesses can identify patterns and trends that help in segmenting customers.

2. Cluster Analysis: Cluster analysis is a statistical technique used to identify natural groupings within a dataset. It helps businesses discover customer segments based on similarities in their attributes or behaviors.

3. Decision Trees: Decision trees are a visual representation of decision-making processes. They can be used to classify customers into different segments based on specific criteria.

4. Customer Relationship Management (CRM) Systems: CRM systems store and analyze customer data, allowing businesses to create detailed profiles and segment customers based on various criteria.

Benefits of Customer Segmentation

Customer segmentation offers several benefits for businesses:

1. Personalized Marketing: By understanding the unique needs and preferences of each customer segment, businesses can create personalized marketing campaigns that resonate with their target audience, leading to higher conversion rates and sales.

2. Improved Customer Satisfaction: By tailoring products and services to the specific needs of different customer segments, businesses can enhance customer satisfaction and loyalty. Satisfied customers are more likely to become brand advocates and recommend the business to others.

3. Cost Efficiency: Targeted marketing campaigns are more cost-effective than mass marketing efforts. By focusing on specific customer segments, businesses can allocate their resources more efficiently and achieve higher return on investment.

Case Study: Amazon's Customer Segmentation

Amazon, the world's largest online retailer, is known for its sophisticated customer segmentation techniques. By analyzing customer browsing and purchase history, Amazon segments its customers and provides personalized product recommendations. For example, if a customer frequently purchases books about cooking, Amazon will display targeted ads and recommendations for other cooking-related products. This level of personalization enhances the customer experience and increases the likelihood of repeat purchases.

Ethical Considerations

While customer segmentation can bring significant benefits to businesses, it is important to consider the ethical implications. Businesses must ensure that customer data is collected and used in a responsible and transparent manner. Privacy and data protection regulations should be followed to protect the personal information of customers. Furthermore, businesses should avoid using customer segmentation to discriminate or exclude certain groups based on protected characteristics such as race, gender, or religion.

Conclusion

Customer segmentation is a vital strategy for businesses seeking to understand and meet the unique needs of different customer groups. By dividing customers into segments based on key characteristics, businesses can personalize their marketing efforts, improve customer satisfaction, and ultimately drive business success. However, it is crucial for businesses to handle customer data ethically and avoid discriminatory practices. With the right tools and techniques, businesses can unlock the full potential of customer segmentation and gain a competitive advantage in the market.

Predictive Analytics for Sales

In the fast-paced world of business, staying ahead of the competition is essential. Sales teams are constantly on the lookout for ways to boost their performance and increase revenue. One powerful tool that has revolutionized the way sales are approached is predictive analytics. By harnessing the power of data and advanced algorithms, predictive analytics can provide invaluable insights into customer behavior, market trends, and sales patterns. In this section, we will delve into the world of predictive analytics for sales, exploring its principles, applications, and potential for transforming the sales landscape.

Understanding Predictive Analytics

Predictive analytics is the use of historical data, statistical algorithms, and machine learning techniques to predict future outcomes. In the context of sales, predictive analytics aims to forecast customer behavior, identify potential leads, and optimize sales strategies. By analyzing vast amounts of data, including customer demographics, purchase history, and online interactions, predictive analytics can uncover patterns and make accurate predictions.

The Benefits of Predictive Analytics in Sales

Predictive analytics offers a myriad of benefits to sales teams, including:

1. *Improved Sales Forecasting*: Predictive analytics enables sales teams to forecast sales with greater accuracy. By analyzing historical sales data, market trends, and external factors, such as economic indicators, predictive models can provide realistic sales forecasts, helping sales teams set achievable goals and allocate resources effectively.

2. *Identifying High-Value Leads*: One of the key challenges in sales is identifying leads with the highest potential for conversion. Predictive analytics can analyze customer data to identify patterns and characteristics of high-value leads. By focusing their efforts on these leads, sales teams can maximize their conversion rates and improve overall sales performance.

3. *Optimizing Marketing Strategies*: Marketing campaigns are an integral part of the sales process, and predictive analytics can play a vital role in optimizing these strategies. By analyzing customer data, predictive models can provide insights into customer preferences, behaviors, and buying patterns. This information can guide marketers in tailoring their campaigns to target specific customer segments, resulting in higher engagement and conversion rates.

4. *Reducing Sales Cycle Time*: Predictive analytics can help sales teams streamline their sales processes and reduce the time it takes to close deals. By identifying leads that are most likely to convert and providing insights into the best timing and approach for engagement, predictive analytics can help sales teams prioritize their efforts and focus on the deals that have the highest likelihood of success.

5. *Enhancing Customer Relationship Management*: Predictive analytics can provide valuable insights into customer behavior, enabling sales teams to personalize their interactions and build stronger relationships. By understanding customer preferences, needs, and pain points, sales teams can tailor their sales pitches and recommendations, increasing customer satisfaction and loyalty.

Implementing Predictive Analytics in Sales

To successfully implement predictive analytics in sales, organizations need to follow a systematic approach:

1. *Define Objectives*: The first step is to clearly define the objectives of the predictive analytics initiative. Are you looking to improve sales forecasting, identify high-value leads, optimize marketing strategies, or all of the above? Having well-defined objectives will guide the data collection and analysis processes.

2. *Data Collection and Preparation*: The success of predictive analytics relies heavily on the quality and quantity of data available. Organizations need to collect relevant data from various sources, such as CRM systems, transaction records, and online interactions. The data should then be cleaned, validated, and properly prepared for analysis.

3. *Choose the Right Tools and Algorithms*: There are a plethora of tools and algorithms available for conducting predictive analytics. Organizations need to choose the ones that best align with their objectives and data. Commonly used algorithms in sales predictive analytics include linear regression, decision trees, and neural networks.

4. *Model Development and Training*: Once the tools and algorithms are selected, the next step is to develop and train the predictive models. This involves feeding the historical data into the models, tuning the parameters, and validating the models against known outcomes. This iterative process helps refine the models and improve their accuracy.

5. *Integration with Sales Processes*: To fully leverage the power of predictive analytics, organizations should integrate it with their existing sales processes and systems. This ensures that the insights generated from predictive analytics are seamlessly incorporated into the sales workflow, enabling sales teams to take timely and informed actions.

Challenges and Limitations

While predictive analytics has tremendous potential in sales, it is not without its challenges and limitations. Some of the key challenges include:

1. *Data Quality and Accessibility*: Predictive analytics heavily relies on the availability of high-quality data. Poor data quality or limited access to data can hamper the accuracy and effectiveness of predictive models. Organizations must prioritize data governance and invest in data infrastructure to ensure the availability and reliability of data.

2. *Model Accuracy and Interpretability*: Predictive models are not infallible and can sometimes produce inaccurate predictions. Additionally, some models, such as deep learning neural networks, are often considered black boxes, making it challenging to interpret how they arrive at their predictions. Organizations must strike a balance between model accuracy and interpretability.

3. *Privacy and Ethical Concerns*: Predictive analytics relies on collecting and analyzing vast amounts of customer data, raising concerns about privacy and ethical use of data. Organizations must adhere to ethical guidelines and privacy regulations to ensure that customer data is protected and used responsibly.

Despite these challenges, the potential benefits that predictive analytics brings to the sales process outweigh the limitations. By harnessing the power of data, algorithms, and machine learning, sales teams can gain a competitive edge, boost their productivity, and drive revenue growth.

Real-World Example: Predictive Analytics in E-commerce

Consider an e-commerce company that sells a wide range of products online. The company wants to optimize its sales strategy and increase customer conversion rates. Using predictive analytics, the company collects and analyzes customer data, including browsing history, purchase patterns, and demographic information. By employing machine learning algorithms, the company can identify customers with a high likelihood of making a purchase and personalize their online experience. For instance, the company can recommend products based on the customer's browsing history, send personalized promotions, or offer targeted discounts. By leveraging the power of predictive analytics, the company can significantly improve its sales performance and customer satisfaction.

Further Reading and Resources

To further explore the topic of predictive analytics in sales, the following resources can be helpful:

1. "Predictive Analytics for Sales and Marketing Effectiveness: Best Practices" by Eric Siegel 2. "Sales Analytics: A Guide to Using Data for Better Sales Performance Management" by Tom Nessen 3. "Predictive Analytics: The Power to Predict Who Will Click, Buy, Lie, or Die" by Eric Siegel 4. Salesforce Predictive Analytics: A complete guide to Salesforce Einstein Analytics 5. Data Science for Business: What You Need to Know about Data Mining and Data-Analytic Thinking by Foster Provost and Tom Fawcett

By diving into these resources, sales professionals can deepen their understanding of predictive analytics and unlock its full potential in driving sales success.

Exercises

1. Think of a company or industry where predictive analytics can be applied to improve sales performance. Describe the potential benefits and challenges specific to that context.

2. Suppose you are a sales manager for an online retail company. How would you use predictive analytics to optimize your marketing strategies and improve customer conversion rates? Provide a step-by-step plan.

3. Research and identify a real-world case study where a company successfully implemented predictive analytics in sales. Discuss the outcomes and impact on the company's sales performance.

4. Explore the ethical considerations associated with the use of predictive analytics in sales. Discuss the potential risks and guidelines for responsible use of customer data.

5. Investigate the latest advancements in predictive analytics for sales, such as the integration of artificial intelligence and machine learning. Discuss the potential implications and future trends.

These exercises will help reinforce the concepts covered in this section and provide practical insights into the world of predictive analytics for sales.

AI Applications in Finance

Robo-advisory

Robo-advisory is a cutting-edge application of artificial intelligence (AI) in the field of finance. It combines the power of data analysis and machine learning algorithms to provide automated investment advice and portfolio management services. This section will explore the principles of robo-advisory, its benefits, challenges, and real-world examples.

Principles of Robo-advisory

Robo-advisory platforms utilize sophisticated algorithms and data-driven models to offer investment recommendations tailored to individual investors' goals and risk tolerance. The principles underlying robo-advisory can be summarized as follows:

- **Data Gathering:** Robo-advisory platforms collect extensive information from investors, including their financial goals, investment horizon, risk appetite, and existing portfolio details. This data forms the foundation for generating customized investment strategies.

- **Risk Profiling:** Robo-advisors use advanced risk assessment tools to evaluate an investor's risk tolerance and capacity to bear losses. Based on this analysis, the platform generates a risk profile for each investor, which serves as a blueprint for constructing an appropriate investment portfolio.

- **Algorithmic Portfolio Construction:** Robo-advisors employ advanced optimization algorithms to generate optimized investment portfolios based on the investor's risk profile. These algorithms balance various factors, such as asset allocation, diversification, and cost efficiency, to create a well-rounded portfolio tailored to individual needs.

- **Automated Rebalancing:** Robo-advisory platforms continuously monitor the performance of the investment portfolio and automatically rebalance it when necessary. Rebalancing ensures that the portfolio remains aligned with the investor's goals and risk tolerance, reducing the impact of market fluctuations.

- **Cost Efficiency:** Robo-advisors leverage technology to operate with lower overhead costs compared to traditional human advisors. This cost efficiency enables them to offer their services at lower fees, making professional investment advice accessible to a broader segment of the population.

Benefits of Robo-advisory

Robo-advisory offers numerous advantages over traditional human advisors. Let's explore some of the key benefits:

- **Accessibility:** Robo-advisory platforms provide individuals with easy access to professional investment advice without requiring a large initial investment. This accessibility empowers individuals who may have previously been excluded from traditional financial advisory services.

- **Diversification:** Robo-advisors excel at generating well-diversified portfolios by leveraging advanced algorithms. Diversification reduces the overall risk associated with investing by allocating assets across different asset classes, industries, and geographic regions.

- **Cost Efficiency:** As mentioned earlier, robo-advisory platforms operate with lower costs compared to human advisors. This cost advantage allows them to offer their services at a fraction of the cost, making professional investment advice affordable for small investors.

- **Transparency:** Robo-advisory platforms provide investors with transparency by offering detailed information about the investment strategies, underlying assets, and associated fees. This transparency promotes trust and enables investors to make informed decisions.

- **Automation:** By automating portfolio management tasks, robo-advisors free up investors' time and eliminate the need for constant monitoring and manual intervention. Investors can focus on other aspects of their financial planning while the robo-advisor takes care of the investment management process.

Challenges and Considerations

While robo-advisory presents numerous benefits, there are certain challenges and considerations to keep in mind:

- **Limited Human Interaction:** Robo-advisory platforms lack the personalized touch and emotional intelligence offered by traditional human advisors. Some investors may still prefer the human interaction and guidance provided by experienced financial professionals.

- **Algorithmic Risks:** The performance of robo-advisory platforms relies heavily on the accuracy of their algorithms and data inputs. Errors in predictions or faulty data can lead to suboptimal investment decisions and potential financial losses. Regular monitoring and quality assurance of the algorithms are therefore crucial.

- **Regulatory Compliance:** Robo-advisory platforms must comply with strict financial regulations to protect investors and ensure fair practices. As the technology evolves, regulators are continuously adapting and updating rules to address potential risks and concerns associated with AI-driven financial services.

- **Loss of Control:** Some investors may feel a loss of control when entrusting their investments to a machine-driven platform. It is essential for investors to understand the underlying investment principles and have confidence in the robo-advisor's ability to generate optimal investment strategies.

Real-world Examples

Robo-advisory has gained significant traction in the financial industry, with several prominent players leading the way. Let's take a look at two notable examples:

- **Betterment:** Betterment is a well-established robo-advisory platform that offers a range of investment products and services. It uses a combination of data-driven algorithms and human expertise to provide personalized investment advice and diversified portfolios. Betterment has garnered attention for its user-friendly interface and transparent fee structure.

- **Wealthfront:** Wealthfront is another popular robo-advisory platform that emphasizes low-cost, passive investing. It utilizes advanced algorithms to construct and rebalance investment portfolios, offering features such as tax-loss harvesting and direct indexing. Wealthfront has a strong focus on long-term financial goals and aligning investments with an individual's risk tolerance.

These examples demonstrate how robo-advisory platforms have disrupted the traditional financial advisory landscape by providing accessible, cost-effective, and transparent investment solutions.

Conclusion

Robo-advisory represents an exciting application of AI technology in the domain of finance. By leveraging data analysis, machine learning algorithms, and automation, robo-advisors offer personalized investment advice, diversification, and cost efficiency to investors of all levels. While challenges and considerations exist, the benefits of robo-advisory, such as accessibility and transparency, make it a compelling option in the modern financial landscape. As technology continues to advance, robo-advisory is likely to play an increasingly significant role in shaping the future of investment management.

Algorithmic Trading

In the dynamic and fast-paced world of financial markets, algorithmic trading has emerged as a powerful tool for traders and investors. This section explores the concept of algorithmic trading, its benefits and applications, and the underlying principles that drive this automated approach to trading.

Introduction to Algorithmic Trading

Algorithmic trading, also known as algo trading or black-box trading, refers to the use of computer algorithms to execute trades in financial markets. These algorithms are designed to analyze vast amounts of data, identify trading opportunities, and execute trades at high speeds.

One of the key advantages of algorithmic trading is its ability to eliminate human bias and emotions from the trading process. By relying on predefined rules and algorithms, algorithmic trading enables consistent and disciplined execution of trades, free from emotional and irrational decision-making.

Principles of Algorithmic Trading

There are several key principles that underpin algorithmic trading:

- **Market Efficiency:** Algorithmic trading assumes that markets are semi-efficient and that prices reflect all available information. The algorithms used in this approach aim to capitalize on short-lived market inefficiencies by executing trades at optimal times and prices.
- **Data Analysis:** Algorithmic trading relies heavily on data analysis. Historical data, including price movements, trading volumes, and news sentiment, is used to develop models and strategies that guide trading decisions. Advanced statistical and machine learning techniques are applied to identify patterns and trends in the data for predictive purposes.
- **Risk Management:** Effective risk management is crucial in algorithmic trading. Algorithms are designed to incorporate risk parameters, such as stop-loss orders and position sizing, to protect against significant losses. Additionally, risk management protocols ensure that trades are executed within predefined risk tolerances.
- **Low Latency:** Speed is a critical factor in algorithmic trading. To capitalize on fleeting market opportunities, algorithms are designed to execute trades within milliseconds. This requires sophisticated infrastructure, including high-speed connections to exchanges and sophisticated order routing systems.

Types of Algorithmic Trading Strategies

There are various types of algorithmic trading strategies, each with its own approach and objectives. Here are a few commonly used strategies:

- **Trend Following:** This strategy aims to identify and capitalize on market trends. Algorithms analyze historical data, such as moving averages and price patterns, to determine if a trend is developing. Trades are then executed in the direction of the identified trend.

- **Arbitrage:** Arbitrage strategies aim to profit from price discrepancies between different markets or assets. Algorithms monitor multiple markets and execute trades to exploit temporary price differences, thereby generating risk-free profits.

- **Mean Reversion:** This strategy is based on the belief that prices tend to revert to their mean or average values over time. Algorithms identify situations where prices have deviated significantly from their mean and execute trades to take advantage of the expected reversion.

- **Statistical Arbitrage:** In statistical arbitrage, algorithms use complex statistical models to identify relationships or correlations between different assets. Trades are executed based on deviations from these relationships, allowing for profit opportunities.

Challenges and Risks

While algorithmic trading offers numerous benefits, it is not without challenges and risks. Here are a few key considerations:

- **Technical Risks:** Algorithmic trading relies on cutting-edge technology and infrastructure. Any technical failures or glitches can have severe consequences, leading to significant losses. Robust monitoring systems and fail-safe mechanisms are essential to mitigate these risks.

- **Regulatory Compliance:** Algorithmic trading is subject to strict regulations to ensure fair and orderly markets. Traders and firms involved in algorithmic trading must comply with rules related to market manipulation, unfair trading practices, and risk management. Failure to comply can result in regulatory scrutiny and penalties.

- **Market Liquidity:** Algorithmic trading can impact market liquidity, particularly during periods of extreme volatility. Large-scale algorithmic trading can exacerbate price movements and lead to market disruptions. It is crucial to monitor liquidity conditions and adjust trading strategies accordingly.

- **Model Risks:** The success of algorithmic trading depends on the accuracy and effectiveness of the underlying models. If the models fail to capture relevant market dynamics or if the assumptions underlying the models are flawed, significant losses can occur. Regular model validation and refinement are necessary to mitigate these risks.

Real-World Example: Flash Crash

One notable example of the risks associated with algorithmic trading is the "Flash Crash" of May 6, 2010. Within minutes, the U.S. stock market experienced a rapid and severe decline, followed by a swift recovery.

The Flash Crash was triggered by a combination of high-frequency trading algorithms and market conditions. As these algorithms reacted to market movements, selling pressure intensified. The decline in prices triggered further algorithms to sell, amplifying the downward spiral. Ultimately, the market rebounded, but not before wiping out billions of dollars in market value.

This incident highlighted the need for enhanced risk controls and safeguards in algorithmic trading to prevent such extreme market disruptions.

Resources

For those interested in delving deeper into the world of algorithmic trading, here are some recommended resources:

- Book: "Algorithmic Trading: Winning Strategies and Their Rationale" by Ernie Chan
- Online Course: "Machine Learning for Trading" on Coursera
- Research Paper: "High-Frequency Trading and Its Impact on Market Quality" by Terrence Hendershott, Charles M. Jones, and Albert J. Menkveld

Summary

Algorithmic trading has transformed the landscape of financial markets, enabling traders to capitalize on opportunities with speed, precision, and efficiency. By leveraging advanced data analysis techniques and predefined trading strategies, algorithmic trading has the potential to generate consistent returns and reduce human biases. However, it is not without risks, and careful risk management, robust infrastructure, and regulatory compliance are essential for success in this domain.

Exercises

1. What are the key advantages of algorithmic trading compared to traditional manual trading?

2. Explain the concept of market efficiency in the context of algorithmic trading.

3. How does risk management play a role in algorithmic trading? Provide specific examples of risk management techniques used in this approach.

4. Discuss the challenges associated with algorithmic trading and how they can be mitigated.

5. Research and explain another real-world example of a significant event or incident related to algorithmic trading.

AI Applications in Healthcare

Medical Diagnosis and Treatment

In the world of medicine, Artificial Intelligence (AI) has emerged as a powerful tool that has the potential to revolutionize medical diagnosis and treatment. With its ability to process massive amounts of data and identify patterns, AI is helping doctors and healthcare professionals make more accurate diagnoses, develop personalized treatment plans, and improve patient outcomes.

The Need for AI in Medical Diagnosis

Medical diagnosis is a complex and challenging task that relies on the knowledge and experience of healthcare professionals. However, due to the vast amount of medical literature and research, it is impossible for a single individual to stay up-to-date with all the latest advancements. This is where AI comes in, by leveraging cutting-edge algorithms to analyze medical data and generate insights that can aid in diagnosis.

AI can process a wide range of medical data, including electronic health records, medical images, genetic information, and patient-reported data. By combining this data with machine learning algorithms, AI systems can identify subtle patterns and correlations that humans may overlook. This can lead to earlier and more accurate diagnoses, enabling timely intervention and treatment.

Machine Learning in Medical Diagnosis

Machine learning techniques play a crucial role in medical diagnosis. These algorithms learn from large datasets and use statistical models to make predictions based on the input data.

One common machine learning technique used in medical diagnosis is classification. Classification algorithms can categorize patients into different groups based on their symptoms, medical history, and test results. For example, in cancer diagnosis, machine learning algorithms can analyze tumor imaging data and predict whether a tumor is benign or malignant with high accuracy.

Another important machine learning technique in medical diagnosis is regression analysis. Regression algorithms can analyze the relationship between different variables and predict the value of a target variable. For instance, these algorithms can predict the progression of a disease based on patient-specific factors such as age, gender, and genetic markers.

Deep Learning in Medical Imaging

Medical imaging plays a critical role in diagnosing and monitoring diseases. However, interpreting medical images can be challenging and time-consuming for human radiologists. This is where deep learning, a subset of machine learning, has shown tremendous promise.

Deep learning algorithms, particularly Convolutional Neural Networks (CNNs), have demonstrated exceptional performance in medical image analysis. These networks are designed to mimic the organization of the visual cortex in the human brain, enabling them to extract intricate features from images.

In medical diagnosis, CNNs can analyze various types of medical images, including X-rays, CT scans, MRIs, and histopathological slides. These algorithms can detect abnormalities, segment organs and tumors, and classify images into different disease categories. For example, in dermatology, CNNs can accurately classify skin lesions as benign or malignant, aiding in the early detection of skin cancer.

Enhancing Treatment Decisions with AI

Beyond diagnosis, AI can also assist in developing personalized treatment plans for patients. By analyzing a patient's medical history, genetic information, and treatment response data, AI algorithms can identify the most effective treatments for specific individuals.

One area where AI is making significant contributions is in the field of precision medicine. Precision medicine aims to deliver tailored treatments based on an individual's unique genetic makeup. AI can analyze genetic data and identify genetic markers associated with specific diseases or treatment responses. This information can help doctors select the most appropriate medication or therapy, leading to improved patient outcomes and reduced adverse effects.

Furthermore, AI can also help streamline treatment decision-making through clinical decision support systems. These systems analyze patient data, clinical guidelines, and scientific literature to provide evidence-based recommendations to healthcare professionals. By leveraging AI, doctors can make more informed decisions about treatment options, dosage recommendations, and potential drug interactions.

Challenges and Ethical Considerations

While the potential of AI in medical diagnosis and treatment is exciting, it is essential to address the challenges and ethical considerations associated with its implementation.

One major challenge is the need for high-quality and diverse medical datasets for training AI algorithms. Without representative datasets, AI models may be biased or fail to generalize to different populations. Another challenge is ensuring the interpretability and transparency of AI algorithms. Explainable AI is crucial in the medical field, as doctors need to understand the reasoning behind AI recommendations.

Ethical considerations also come into play when implementing AI in healthcare. Patient privacy and data security are paramount, as AI systems rely on sensitive medical information. Additionally, there is a concern about the impact of AI on the doctor-patient relationship. While AI can enhance diagnosis and treatment decisions, it should not replace the human touch and empathy that patients expect from their healthcare providers.

Case Study: AI in Radiology

To illustrate the impact of AI in medical diagnosis, let's consider a case study in radiology. In traditional radiology, radiologists manually review medical images to detect abnormalities and assist in diagnosis. However, this manual process is time-consuming and prone to human error.

By implementing AI, radiologists can leverage deep learning algorithms to analyze medical images more efficiently and accurately. For example, a deep learning model can identify minute changes in lung X-rays that may indicate the early stages of lung cancer, allowing for timely intervention.

Moreover, AI can be used to improve workflows in radiology departments. AI algorithms can automatically triage incoming scans, prioritizing urgent cases and reducing the workload on radiologists. This can lead to faster diagnosis and treatment initiation for patients.

Conclusion

AI is transforming medical diagnosis and treatment by augmenting the capabilities of healthcare professionals, improving diagnostic accuracy, and enabling personalized treatment plans. Machine learning and deep learning algorithms are empowering doctors to make data-driven decisions and providing patients with more effective and tailored care.

However, the integration of AI in healthcare comes with challenges and ethical considerations that need to be addressed. It is crucial to ensure the quality and representativeness of medical datasets, promote transparency and explainability of AI algorithms, and safeguard patient privacy and data security.

As AI continues to evolve and improve, we can expect further advancements in medical diagnosis and treatment, ultimately leading to enhanced patient outcomes and a brighter future for healthcare.

Drug Discovery and Development

In this section, we will dive into the fascinating world of drug discovery and development, exploring how artificial intelligence (AI) is revolutionizing this field. We will discuss the challenges faced in discovering new drugs, the role of AI in streamlining the process, and the social implications of AI-driven drug development.

The Challenge of Drug Discovery

Drug discovery is an intricate and time-consuming process that involves identifying and developing compounds that can effectively treat diseases. Traditionally, this process has relied on trial and error and has been hindered by its high cost, low success rate, and lengthy timelines. To put it simply, drug discovery is a bit like searching for a needle in a haystack.

The journey starts with target identification, where scientists identify specific molecular targets, such as proteins or genes, that play a key role in a disease. Once a target is identified, researchers perform high-throughput screening, testing thousands or even millions of compounds to find potential candidates that can interact with the target.

After the initial screening, the selected compounds undergo further testing through a series of stages: hit-to-lead optimization, preclinical development, clinical trials, and finally, regulatory approval. This entire process can take up to 10-15 years and costs billions of dollars.

AI in Drug Discovery

AI has emerged as a powerful tool to accelerate and optimize the drug discovery process. By leveraging machine learning algorithms, AI systems can analyze vast amounts of data, identify patterns, and make predictions with unprecedented speed and accuracy. Let's explore some key areas where AI is making a significant impact.

Virtual Screening Virtual screening involves using computational models to predict the binding affinity of compounds to a specific target. AI algorithms can analyze the chemical structure and properties of millions of compounds and prioritize those that are most likely to exhibit the desired therapeutic effects. This approach significantly reduces the number of compounds that need to be experimentally tested, saving time and resources.

De Novo Drug Design De novo drug design is the process of creating new molecules that possess certain desired properties. AI can generate novel drug-like molecules by exploring the vast chemical space and optimizing them based on target interactions, safety, and drug-like properties. This enables the discovery of potentially innovative and effective drug candidates that may not have been identified through traditional methods.

Drug Repurposing Drug repurposing involves finding new therapeutic uses for existing drugs. AI algorithms can analyze large-scale biomedical data, including genomics, proteomics, and clinical data, to uncover hidden relationships between drugs and diseases. By identifying new indications for approved drugs, AI can expedite the process of finding effective treatments for diseases, potentially bypassing years of preclinical and early clinical development.

Clinical Trial Optimization AI can also optimize the design and execution of clinical trials, a critical step in drug development. By analyzing patient data, electronic health records, and historical trial data, AI algorithms can identify patient populations that are more likely to respond positively to a particular drug. This enables more targeted and efficient clinical trials, reducing costs and accelerating the time it takes to bring a drug to market.

Ethical Considerations and Challenges

While the integration of AI in drug discovery offers immense potential, it also raises ethical considerations and challenges that need to be addressed. Let's explore some of the key concerns:

Data Privacy and Bias Access to large datasets is crucial for training AI models. However, the use of personal health data for drug discovery raises concerns about privacy and security. Transparent and secure data governance frameworks are essential to protect patient privacy while ensuring adequate data access for research purposes.

Moreover, AI algorithms are only as good as the data they are trained on. Biases present in the training data can lead to biased predictions and discriminatory practices. It is crucial to ensure that diverse and representative datasets are used and that algorithms are regularly evaluated for fairness to prevent unintended consequences.

Regulatory and Safety Considerations The regulatory landscape for AI-driven drug development is still evolving. Regulatory bodies must strike a balance between facilitating innovation and ensuring patient safety. Robust frameworks are needed to evaluate the safety and efficacy of AI-generated drug candidates and to address the potential risks associated with algorithms making critical decisions in healthcare.

Case Study: DeepMind's AlphaFold

A groundbreaking example of AI in drug discovery is DeepMind's AlphaFold, an AI system that uses deep learning to predict protein structures. Understanding the 3D structure of proteins is crucial for drug discovery, as it allows researchers to design drugs that specifically target proteins involved in diseases.

AlphaFold's ability to accurately predict protein structures has the potential to revolutionize drug development. By providing researchers with valuable insights into protein folding and structure-function relationships, this AI system can accelerate the discovery of new drugs and cut down on experimental guesswork.

The success of AlphaFold was demonstrated in the 2020 Critical Assessment of Structure Prediction (CASP) competition, where it outperformed other methods in predicting protein structures. This achievement has garnered significant attention and holds great promise for the future of drug discovery.

Conclusion

AI is transforming the field of drug discovery and development. Through virtual screening, de novo drug design, and drug repurposing, AI algorithms can expedite the identification of potential drug candidates. Additionally, AI optimization of clinical trials can enhance efficiency and reduce costs.

However, the integration of AI in drug development also poses ethical challenges, such as data privacy, bias, and regulatory considerations. Addressing these concerns is crucial to ensure the responsible and safe implementation of AI in healthcare.

As we look ahead, the synergy between AI and drug discovery holds tremendous potential for finding innovative treatments and improving patient outcomes. By harnessing the power of AI intelligently and ethically, we can unlock a new era of drug discovery and development, enabling us to tackle some of the world's most pressing health challenges.

Healthcare Robotics

In recent years, healthcare has seen a significant growth in the implementation of robotic technologies to improve patient care, enhance medical procedures, and streamline healthcare operations. Healthcare robotics combines the power of artificial intelligence and automation to revolutionize the healthcare industry and assist healthcare professionals in various tasks. In this section, we will explore the applications and benefits of healthcare robotics, as well as the challenges that need to be addressed for successful integration.

Robotic Surgery

One of the most prominent applications of healthcare robotics is in the field of robotic surgery. Robotic surgical systems, such as the da Vinci Surgical System, have transformed the way surgeries are performed by providing higher precision, dexterity, and control to surgeons. These systems consist of robotic arms with surgical instruments attached, controlled by surgeons through a console. The surgeon's hand movements are translated into precise movements of the robotic arms, allowing for minimally invasive surgeries with smaller incisions, reduced pain, and faster recovery times.

The benefits of robotic surgery are numerous. The enhanced visualization and dexterity provided by the robotic arms enable surgeons to perform complex procedures with greater precision, avoiding damage to surrounding tissues. Additionally, robotic surgery offers increased range of motion, eliminating natural hand tremors and allowing for fine-tuned movements. Robotic systems also provide a 3D visualization of the surgical site, improving depth perception and enhancing surgical accuracy.

Despite its advantages, robotic surgery also presents challenges. The high cost of robotic systems, including the initial investment and ongoing maintenance, limits their accessibility to larger healthcare institutions. Training and certification for robotic surgery are also essential, as surgeons need to acquire specific skills to operate the systems effectively. Moreover, the lack of haptic feedback in robotic surgery remains a challenge, as surgeons rely on touch and feel during traditional surgeries. Ongoing research aims to address these challenges by improving haptic feedback and reducing costs to make robotic surgery more widely available.

Assistance and Rehabilitation

Healthcare robotics also plays a vital role in assisting patients with limited mobility and physical disabilities. Robotic exoskeletons, for example, provide support and strength to individuals with spinal cord injuries, allowing them to stand and walk. These exoskeletons use sensors and motors to detect body movements and provide the necessary assistance to help patients regain functionality and improve their quality of life.

Another area where healthcare robotics is making an impact is in rehabilitation therapy. Robotic devices, such as robotic arms and legs, are used to guide and assist patients in regaining motor control and relearning movements. These devices incorporate motion sensors and actuators to deliver precise movements and adjust therapy intensity based on individual needs. By providing repetitive and customized rehabilitation exercises, robotic devices can accelerate the recovery process and improve functional outcomes for patients.

One of the main advantages of using robotics in assistance and rehabilitation is the ability to provide consistent and standardized care. Robots can deliver therapy with precision and accuracy, ensuring that patients receive the same level of treatment each time and reducing variability in outcomes. Additionally, continuous monitoring of patients' progress allows healthcare providers to track improvements and adjust therapy plans accordingly.

Despite the benefits, challenges exist in the integration of healthcare robotics in assistance and rehabilitation. Cost remains a significant barrier, as acquiring and maintaining robotic devices can be expensive for healthcare facilities. Personalization of therapy is also a challenge, as robotic devices need to adapt to individual needs and preferences. Moreover, the human-robot interaction aspect needs to be carefully considered to ensure patient comfort and acceptance of these technologies.

Robot-Assisted Care

In addition to surgical and rehabilitative applications, healthcare robotics is utilized in various caregiving tasks to assist healthcare professionals and improve patient outcomes. Robot-assisted care includes tasks such as medication administration, patient monitoring, and disinfection of healthcare facilities.

Medication errors can occur due to human factors, such as miscalculations or misinterpretations. Robot-assisted medication administration systems automate the process, reducing the risk of errors and improving medication safety. These systems use barcode scanning or radio-frequency identification (RFID) technology to ensure accurate medication dispensing, reducing the likelihood of administration errors and improving patient care.

Robot-assisted patient monitoring involves the use of sensors and cameras to collect real-time data on patients' vital signs and movements. This data can be analyzed by AI algorithms to detect abnormalities and alert healthcare providers. Monitoring systems equipped with fall detection capabilities, for example, can notify caregivers if a patient falls, allowing for a timely response and prevention of further injuries.

In the wake of the COVID-19 pandemic, robot-assisted disinfection has gained significant attention. Autonomous robots equipped with UV-C lights or disinfectant sprayers can effectively sanitize healthcare facilities, reducing the risk of infections and ensuring a safe environment for patients and healthcare workers. These robots can navigate through the premises autonomously, targeting high-touch surfaces and eliminating pathogens.

Although robot-assisted care offers numerous benefits, challenges need to be addressed for widespread implementation. Interoperability of different robotic systems with existing healthcare infrastructure and electronic health records is crucial to ensure seamless integration. Additionally, patient privacy and data security must be safeguarded to build trust in these technologies. Ongoing research and development are essential to further improve the capabilities and acceptance of robot-assisted care.

Ethical Considerations

The integration of healthcare robotics raises important ethical considerations that need to be addressed for responsible and ethical deployment. One of the key concerns is the impact of robotics on the patient-doctor relationship. It is essential to strike a balance between the use of technology and maintaining the human touch and empathy in healthcare delivery. Healthcare robotics should augment human capabilities rather than replace them entirely, ensuring that patients receive the emotional support and individualized care they need.

Another ethical consideration is the responsibility of healthcare robotics developers and manufacturers to maintain rigorous safety standards. Robust testing and validation procedures are necessary to ensure the safety and reliability of robotic systems used in healthcare settings. Additionally, transparency and accountability in the development and deployment of healthcare robotics are essential to build trust among patients, healthcare professionals, and the general public.

The issue of job displacement also arises with the integration of healthcare robotics. While robotics can automate repetitive tasks and free up healthcare professionals' time, concerns exist regarding potential job losses. It is crucial to prepare healthcare professionals for this shift by providing training and upskilling opportunities to adapt to the changing healthcare landscape and take on more complex roles that require human expertise.

Overall, healthcare robotics holds tremendous potential in transforming the healthcare industry, improving patient outcomes, and enhancing healthcare professionals' capabilities. To harness these benefits, it is vital to address the challenges, ethical considerations, and societal implications associated with the integration of healthcare robotics. With responsible development, collaboration between humans and robots can lead to a future where healthcare is more efficient, accessible, and patient-centered.

AI Ethics and Social Implications

Bias and Fairness in AI

Algorithmic Bias

Algorithmic bias refers to the phenomenon where artificial intelligence (AI) systems exhibit unfair or discriminatory behavior towards certain individuals or groups. Despite the promise of AI to provide objective and unbiased decision-making, these systems can inadvertently reflect the biases present in the data used to train them or in the algorithms themselves. This can lead to biased outcomes in areas such as employment, law enforcement, and lending.

Understanding Algorithmic Bias

Algorithmic bias can arise from various sources, including biased training data, biased algorithms, and biased human decisions during model development. Biased training data occurs when the data used to train an AI system is unrepresentative or reflects historical disparities. For example, if an AI system is trained on historical hiring data that reflects gender biases, it may perpetuate those biases when making hiring recommendations.

Biased algorithms can also contribute to algorithmic bias. Algorithms are designed based on assumptions and decision rules that can introduce subjective biases. For example, an algorithm that uses zip codes as a proxy for race or socioeconomic status may inadvertently discriminate against certain groups.

Furthermore, biased decisions made by humans during the development of AI models can influence the presence of algorithmic bias. If human biases are not addressed during the design and development process, AI systems may perpetuate these biases when making decisions.

Types of Algorithmic Bias

There are different types of algorithmic bias that can manifest in AI systems:

1. Selection bias: This occurs when the training data used to build the AI model is not representative of the population it should generalize to. For example, if an AI model for job screening is trained using data from predominantly male applicants, it may not accurately assess the qualifications of female applicants.

2. Prejudice bias: Prejudice bias refers to discrimination or favoritism towards certain groups. This can occur when an AI system includes factors that are correlated with protected attributes such as race, gender, or age. For instance, facial recognition systems have been found to perform poorly for people with darker skin tones, leading to higher rates of misidentification and false arrests among minority communities.

3. Stereotyping bias: Stereotyping bias occurs when an AI system generalizes assumptions or stereotypes about certain groups. For example, if an AI system is trained on data that associates certain professions with specific genders, it may perpetuate gender stereotypes when making recommendations or predictions.

Impact and Challenges

Algorithmic bias can have significant societal and ethical implications. It can perpetuate existing inequalities, reinforce discrimination, and hinder social progress. Biased AI systems can result in unfair treatment, limited opportunities, and marginalization of already disadvantaged groups. For instance, biased facial recognition systems can lead to wrongful arrests or biased hiring algorithms can perpetuate gender and racial disparities in employment.

Addressing algorithmic bias poses several challenges. Firstly, identifying and measuring bias is complex. Bias can be subtle, indirect, or context-dependent, making it difficult to detect. Additionally, biases can be amplified or obscured when AI systems are deployed in real-world settings, further complicating efforts to address them.

Secondly, addressing bias in AI systems requires a multidisciplinary approach. It involves expertise from fields such as computer science, ethics, law, sociology, and public policy. Collaboration between these disciplines is crucial to understand the nuances of bias, design fair algorithms, and develop appropriate safeguards.

Addressing Algorithmic Bias

Addressing algorithmic bias is an ongoing area of research and development. Here are some strategies to mitigate and minimize bias in AI systems:

1. **Data collection and preprocessing:** Ensuring diverse and representative training data is essential for reducing bias. Data collection methods should account for potential biases and actively seek to include underrepresented groups. Additionally, data preprocessing techniques can be employed to identify and remove biased or discriminatory patterns from the data.

2. **Algorithmic transparency and accountability:** Increasing transparency in AI systems can help identify and address biases. Organizations should document and disclose information about the algorithms used in their systems, including the variables considered and the decision-making process. Accountability mechanisms, such as third-party audits or regulatory frameworks, can also contribute to detecting and rectifying bias.

3. **Regular testing and evaluation:** Continuously monitoring and evaluating AI systems for bias is essential. Organizations should conduct regular audits and tests to assess the fairness and accuracy of their algorithms. This can involve benchmarking against predefined metrics, analyzing outcomes across different demographic groups, and soliciting feedback from diverse stakeholders.

4. **Diverse and inclusive development teams:** Having diverse teams involved in the development of AI systems can help identify and address bias. Different perspectives and experiences can bring attention to potential biases and contribute to more inclusive approaches to AI development.

Case Study: Bias in Predictive Policing

One prominent example of algorithmic bias is its impact on predictive policing systems. Predictive policing algorithms use historical crime data to predict where crimes are likely to occur in the future. However, if the training data used to build these algorithms is biased, it can perpetuate discriminatory policing practices.

For instance, if police patrols have historically targeted certain neighborhoods due to racial profiling, the data used to train the predictive policing algorithm will reflect this bias. As a result, the algorithm will likely recommend increased police presence in those neighborhoods, further reinforcing discriminatory practices.

To address this bias, it is crucial to ensure that training data is representative and free from biased policing practices. Additionally, predictive policing algorithms should be evaluated regularly to detect and mitigate any biases that may arise during their deployment.

Conclusion

Algorithmic bias is a critical issue that needs to be addressed to ensure fairness, equity, and trust in AI systems. It requires a collective effort from researchers, policy-makers, and practitioners to develop and implement strategies that mitigate bias and uphold ethical principles. By recognizing the existence of algorithmic bias and taking proactive steps to address it, we can harness the potential of AI to benefit all members of society.

Fairness in AI Decision-making

Fairness is a crucial aspect of decision-making in the context of Artificial Intelligence (AI). As AI systems become increasingly integrated into our daily lives, it is essential to ensure that these systems make fair and unbiased decisions. However, achieving fairness in AI decision-making is not a straightforward task. It requires a deep understanding of the underlying biases in the data, the algorithms used, and the social implications of their application.

The Challenge of Bias

Bias in AI decision-making arises when the outcomes or predictions of an AI system disproportionately favor or disadvantage certain individuals or groups. This bias can be unintentional, as the algorithms used in AI systems are typically trained on historical data that reflects societal biases. However, this can perpetuate and even amplify existing inequalities and injustices, leading to unfair outcomes.

Identifying Bias

To address bias in AI decision-making, the first step is to identify and understand its presence. This involves conducting a comprehensive analysis of the data, the algorithm, and the decision-making process. It is crucial to examine the training data carefully and identify any existing biases or underrepresented groups. Additionally, the algorithms themselves need to be thoroughly examined to ensure they are not implicitly biased.

Measuring Fairness

Once bias has been identified, it is essential to develop measures of fairness to evaluate the performance of AI systems. There are different approaches to measuring fairness, depending on the context and the desired outcomes. Some common fairness metrics include:

- **Statistical Parity:** This metric measures whether the outcomes of an AI system are distributed equally among groups. For example, if an AI system is used for predicting loan approval, statistical parity ensures that the approval rate is similar across different racial or gender groups.

- **Equal Opportunity:** This metric focuses on the ratio of true positives to the total number of actual positive instances for each group. It ensures that the AI system does not disproportionately miss positive instances for any particular group.

- **Predictive Parity:** This metric assesses whether the predictions of an AI system have similar predictive accuracy across different groups. It aims to achieve equal error rates across all groups.

Mitigating Bias and Ensuring Fairness

Achieving fairness in AI decision-making requires proactive steps to mitigate bias. Here are some strategies that can be implemented to ensure fairness:

- **Diverse and Representative Training Data:** Ensuring that the training data used for AI systems is diverse and representative of the entire population is crucial. Data collection should include various demographic groups to avoid underrepresentation and bias.

- **Regular Monitoring and Auditing:** Continuously monitoring and auditing AI systems for bias and unfair outcomes is essential. This involves regular testing and evaluation to identify and mitigate any emerging biases.

- **Algorithmic Transparency:** Increasing transparency in AI decision-making can help identify and rectify biases. Understanding the inner workings of algorithms allows for a deeper analysis of their decision-making processes.

- **Post-Hoc Adjustments:** After the development of AI systems, post-hoc adjustments can be made to address any observed biases. These adjustments can help calibrate the system to achieve fairness.

Ethical Implications

The discussion of fairness in AI decision-making is not complete without considering the ethical implications. Fairness is not an objective concept and may vary depending on the context and values of different stakeholders. It requires making value-based decisions and striking a balance between different competing objectives.

Moreover, fairness should not be the sole responsibility of AI developers or data scientists. It requires collaboration with experts from diverse disciplines, including social scientists, ethicists, and legal professionals. Engaging with affected communities and incorporating their perspectives is essential to avoid perpetuating systemic biases.

Case Study: Predictive Policing

One example that highlights the importance of fairness in AI decision-making is the use of predictive policing algorithms. These algorithms aim to identify potential crime hotspots and allocate police resources accordingly. However, studies have shown that these algorithms can reinforce existing biases in the criminal justice system, leading to over-policing in marginalized communities.

To address this issue, fairness measures can be implemented. For example, by considering additional factors such as income or education level in the algorithm, a more balanced and fair distribution of police resources can be achieved.

Conclusion

Ensuring fairness in AI decision-making is critical for the responsible and ethical development and deployment of AI systems. Addressing bias, measuring fairness, and implementing strategies to mitigate biases are essential steps in achieving fairness. However, fairness is a complex and multifaceted concept that requires ongoing evaluation, dialogue, and engagement with diverse stakeholders. By striving for fairness, we can harness the power of AI to create a more just and equitable world.

Addressing Bias in AI Systems

Bias is a pervasive issue in artificial intelligence (AI) systems that can have far-reaching consequences. In this section, we will explore the various forms of bias that can arise in AI, understand their implications, and discuss strategies to address and mitigate them.

Understanding Bias in AI

In the context of AI, bias refers to the systematic favoritism or unfair treatment of certain groups or individuals. Bias can occur at various stages of the AI lifecycle, including data collection, algorithm design, and decision-making processes. Understanding the different types of bias is crucial in developing effective strategies to address them.

1. Representation Bias: This occurs when the training data used to build AI models is not representative of the real-world population. For example, if a facial recognition system is trained primarily on data of light-skinned individuals, it will likely exhibit lower accuracy for people with darker skin tones.

2. Measurement Bias: Measurement bias happens when certain attributes or variables are not accurately captured or represented in the data. For instance, if an AI system is trained on historical hiring data that reflects gender discrimination, it may perpetuate biased decisions when selecting job candidates.

3. Prejudice Bias: Prejudice bias occurs when AI models learn and reinforce societal biases that are reflected in the training data. For instance, if an AI-powered loan approval system is trained on data that shows bias against certain racial or ethnic groups, it may perpetuate discriminatory lending practices.

Implications of Bias in AI

Bias in AI systems can lead to serious consequences, including perpetuating discrimination, reinforcing social inequalities, and undermining trust in AI technologies. It is essential to recognize the implications of bias and its potential harm.

1. Discrimination: Biased AI systems can unfairly discriminate against certain groups, denying them opportunities or subjecting them to undue scrutiny. For example, if a predictive policing algorithm is biased against certain neighborhoods, it can lead to over-policing and disproportionate targeting of specific communities.

2. Reinforcement of Inequality: Biased AI systems can perpetuate existing social inequalities by replicating and amplifying biased decisions and behaviors.

This can further marginalize underrepresented groups and hinder progress towards a more equitable society.

3. **Lack of Trust:** Bias erodes trust in AI systems and can lead to skepticism and resistance towards their adoption. If users perceive AI systems to be biased or unfair, they may disengage from using them, limiting their potential benefits.

Strategies for Bias Mitigation

Addressing bias in AI systems requires a comprehensive approach that encompasses all stages of the AI lifecycle. Here, we discuss some strategies to mitigate bias and develop more fair and trustworthy AI systems.

1. **Diverse and Representative Data:** To reduce representation bias, it is crucial to ensure that training data is diverse and representative of the target population. This may involve collecting data from a wide range of sources and actively seeking to include underrepresented groups.

2. **Data Preprocessing and Cleaning:** Rigorous data preprocessing and cleaning techniques are essential to identify and mitigate measurement bias. This may include removing or anonymizing sensitive attributes, correcting data anomalies, and ensuring data quality and reliability.

3. **Algorithmic Fairness:** Algorithmic fairness techniques aim to mitigate prejudice bias by explicitly accounting for protected attributes (such as race or gender) during model training. This ensures that the AI system does not make discriminatory decisions based on these attributes.

4. **Evaluation and Auditing:** Regular evaluation and auditing of AI systems can help identify and address bias. This involves assessing the impact of AI algorithms on different groups, monitoring outcomes, and making necessary adjustments to achieve fairness.

5. **Diversity in AI Development:** Ensuring diversity in AI development teams can help uncover and address bias more effectively. Different perspectives and experiences can contribute to the identification of overlooked biases and the design of fairer AI systems.

Case Study: Gender Bias in Hiring Algorithms

An example of bias in AI systems is gender bias in hiring algorithms. Several studies have shown that AI-powered resume screening tools often exhibit gender bias, favoring male candidates over equally qualified female candidates.

This bias can occur due to historical imbalances in the data used for training, where male candidates are overrepresented. Additionally, language patterns and biases present in job descriptions and historical hiring data can also contribute to this bias.

Addressing this bias requires a combination of strategies. First, it is necessary to ensure diversity in the training data, including equal representation of male and female candidates. Second, the algorithmic design should account for gender fairness, considering the impact of protected attributes (like gender) during candidate evaluation. Regular evaluation and auditing of the algorithm's outcomes can help identify and correct any biases that may arise.

Conclusion

Bias is a significant and complex challenge in AI systems, requiring careful consideration and proactive measures to address. By understanding the different types of bias, recognizing their implications, and adopting strategies for bias mitigation, we can develop AI systems that are fair, inclusive, and trustworthy.

Privacy and Data Protection

Data Governance

Data governance plays a crucial role in the responsible and ethical use of data within the context of artificial intelligence (AI). It provides a framework for organizations to ensure the quality, integrity, and security of data, as well as compliance with relevant laws and regulations. In this section, we will explore the key concepts and principles of data governance, along with its importance in the AI landscape.

Defining Data Governance

Data governance refers to the overall management of the availability, integrity, usability, and security of data within an organization. It encompasses the policies, procedures, and controls that govern data-related activities and ensure that data is handled in a consistent, controlled, and compliant manner.

In the context of AI, data governance becomes even more critical. AI systems rely heavily on large volumes of data for training, testing, and decision-making. Without effective data governance, AI algorithms may produce biased results, compromise privacy, or fail to meet legal and ethical standards.

Principles of Data Governance

There are several key principles that underpin effective data governance:

1. **Accountability**: Organizations should assign clear roles and responsibilities for data governance, ensuring that individuals or teams are accountable for the quality, protection, and appropriate use of data.

2. **Data Integrity**: Data must be accurate, consistent, and reliable. Organizations should establish controls and processes to ensure data integrity throughout its lifecycle, including data collection, storage, processing, and analysis.

3. **Transparency**: Organizations should be transparent about their data governance practices, including how data is collected, used, and shared. Transparency builds trust with stakeholders and helps to mitigate concerns about data misuse.

4. **Compliance**: Data governance should align with applicable laws, regulations, and industry standards. Organizations must ensure that data management practices adhere to legal requirements and ethical guidelines.

5. **Privacy and Security**: Data governance should prioritize the protection of personal and sensitive information. Organizations should implement appropriate security measures to safeguard data against unauthorized access, breaches, or misuse.

6. **Data Quality Management**: Effective data governance requires organizations to establish processes for data quality management. This involves defining data quality standards, conducting regular data quality assessments, and implementing measures to correct or prevent data errors.

Challenges in Data Governance

Implementing robust data governance practices can be challenging. Organizations may face the following difficulties:

1. **Data Silos**: Many organizations struggle with data silos, where data is fragmented across different systems or departments. This makes it difficult to establish a cohesive data governance framework and maintain consistent data standards.

2. **Data Ownership**: Determining data ownership can be complex, especially in organizations with multiple stakeholders. Clear policies and guidelines must be established to define who has the right to access, use, and manage specific data sets.

3. **Lack of Awareness**: Many employees may not fully understand the importance of data governance or may not be aware of the policies and procedures in place. Ongoing training and awareness programs are essential to promote a data-driven culture and ensure adherence to data governance principles.

4. **Rapid Technological Advancements**: The fast-paced nature of technological advancements poses challenges for data governance. New technologies like AI, big

data, and cloud computing introduce complexities that may require organizations to update their data governance practices.

Best Practices in Data Governance

To overcome the challenges in data governance, organizations can adopt best practices:

1. Data Governance Framework: Establish a comprehensive data governance framework that defines roles, responsibilities, and processes for data management. This framework should align with the organization's overall strategy and objectives.

2. Data Inventory: Conduct a thorough inventory of data assets, including their sources, formats, and intended uses. This helps organizations gain visibility into their data landscape and identify areas that require improvement.

3. Data Classification and Categorization: Classify and categorize data based on its sensitivity, criticality, and regulatory requirements. This allows organizations to apply appropriate security measures, access controls, and retention policies.

4. Data Governance Council: Form a data governance council or committee comprising representatives from various departments and stakeholders. This council can oversee data governance initiatives, make decisions, and resolve conflicts related to data management.

5. Data Stewardship: Appoint data stewards who are responsible for ensuring data quality, integrity, and compliance within their respective areas. Data stewards act as advocates for data governance and promote its principles throughout the organization.

6. Continuous Monitoring: Regularly monitor and audit data governance processes to ensure their effectiveness. This may involve conducting data quality checks, reviewing access logs, and assessing compliance with data privacy regulations.

7. Collaborative Approach: Foster collaboration between IT, legal, compliance, and business units to ensure that data governance initiatives are holistic and aligned with the organization's goals.

Case Study: Data Governance in the Healthcare Industry

The healthcare industry faces unique challenges in data governance due to the sensitive nature of patient data and regulatory requirements. Let's consider an example to illustrate the importance of data governance in this context.

Imagine a large healthcare system that wants to implement AI algorithms for improving diagnostic accuracy. To ensure data governance, the organization establishes clear policies and procedures for data collection, storage, and sharing. They also create a data governance council consisting of representatives from clinical, IT, and legal departments.

The organization implements data classification and categorization, classifying patient data based on its sensitivity and regulatory requirements. They carefully control access to patient data, enforce strict security measures, and regularly monitor data usage to detect any unauthorized activity.

To address challenges related to data silos, the healthcare system invests in interoperability solutions that enable seamless data exchange between various departments and systems. They also provide ongoing training and awareness programs for employees, ensuring that everyone understands the importance of data governance in protecting patient privacy and ensuring quality care.

By implementing robust data governance practices, the healthcare system ensures the responsible use of AI algorithms, improving diagnostic accuracy while maintaining compliance with privacy regulations and ethical standards.

Conclusion

Data governance is a critical component of responsible and ethical AI. It provides a framework for organizations to manage data effectively, ensuring its quality, integrity, and security. By implementing best practices in data governance, organizations can mitigate risks, build trust with stakeholders, and maximize the value of data in the AI-driven world.

Key Takeaways

- Data governance involves managing the availability, integrity, usability, and security of data within an organization.
   - Key principles of data governance include accountability, data integrity, transparency, compliance, privacy and security, and data quality management.
   - Challenges in data governance include data silos, data ownership, lack of awareness, and rapid technological advancements.
   - Best practices in data governance include establishing a data governance framework, conducting data inventory, classifying and categorizing data, forming a data governance council, appointing data stewards, continuous monitoring, and fostering collaboration.
   - Healthcare organizations face unique challenges in data governance due to patient data sensitivity and regulatory requirements. Proper data governance ensures the responsible use of AI in healthcare.

Exercises

1. Explain why data governance is important in the context of AI.

2. Discuss the key principles of data governance and their significance.

3. What are the challenges commonly faced in implementing data governance practices? Provide examples.

4. How can organizations overcome the challenges in data governance? Discuss best practices with relevant examples.

5. Explore data governance practices in an industry of your choice other than healthcare. Highlight the challenges and best practices specific to that industry.

Privacy Regulations

Privacy regulations play a crucial role in governing the collection, use, and protection of personal data in the age of artificial intelligence. As AI systems become increasingly sophisticated and capable of processing massive amounts of data, privacy regulations aim to strike a balance between enabling innovation and safeguarding the privacy rights of individuals. In this section, we will explore the key concepts and principles of privacy regulations and their implications for AI applications.

Data Protection Principles

The foundation of privacy regulations lies in a set of data protection principles that govern the lawful processing of personal data. These principles provide a framework for organizations to ensure that personal data is handled responsibly. Let's dive into the key principles:

1. **Lawfulness, fairness, and transparency:** Organizations must process personal data in a lawful and fair manner, with transparency towards individuals regarding the collection and use of their data. This means ensuring that individuals are aware of how their data is being used and have given their consent where necessary.

2. **Purpose limitation:** Personal data should be collected for specified, explicit, and legitimate purposes. It should not be further processed in a manner that is incompatible with those purposes.

3. **Data minimization:** Organizations should only collect and process personal data that is necessary for the intended purpose. They should avoid collecting excessive or irrelevant data.

4. **Accuracy:** Personal data should be accurate and kept up to date. Organizations should take reasonable steps to rectify inaccurate or incomplete data.

5. **Storage limitation:** Personal data should be kept in a form that allows identification of individuals for no longer than necessary. It should be securely deleted or anonymized once it is no longer needed.

6. **Integrity and confidentiality:** Personal data should be processed in a manner that ensures its security, integrity, and confidentiality. Organizations must implement appropriate technical and organizational measures to protect personal data against unauthorized access, loss, or disclosure.

7. **Accountability:** Organizations are responsible and accountable for ensuring compliance with privacy regulations. They should be able to demonstrate their compliance and have mechanisms in place to handle data subject requests and data breaches.

By adhering to these principles, organizations can establish a strong foundation for privacy protection in the context of AI systems.

General Data Protection Regulation (GDPR)

One of the most significant and comprehensive privacy regulations is the General Data Protection Regulation (GDPR), which came into effect in the European Union (EU) in 2018. The GDPR sets strict rules for the collection, processing, and storage of personal data, including explicit provisions related to AI. Let's explore some key aspects of the GDPR:

1. **Consent and lawful basis:** The GDPR emphasizes the importance of obtaining valid consent from individuals for the processing of their personal data. It also recognizes several lawful bases for processing, including the necessity for the performance of a contract, compliance with a legal obligation, protection of vital interests, and legitimate interests pursued by the data controller or a third party.

2. **Data subject rights:** The GDPR grants individuals certain rights over their personal data, such as the right to access, rectify, erase, and restrict the processing of their data. It also introduces the right to data portability,

allowing individuals to obtain a copy of their data in a commonly used and machine-readable format.

3. **Data protection impact assessment (DPIA):** The GDPR mandates conducting a DPIA for AI projects involving high-risk processing of personal data. A DPIA helps identify and minimize privacy risks associated with the project and allows organizations to implement appropriate safeguards.

4. **Profiling and automated decision-making:** The GDPR imposes specific requirements for profiling and automated decision-making, including the right to obtain meaningful information about the logic involved, as well as the significance and consequences of such processing. It also introduces safeguards for individuals, such as the right to opt-out of automated decision-making in certain cases.

5. **Data breach notification:** The GDPR introduces mandatory data breach notification requirements, whereby organizations must notify the relevant supervisory authority and affected individuals within a specified timeframe when a personal data breach occurs.

The GDPR has had a significant impact on privacy practices not only in the EU but also globally. Organizations that process personal data of EU residents, irrespective of their location, are subject to the GDPR's provisions, thus influencing the way AI systems handle personal data.

California Consumer Privacy Act (CCPA)

In the United States, the California Consumer Privacy Act (CCPA) stands as one of the most comprehensive privacy laws. Enacted in 2018 and becoming effective in 2020, the CCPA aims to enhance privacy rights and consumer protection for residents of California. While the CCPA focuses on the rights of Californian consumers, its impact extends beyond state borders due to its extraterritorial applicability. Here are some key features of the CCPA:

1. **Consumer rights:** The CCPA grants Californian consumers various rights, including the right to know what personal information is being collected, the right to delete their personal information, and the right to opt-out of the sale of their personal information. It requires organizations to provide clear and conspicuous notices about consumer data collection and processing practices.

2. **Business obligations:** The CCPA applies to businesses that meet certain criteria, such as having annual gross revenues above a specified threshold or handling large amounts of consumer data. Covered businesses are required to implement mechanisms for consumers to exercise their rights and must also maintain reasonable security practices to protect consumer data.

3. **Service provider obligations:** The CCPA places obligations on businesses that disclose personal information to service providers. Businesses must have agreements in place to restrict service providers' use of personal information and ensure its protection.

4. **Private right of action:** The CCPA grants consumers the right to bring a private right of action against businesses in the event of a data breach, where nonencrypted and nonredacted personal information is exposed as a result of the business's failure to implement reasonable security measures.

The CCPA has prompted organizations to reassess their data protection practices not only in California but also in other states and countries where similar privacy regulations are being considered.

International Data Transfers

In the era of global data flow, privacy regulations also address the transfer of personal data across international borders. These regulations aim to ensure that when personal data is transferred to a country or organization outside the jurisdiction of the data's origin, an adequate level of protection is maintained. Let's explore some mechanisms for facilitating international data transfers:

1. **European Commission's adequacy decisions:** The European Commission assesses the level of protection offered by a country and, if deemed adequate, issues an adequacy decision. This decision allows for the free flow of personal data from the EU to that country without the need for additional safeguards.

2. **Standard contractual clauses (SCCs):** SCCs are pre-approved sets of contractual terms and conditions issued by the European Commission. They provide a legal framework for transferring personal data from the EU to countries without adequacy decisions. Organizations can incorporate SCCs into their contracts as a means of ensuring appropriate protection of personal data.

3. **Binding Corporate Rules (BCRs):** BCRs are internal rules adopted by multinational organizations that define their global data protection obligations. They ensure that personal data transfers within the organization meet the requisite standards of protection.

4. **Privacy Shield:** Privacy Shield was a framework designed to facilitate data transfers between the EU and the United States. However, the European Court of Justice invalidated the Privacy Shield in 2020, citing concerns about U.S. surveillance practices. Organizations now need to explore alternative mechanisms for transferring data between the EU and the United States.

These mechanisms provide a legal framework for transferring personal data globally, ensuring that it is adequately protected even when moving across national boundaries.

Additional Considerations

While privacy regulations provide a comprehensive framework to protect personal data and address the challenges posed by AI, there are still some considerations that require attention:

- **Emerging technologies:** Privacy regulations may struggle to keep pace with the rapid advancements in AI and emerging technologies. Continuous efforts are needed to address the privacy implications of evolving technologies such as facial recognition, biometric data processing, and AI-driven analytics.

- **Algorithmic transparency:** The interpretability and explainability of AI algorithms present challenges in meeting privacy regulations. Striking the right balance between privacy and explainability is crucial, as individuals have the right to understand the logic behind the decisions made by AI systems that impact them.

- **Global harmonization:** Privacy regulations vary across countries, posing challenges for global organizations to comply with multiple regulatory regimes. Harmonization efforts to establish global privacy standards could facilitate cross-border data flows while maintaining high standards of privacy protection.

Addressing these considerations will ensure that privacy regulations remain relevant and effective in the face of evolving AI technologies and global data flow.

Exercises

1. Research and discuss a recent case where a company's violation of privacy regulations led to significant consequences. Explain the privacy principles that were breached and the impact of the violation.

2. Select a country without an adequacy decision from the European Commission and describe its mechanisms for facilitating international data transfers. Discuss any challenges that organizations face when transferring personal data to that country.

3. Investigate recent developments in privacy regulations related to emerging technologies such as facial recognition and biometric data processing. Discuss the privacy concerns associated with these technologies and the steps being taken to address them.

4. Form a small group and conduct a mock data protection impact assessment (DPIA) for an AI project that involves high-risk processing of personal data. Identify potential privacy risks and propose appropriate mitigations to ensure compliance with privacy regulations.

Additional Resources

- European Union General Data Protection Regulation (GDPR): https://gdpr-info.eu/

- California Consumer Privacy Act (CCPA): https://oag.ca.gov/privacy/ccpa

- European Commission - International Data Transfers: https://ec.europa.eu/info/law/law-topic/data-protection/international-dimension-data-protection_en

---

In this section, we explored the significance of privacy regulations in the context of artificial intelligence. We covered the fundamental data protection principles, examined two prominent privacy regulations (GDPR and CCPA), discussed international data transfers, and highlighted additional considerations. Understanding and complying with privacy regulations is essential for AI practitioners and organizations to ensure ethical and responsible handling of personal data. By incorporating privacy into the design and development of AI systems, we can address societal concerns and foster trust in the field of artificial intelligence.

Secure AI Systems

As we venture further into the world of artificial intelligence (AI), we must also address the pressing concern of securing these powerful systems. AI systems are increasingly being used in critical applications, such as autonomous vehicles, financial transactions, and healthcare, making it crucial to protect them from potential vulnerabilities and attacks. In this section, we will explore the challenges and best practices for securing AI systems.

Understanding the Security Landscape

Securing AI systems requires a thorough understanding of the security landscape and the potential risks involved. Let's take a moment to delve into some key concepts related to AI security.

Threat Modeling: Threat modeling is a crucial step in analyzing potential threats and vulnerabilities in AI systems. It involves identifying the assets to be protected, potential threats to those assets, and the impact of a successful attack. By understanding the threat landscape, developers can design robust security measures.

Adversarial Attacks: Adversarial attacks are intentional actions designed to deceive or mislead AI systems. These attacks exploit vulnerabilities in AI models, leading to incorrect or manipulated outputs. For example, an attacker can modify input data to trick an AI image recognition system into misclassifying objects. Understanding adversarial attacks is essential in developing defenses against them.

Data Poisoning: Data poisoning involves maliciously manipulating training data to corrupt or compromise AI models. Attackers may inject crafted or manipulated data during the training phase, leading to biased or misleading results. Robust data validation and cleansing techniques are necessary to mitigate the risk of data poisoning.

Securing AI Models

Securing AI models is a critical aspect of building secure AI systems. Here are some key considerations:

Model Architecture: The choice of model architecture can impact the security of an AI system. Complex models with a large number of parameters are more susceptible to adversarial attacks. It is important to strike a balance between model complexity and security, considering the specific use-case requirements.

Regularization Techniques: Regularization techniques, such as dropout and weight decay, can help improve the robustness of AI models. They prevent overfitting and make the model more resilient to adversarial attacks. Regularization should be an integral part of the model training process.

Adversarial Training: Adversarial training involves augmenting the training data with adversarial examples to make the model more robust against adversarial attacks. This technique exposes the model to various attack scenarios, helping it learn to distinguish between genuine and adversarial inputs. Adversarial training should be conducted iteratively to enhance the model's robustness.

Model Monitoring: Continuous monitoring of AI models is essential to detect any signs of unusual behavior or compromise. Monitoring can involve analyzing input-output patterns, checking for unexpected outputs, and comparing the model's performance against predefined thresholds. Any anomalies should trigger alerts for further investigation.

Data Security and Privacy

Data security and privacy are key components of securing AI systems. Consider the following aspects:

Data Encryption: To ensure data confidentiality, sensitive data used in AI systems should be encrypted both during storage and transmission. Encryption techniques such as symmetric key encryption, asymmetric key encryption, and homomorphic encryption provide different levels of security and should be used based on the specific requirements.

Access Control: Strict access control mechanisms should be put in place to limit data access to authorized individuals or processes. Role-based access control (RBAC), multi-factor authentication, and other access control techniques should be implemented to prevent unauthorized data access.

Secure Data Storage: Securely storing data involves protecting it from unauthorized access, tampering, and accidental loss. Techniques like hashing, data backups, and redundancy can be employed to ensure data integrity and availability.

Data De-identification: In situations where personally identifiable information (PII) is involved, data de-identification techniques, such as anonymization or pseudonymization, should be applied to protect user privacy. This helps prevent the unintended disclosure of sensitive information while still enabling data analysis and AI model training.

Securing the Deployment Environment

Securing the deployment environment of AI systems is crucial to ensure their integrity and availability. Consider the following measures:

Secure Infrastructure: The underlying infrastructure supporting AI systems must be secure. This includes secure server rooms, firewalls, intrusion detection systems, and regular security audits. Additionally, keeping all software, firmware, and operating systems up to date with security patches is critical.

Network Security: Secure network configurations, such as network segmentation, isolated AI system networks, and encrypted communication channels, are vital to protect against network-based attacks. Regular vulnerability assessments and penetration testing can help identify and address network vulnerabilities.

Secure Model Deployment: Proper security measures must be implemented when deploying AI models to production environments. This includes running models in isolated containers, using secure APIs for communication, and employing strong authentication and authorization techniques.

Ethics and Safeguarding against Bias

As AI systems increasingly affect our lives, it is crucial to ensure that they are fair and free from bias. Consider the following aspects:

Algorithmic Bias: AI models can inherit, amplify, or introduce biases, leading to unfair outcomes. Bias identification and mitigation techniques should be implemented to ensure fairness across different demographic groups and mitigate the impact of biased decisions.

Diverse and Representative Data: Training AI models with diverse and representative datasets helps mitigate bias. Care should be taken to collect data from different population groups to ensure fairness and avoid skewed or discriminatory outcomes.

Independent Auditing: Independent audits of AI systems should be conducted to evaluate their fairness and identify biases. These audits should involve external experts who can assess the models, algorithms, and datasets used.

Resources and Further Reading

Securing AI systems is a multidisciplinary field that requires knowledge and expertise across various domains. Here are some resources to explore further:

- "Adversarial Machine Learning" by Battista Biggio and Fabio Roli
- "Artificial Intelligence Safety and Security" by Roman V. Yampolskiy
- "AI Security: Analyses, Requirements, and Methods" by Richard Röttger, Sven Wohlgemuth, and Utz Roedig

- "Building Machine Learning Powered Applications" by Emmanuel Ameisen
- "Fairness and Machine Learning" by Solon Barocas, Moritz Hardt, and Arvind Narayanan

Be sure to explore these resources for a deeper understanding of secure AI systems and ethical considerations.

Conclusion

Securing AI systems is a critical step in harnessing the full potential of AI while mitigating the risks it poses. By understanding the security landscape, employing robust model training techniques, ensuring data privacy, securing the deployment environment, and addressing ethics and bias, we can build AI systems that are not only powerful but also safe and reliable. As AI technology continues to evolve, it is essential to stay updated with the latest security practices and continuously evaluate and enhance the security measures in place.

Impact on Employment and Society

Automation and Job Displacement

In our ever-evolving world, the rapid advancement of Artificial Intelligence (AI) and automation has raised concerns about the potential displacement of jobs. Automation is the process by which tasks previously carried out by humans are now performed by machines or AI systems. This section will explore the impact of automation on the job market, the types of jobs at risk, and the potential solutions to mitigate the negative consequences.

The Rise of Automation

Automation has a long history, starting with the Industrial Revolution, where machines replaced manual labor in factories. However, the recent advancements in AI technology have significantly accelerated the automation process. With the advent of machine learning and deep learning algorithms, machines can now perform complex cognitive tasks, leading to the automation of jobs that were previously considered safe from technological disruption.

The Jobs at Risk

The potential scope of automation is vast, with jobs across various industries facing the risk of displacement. Repetitive and routine tasks are most vulnerable, such as those in manufacturing, data entry, and customer service. For example, chatbots can now handle basic customer inquiries, reducing the need for human customer support representatives. Similarly, self-checkout systems in supermarkets have replaced traditional cashiers.

Even jobs requiring specialized skills are not immune to automation. AI-powered algorithms can analyze large sets of data and make predictions, threatening professions like financial analysis, legal research, or medical diagnostics. However, it is important to note that automation does not necessarily mean complete job eradication. Instead, certain tasks within a job may be automated, leading to job transformation rather than outright elimination.

The Impact on the Workforce

The automation of jobs can have significant consequences on the workforce. Job displacement due to automation can lead to unemployment and income inequality. Workers who lose their jobs may struggle to find suitable replacements, especially if their skills are outdated or not easily transferable to other industries.

Additionally, the fear of job loss creates anxiety and uncertainty among workers, negatively impacting their job satisfaction and overall well-being. The psychological toll of automation must not be overlooked, as it can have far-reaching implications for individuals and society as a whole.

Solutions and Reskilling

While automation poses challenges, there are also opportunities to adapt and thrive in a changing job market. Reskilling and upskilling programs play a pivotal role in preparing the workforce for the digital age. Governments, educational institutions, and businesses should collaborate to offer training programs that provide workers with new skills and knowledge. This will enable individuals to transition into roles that are less susceptible to automation.

Promoting entrepreneurship and innovation can create new job opportunities that align with the changing landscape. Encouraging the development of AI startups or supporting existing businesses in adopting AI technologies can lead to job creation and economic growth.

Furthermore, policies that focus on income redistribution and social safety nets can help mitigate the negative effects of job displacement. Universal basic income, for instance, provides a guaranteed income to individuals, regardless of their employment status, ensuring a basic standard of living.

Embracing Change

As new technologies continue to reshape the job market, it is crucial to adapt and embrace change rather than resist it. Lifelong learning becomes essential, as individuals must be prepared to continuously update their skills and knowledge. The ability to adapt and learn new things will become a critical competitive advantage in the future job market.

In conclusion, automation and AI have the potential to disrupt existing job roles, leading to job displacement. However, by recognizing the challenges posed by automation, implementing reskilling programs, and embracing change, we can navigate the changing job landscape and build a future where humans and AI technology work in harmony. The key lies in striking a balance between technological progress and ensuring a just and equitable society for all.

Workforce Reskilling and Upskilling

In the ever-evolving landscape of artificial intelligence (AI), one of the most pressing concerns is the impact it will have on the workforce. As AI and automation technologies continue to advance, there is a growing concern about the potential displacement of jobs. However, AI also presents new opportunities for individuals to acquire new skills and adapt to the changing demands of the job market. This section will explore the concept of workforce reskilling and upsilling, the importance of lifelong learning, and the strategies and resources available to individuals to navigate the AI-enabled future.

The Need for Reskilling and Upskilling

As AI technology continues to mature, it has the potential to automate a wide range of tasks previously performed by humans. This could result in job displacement and changes in the composition of the workforce. However, it is essential to recognize that AI is not intended to replace humans but rather augment their capabilities. By automating mundane and repetitive tasks, AI frees up human workers to focus on higher-value and more complex work that requires creativity, critical thinking, and problem-solving skills.

To leverage the opportunities of the AI-enabled future, individuals need to reskill and upskill themselves continuously. Reskilling refers to acquiring new skills that are different from one's current skill set, while upskilling refers to enhancing existing skills to adapt to new technologies and demands. The traditional model of education that focuses on formal degrees or certifications is no longer sufficient. Lifelong learning has become the key to remaining relevant and competitive in the job market.

The Role of Lifelong Learning

Lifelong learning refers to the ongoing process of acquiring knowledge, skills, and competencies throughout one's life. In the context of AI, it is crucial for individuals to adopt a mindset of continuous learning and personal growth. Lifelong learning enables individuals to adapt to new technologies, reinvent their careers, and seize emerging opportunities.

One of the essential elements of lifelong learning is self-directed learning. With the abundance of online resources and learning platforms, individuals have the power to take ownership of their learning journey. They can choose the skills they want to acquire, the pace at which they learn, and the method of learning that suits them best. The democratization of knowledge through the internet has made lifelong learning accessible to anyone with an internet connection.

Strategies for Reskilling and Upskilling

Reskilling and upskilling require a thoughtful approach and a clear understanding of one's goals and interests. Here are some strategies to navigate the process effectively:

1. Identify Future-Proof Skills: It is essential to identify skills that are expected to be in high demand in the AI-enabled future. These skills typically include complex problem-solving, critical thinking, creativity, emotional intelligence, and the ability to work collaboratively with AI systems. By focusing on these skills, individuals can position themselves for roles that are less likely to be automated.

2. Embrace Technology: To thrive in an AI-dominated world, individuals need to embrace technology and develop digital literacy. This includes developing an understanding of AI concepts, learning programming languages, and gaining familiarity with tools and platforms that support AI development and deployment. Online courses and tutorials are excellent resources for acquiring these technical skills.

3. Cultivate Soft Skills: While technical skills are crucial, individuals must not neglect the development of soft skills. Skills such as effective communication, empathy, adaptability, and leadership, are highly valued in the workplace and are less likely to be automated. Enhancing these skills through courses, workshops, and real-world experiences can significantly enhance one's employability.

4. Engage in Collaborative Learning: Learning from others and collaborating on projects is an effective way to build new skills. Joining communities of practice, participating in hackathons or coding competitions, and working on open-source projects can provide valuable learning experiences and opportunities for networking with like-minded individuals.

5. Leverage Online Learning Platforms: Online learning platforms such as Coursera, Udemy, and LinkedIn Learning offer a vast array of courses on various topics. These platforms provide flexibility and convenience, allowing individuals to learn at their own pace and fit learning into their busy schedules. Furthermore, some platforms offer certifications that validate one's newfound skills, providing a credential to showcase to potential employers.

6. Seek Mentorship and Networking: Mentors play a crucial role in guiding individuals through their reskilling and upskilling journeys. Connect with professionals in your desired field or industry who can provide guidance, support, and advice. Networking events, industry conferences, and online communities are excellent avenues for building professional relationships and expanding your network.

Real-World Examples

Let's dive into a few real-world examples to illustrate the importance of reskilling and upskilling in the AI era:

Example 1: Bridging the Skills Gap A manufacturing company is implementing AI-powered robots to automate their production line. To ensure a smooth transition, the company invests in reskilling programs for its employees. By providing training in programming and robotics, the company equips its workforce with the skills needed to operate, maintain, and program the AI-driven robots. This not only prevents job displacement but also increases the efficiency and productivity of the manufacturing process.

Example 2: Upskilling for Data Analytics A marketing professional wants to leverage AI in their role to gain deeper insights from customer data. They enroll in an online course on data analytics, learning techniques such as data visualization, statistical analysis, and machine learning. Armed with these skills, the professional is now able to analyze large datasets, identify patterns, and make informed data-driven decisions, leading to improved marketing strategies and business outcomes.

Example 3: Career Transition into AI Development A software engineer realizes the potential of AI and decides to transition into AI development from their previous role. They embark on a self-directed learning journey, enrolling in online courses and reading books on machine learning and neural networks. Throughout the process, they also participate in online coding communities, collaborating and receiving feedback on their AI projects. This practical experience, combined with their existing programming skills, helps them to secure an AI developer role, opening up new career opportunities.

Conclusion

The AI-enabled future demands a proactive approach to reskilling and upskilling. Lifelong learning, in combination with the development of future-proof skills, technology adoption, and continuous personal growth, is the key to remaining valuable in an evolving job market. By embracing the challenges and opportunities presented by AI, individuals can adapt, thrive, and shape their own future. Remember, it's never too late to learn and grow – the power to transform your career lies in your hands.

Additional Resources:

- *"AI Superpowers: China, Silicon Valley, and the New World Order"* by Kai-Fu Lee

- *"The Industries of the Future"* by Alec Ross

- *"Learning How to Learn: Powerful Mental Tools to Help You Master Tough Subjects"* on Coursera

- *"How to Become a Data Scientist"* on Coursera

Societal Impact and Policy Considerations

In recent years, the rapid advancement of artificial intelligence (AI) has sparked widespread excitement and concern. As AI continues to permeate various aspects of our lives, it is crucial to examine its societal impact and consider the policy implications. In this section, we will explore the potential benefits and challenges of AI, discuss its impact on employment, and delve into important ethical considerations.

Benefits and Challenges of AI

AI has the potential to revolutionize industries and improve the overall quality of life. It can augment human capabilities, automate repetitive tasks, and enhance decision-making processes. For example, AI-powered medical diagnosis systems can assist doctors in identifying diseases more accurately and efficiently.

However, along with these benefits come challenges. The widespread adoption of AI may lead to job displacement, as automation replaces certain tasks currently performed by humans. It is crucial to address this issue through policies that focus on reskilling and upskilling the workforce to ensure a smooth transition into a technology-driven economy.

Furthermore, AI algorithms are susceptible to biases, which can perpetuate societal inequalities. For instance, AI-powered hiring systems may inadvertently favor certain demographics, leading to discrimination in employment. Policymakers must actively work towards ensuring the fairness and accountability of AI systems to mitigate these biases.

AI and Employment

One of the most significant concerns surrounding AI is its impact on employment. As AI-driven automation continues to advance, some jobs will become obsolete, leading to job displacement. However, AI will also create new job opportunities. For example, AI specialists, data scientists, and machine learning engineers will be in high demand.

To mitigate the negative effects of job displacement, policymakers must focus on workforce reskilling and upskilling initiatives. Providing training programs and educational opportunities for individuals whose jobs are at risk can help them transition into AI-related roles. Additionally, policies promoting lifelong learning and continuous skill development can ensure that the workforce remains adaptable in the face of technological advancements.

Ethical Considerations

While AI brings numerous benefits, it also presents ethical challenges that must be addressed. One major concern is the potential for AI systems to make biased decisions. Biases can emerge from the underlying data used to train AI algorithms, perpetuating inequalities and discriminating against certain individuals or groups. Policymakers need to develop regulatory frameworks that hold AI systems accountable for fair and unbiased decision-making.

Another ethical consideration is the privacy and security of data. AI systems often rely on large amounts of personal data to generate insights and predictions. It is crucial to establish robust data governance and privacy regulations that protect individuals' sensitive information from misuse or unauthorized access. Additionally, policymakers should ensure that AI systems are secure against cyberattacks to prevent potential breaches that could have far-reaching consequences.

Finally, transparency and explainability are crucial for building trust in AI systems. Users should have a clear understanding of how AI algorithms make decisions and what data they are based on. Policymakers should encourage the development of explainable AI techniques and mandate transparency requirements to ensure that AI systems are not "black boxes" that operate without accountability.

Examples and Real-World Implications

To illustrate the societal impact and policy considerations of AI, let's consider a few examples:

1. Algorithmic hiring systems: AI-powered recruiting platforms may inadvertently discriminate against certain demographics if the historical hiring data used to train them exhibits biased patterns. Policymakers should enforce transparency and fairness in these systems to prevent discrimination while encouraging organizations to actively update and diversify their training data.

2. AI in criminal justice: AI algorithms are increasingly being used to inform decisions regarding bail, parole, and sentencing. It is crucial to evaluate and address any biases in these systems to ensure that they do not disproportionately impact marginalized communities.

3. Autonomous vehicles: The widespread adoption of self-driving cars raises questions about liability and safety. Policymakers must establish regulations and standards that govern the ethical behavior and decision-making of autonomous vehicles to ensure public safety and prevent potential misuse.

It is essential for policymakers to engage in meaningful discussions with experts from various domains, including AI researchers, ethicists, and industry leaders, to develop informed policies that address the societal impact of AI while fostering innovation.

Resources and Further Reading

To delve deeper into the societal impact and policy considerations of AI, the following resources are recommended:

1. "Weapons of Math Destruction" by Cathy O'Neil provides insights into the ethical concerns and biases associated with AI algorithms in different domains.

2. "Artificial Unintelligence: How Computers Misunderstand the World" by Meredith Broussard explores the limitations of AI systems and the need for improved transparency and accountability.

3. "The AI Ethics Guidelines Handbook" by European AI Alliance offers a comprehensive guide to building ethical AI systems and provides policy recommendations.

4. The AI Now Institute (https://ainowinstitute.org) and the Partnership on AI (https://www.partnershiponai.org) are valuable resources for keeping up with the latest developments and discussions around AI ethics and policy.

In conclusion, the societal impact of AI and the policy considerations surrounding its adoption are complex and multifaceted. Policymakers must carefully navigate the challenges, address the ethical implications, and develop regulations that promote fairness, transparency, and accountability. By doing so, we can ensure that AI remains a force for positive change while minimizing its potential harms.

The Future of AI

New Frontiers in AI Research

Quantum Computing and AI

In recent years, there has been increasing excitement and buzz around the convergence of quantum computing and artificial intelligence (AI). Although both fields are still in their infancy, their potential synergy is undeniable. Quantum computing, with its ability to process information in a fundamentally different way than classical computing, holds the promise of exponentially faster computations. AI, on the other hand, has revolutionized various industries by enabling machines to learn from data and make intelligent decisions. Combining these two fields has the potential to revolutionize the field of AI, unlocking new possibilities and solving problems that are currently considered computationally intractable.

Basics of Quantum Computing

To understand the potential impact of quantum computing on AI, we must first grasp the basic principles of quantum computing. Classical computers use bits to store and process information, with each bit representing a 0 or a 1. Quantum computers, however, use quantum bits or qubits, which can represent 0, 1, or both simultaneously thanks to a phenomenon called superposition. This unique property allows quantum computers to work on multiple calculations simultaneously, leading to a massive increase in computational power.

Another intriguing property of qubits is entanglement, which allows two or more qubits to become interdependent, regardless of the physical distance between them. This phenomenon could potentially be exploited to create powerful quantum algorithms that leverage entangled states to solve complex problems efficiently.

Quantum Machine Learning

Quantum machine learning (QML) is a young and rapidly evolving subfield that aims to combine quantum computing and AI. The goal of QML is to develop quantum algorithms that can enhance and accelerate traditional machine learning tasks. While still in its early stages, QML has already shown promise in areas such as classification, clustering, and dimensionality reduction.

One example of QML is quantum support vector machines (QSVMs). Like classical support vector machines, QSVMs are used for classification tasks. However, they leverage the quantum nature of computation to find a solution much faster than classical algorithms. Another example is quantum neural networks (QNNs), which utilize the unique properties of qubits to perform computations in parallel and potentially improve training speed.

Quantum Computing for AI Optimization

One of the areas where quantum computing can have a significant impact on AI is optimization. Many real-world problems, such as finding the optimal route for delivery drivers or optimizing the allocation of resources, can be formulated as optimization problems. Traditional optimization algorithms often struggle with finding the global optimum, especially for complex problems with numerous variables and constraints.

Quantum computing's potential for parallel processing and exploration of multiple solutions simultaneously can make it an ideal tool for optimization tasks. Quantum annealing, a specific quantum computing approach, has shown promise in solving combinatorial optimization problems. By mapping a problem to a quantum annealer, we can exploit the inherent parallelism of quantum states and potentially find better solutions faster.

Challenges and Limitations

While the potential of quantum computing for AI is exciting, several challenges and limitations need to be addressed. First and foremost, quantum computers are still in their early stages of development, with limited qubit count and high error rates. These challenges make it difficult to build and execute complex algorithms on current quantum hardware.

Another significant challenge is the integration of classical and quantum systems. Most AI algorithms and frameworks are developed for classical computers, and adapting them to quantum systems is a non-trivial task.

Additionally, quantum algorithms are highly sensitive to noise and require careful error correction techniques.

Furthermore, the overall scalability of quantum computing remains a challenge. As we increase the number of qubits, the complexity of maintaining coherence and managing quantum states grows exponentially. Overcoming this scalability issue is crucial to harness the full potential of quantum computing for AI.

Quantum Computing and AI: The Road Ahead

Despite the challenges, the future of quantum computing and AI holds tremendous potential. As quantum hardware continues to improve, we can expect more sophisticated quantum algorithms specifically designed for AI tasks. These algorithms could lead to significant advancements in fields such as natural language processing, computer vision, and reinforcement learning.

To fully realize the potential of quantum computing for AI, interdisciplinary collaboration between experts in quantum physics and machine learning is essential. This collaboration will enable the development of quantum-inspired algorithms and bridge the gap between classical and quantum approaches.

Additionally, the availability of quantum simulators and cloud-based quantum computing platforms will make it easier for researchers and developers to experiment with quantum algorithms. These resources will help democratize access to quantum computing and foster innovation in the field.

Conclusion

Quantum computing and AI are two cutting-edge fields that, when combined, have the potential to revolutionize the way we approach complex computational problems. From enhancing traditional machine learning tasks to improving optimization techniques, the convergence of these fields opens up new avenues for solving problems that were once considered computationally intractable.

While there are still many technical and practical challenges to overcome, the progress and potential of quantum computing for AI are undeniable. As we continue to push the boundaries of both quantum computing and AI, we can expect exciting developments and a future where the power of quantum and artificial intelligence work hand in hand.

Explainable AI

In recent years, the field of Artificial Intelligence (AI) has seen tremendous advancements in terms of its capabilities. However, one major challenge that has emerged is the lack of transparency and interpretability of AI models. This challenge has given rise to the field of Explainable AI (XAI), which aims to make AI algorithms and models more understandable and interpretable to humans.

The Need for Explainable AI

As AI continues to be integrated into various aspects of our lives, it becomes crucial to understand how AI systems make decisions and recommendations. This is especially important in domains where the impact of these decisions can have significant consequences, such as healthcare, finance, and autonomous vehicles.

Imagine a scenario where an AI system recommends a specific medical treatment for a patient. In such a critical situation, it is essential for doctors and patients to understand the reasoning behind the AI's recommendation. Without explainability, the decision-making process of the AI system remains a "black box," leaving humans uncertain and skeptical about relying on AI.

Explainable AI addresses this challenge by providing insights into the internal workings of AI models, allowing humans to understand why and how AI systems arrive at their decisions. This transparency not only builds trust but also enables human experts to detect potential biases, errors, or inappropriate use of data in the AI systems.

Approaches to Explainable AI

There are various approaches to achieving explainability in AI systems. These approaches can be broadly categorized into two types: interpretable models and post-hoc explanations.

Interpretable Models: In this approach, the AI models themselves are designed to be inherently interpretable. These models are usually simpler and more transparent, allowing humans to understand the decision-making process. Examples of interpretable models include decision trees, rule-based systems, and linear regression models.

Interpretable models provide clear rules and explanations for their predictions, making it easier for humans to understand how the inputs are mapped to the outputs. However, these models may sacrifice some predictive accuracy compared to more complex and opaque models, such as deep neural networks.

Post-hoc Explanations: This approach focuses on explaining the decisions made by complex, black-box AI models after they have been trained. Post-hoc explanations aim to shed light on how the model arrived at a particular decision or prediction.

NEW FRONTIERS IN AI RESEARCH

There are several techniques for generating post-hoc explanations, including:

- Feature Importance: This technique identifies the most important features or variables that influenced the model's decision. For example, in a credit scoring system, the feature importance can reveal which factors, such as income or credit history, had the most impact on the final credit decision.

- Local Explanations: Local explanations provide insights into how the model made a specific decision for an individual instance or data point. Techniques like LIME (Local Interpretable Model-agnostic Explanations) generate simplified and interpretable models that approximate the black-box model's behavior around a particular instance.

- Visual Explanations: Visual explanations use visualization techniques to represent the decision-making process of AI models. For instance, heatmaps can highlight the regions of an image that were most influential in a deep learning model's classification decision, making it easier for humans to understand and verify the model's reasoning.

The Challenges of Explainable AI

While the goal of explainable AI is clear, there are several challenges in achieving a comprehensive and effective explainability framework.

One challenge is balancing model complexity with interpretability. As AI models become more complex and powerful, their interpretability decreases. Techniques that aim to explain these complex models often involve simplifications or approximations, which may not capture the full complexity and reasoning of the original model.

Another challenge is the trade-off between transparency and performance. More transparent models, while easier to interpret, may not achieve the same level of predictive accuracy as their more opaque counterparts. Striking the right balance between these trade-offs is a crucial consideration in developing explainable AI systems.

Additionally, there is the challenge of domain-specific explanations. Different domains may require different types of explanations. For example, in healthcare, explanations need to be provided in terms that medical experts can understand, while in finance, explanations may need to be tailored to suit the needs of financial professionals. Developing domain-specific explanations that are both accurate and meaningful is an ongoing challenge.

Real-World Applications of Explainable AI

Explainable AI has found applications in various domains, where transparency and interpretability are critical. Some notable applications include:

Credit Scoring: Banks and financial institutions use AI models to assess creditworthiness. Explainable AI techniques help explain the factors that contributed to a credit decision, providing transparency and allowing individuals to understand the basis of the decision.

Healthcare: Explainable AI techniques enable clinicians to understand and trust the recommendations made by AI systems in medical diagnosis and treatment planning. It also helps with compliance to ethical guidelines and standards in healthcare.

Autonomous Vehicles: Self-driving cars rely on AI algorithms for decision-making. Explainable AI techniques can help clarify the reasoning behind the decisions made by these vehicles, enhancing safety and trust in autonomous systems.

Ethical Considerations in Explainable AI

While explainability in AI is crucial, it also raises ethical considerations and potential risks. Some key considerations include:

Transparency vs. Confidentiality: Balancing the need for transparency with the protection of sensitive or proprietary information is an ongoing challenge. AI systems may contain confidential or sensitive data that should not be fully exposed in the explanations. Striking the right balance between transparency and confidentiality is essential.

Interpretation Errors: Humans may misinterpret or misjudge AI explanations, leading to incorrect conclusions or biases. It is crucial to validate and test the effectiveness of explanation techniques to ensure that they provide accurate and meaningful insights.

Responsibility and Accountability: Even with explainability, AI systems may still make errors or biased decisions. Determining who is responsible for the decisions made by AI models remains a complex issue. Clear guidelines and regulations are needed to ensure accountability and to address potential risks.

Conclusion

Explainable AI plays a vital role in bridging the gap between AI systems and human users. By providing transparency and interpretability, explainable AI techniques enable humans to understand how AI models arrive at their decisions, fostering trust and preventing biases. As AI continues to transform various industries, the development and adoption of explainable AI will become increasingly important in ensuring the responsible and ethical use of AI systems. So let's dive deeper into the world of Explainable AI and unravel the mysteries of how AI models make decisions!

AI in Space Exploration

Space exploration has always captured the imagination of humanity, and with the advent of Artificial Intelligence (AI), we are empowered to delve even deeper into the mysteries of the cosmos. AI technology has revolutionized space exploration by enabling us to analyze vast amounts of data, improve spacecraft autonomy, and develop innovative solutions for challenges encountered in space missions.

Data Analysis and Decision-Making

Space missions generate an enormous amount of data, ranging from telemetry data to images of celestial objects. AI plays a crucial role in analyzing and extracting valuable insights from this data. Machine learning algorithms can identify patterns, classify objects, and predict outcomes, aiding in the discovery of celestial phenomena or the detection of anomalies.

For example, AI algorithms can be trained to identify and classify different celestial objects, such as stars, galaxies, and asteroids, from astronomical images. This helps astronomers and scientists catalog and study the vast amount of data collected by space telescopes like the Hubble Space Telescope.

Furthermore, AI can assist in real-time decision-making during space missions. Autonomous systems powered by AI can analyze data from various sensors aboard a spacecraft and make critical decisions without human intervention. This capability is especially valuable in scenarios where communication delays make real-time control from Earth impractical, such as Mars rover missions.

Autonomous Navigation

Navigating through the vastness of space is a complex task that requires precise calculations and constant adjustments. AI algorithms can enhance spacecraft autonomy, enabling them to navigate through space with efficiency and accuracy.

AI-based navigation systems use various sources of data, including star maps, deep space network measurements, and onboard sensors, to determine the spacecraft's position and velocity. By incorporating AI, spacecraft can continuously refine their trajectory, optimize fuel usage, and even autonomously avoid obstacles.

One example of AI-enabled navigation is the Deep Space Atomic Clock (DSAC) developed by NASA. DSAC utilizes AI algorithms to autonomously determine the precise position of a spacecraft by analyzing signals from pulsars, which are highly predictable celestial objects. This technology allows for more accurate navigation and reduces dependence on ground-based tracking systems.

Resource Management

Resource management is a critical aspect of space exploration missions. AI can optimize the utilization of resources such as energy, water, and consumables aboard spacecraft and space habitats.

By analyzing data on resource consumption and usage patterns, AI algorithms can predict future needs, identify wasteful practices, and suggest strategies for efficient resource allocation. This not only prolongs mission duration but also reduces the reliance on resupply missions, making space exploration more sustainable.

For instance, AI algorithms can analyze the energy consumption patterns of the International Space Station (ISS) and optimize power usage by adjusting the operation of various systems and equipment. By minimizing energy waste and maximizing efficiency, AI helps ensure the long-term viability of space missions.

Robotic Exploration and Sample Analysis

Robotic exploration of celestial bodies, such as planets, asteroids, and moons, is critical for gathering scientific data and preparing for human missions. AI-powered robotic systems can navigate challenging terrains, conduct scientific experiments, and even extract and analyze samples.

For example, AI algorithms can enable rovers to autonomously analyze the composition of rocks and soil on distant planets. By combining machine learning with spectroscopy techniques, rovers can identify minerals and elements that provide insights into the geological history of the planet.

AI also plays a vital role in sample analysis. For instance, in the recent OSIRIS-REx mission, AI algorithms were used to navigate the spacecraft to asteroid Bennu and collect a sample. These algorithms helped the spacecraft identify safe landing sites and avoid hazards on the asteroid's surface.

Challenges and Future Directions

While AI has made significant contributions to space exploration, several challenges still need to be addressed. One major concern is the robustness and reliability of AI systems in the harsh conditions of space. Radiation, extreme temperatures, and communication delays can affect AI algorithms' performance and reliability, necessitating the development of robust and resilient AI systems.

Moreover, ethical considerations and the potential for AI-driven space militarization must be carefully addressed. International collaborations and regulations are crucial for ensuring the responsible and peaceful use of AI in space exploration.

Looking ahead, the integration of AI with other emerging technologies like quantum computing holds tremendous potential for space exploration. Quantum AI algorithms can solve complex optimization problems and enhance machine learning capabilities, enabling breakthroughs in areas such as interstellar navigation and data analysis.

In conclusion, AI has become an indispensable tool in space exploration, providing us with invaluable assistance in data analysis, autonomous navigation, resource management, and robotic exploration. With ongoing advancements and further research, AI will continue to revolutionize space exploration, pushing the boundaries of our understanding and enabling humanity to reach new frontiers in the cosmos.

AI and Human Augmentation

Brain-Computer Interfaces

In recent years, the field of brain-computer interfaces (BCIs) has made significant strides in merging the powers of the human brain with artificial intelligence (AI) technologies. BCIs are devices or systems that enable direct communication between the brain and external devices, allowing individuals to control these devices solely using their thoughts. This technology holds great promise for enhancing human capabilities, enabling new forms of communication, and assisting individuals with disabilities. In this section, we will delve into the principles, challenges, and future possibilities of brain-computer interfaces.

Principles of Brain-Computer Interfaces

The fundamental principle behind brain-computer interfaces is to decode the brain's electrical signals, known as electroencephalogram (EEG) signals, and translate them into meaningful commands that can control external devices. The human brain consists of billions of neurons that communicate through electrical impulses. BCIs tap into this neural activity by capturing EEG signals through electrodes placed on the scalp or even implanted directly into the brain.

To establish a reliable communication channel, the BCI system needs to accurately distinguish between different brain states or intentions. Signal processing techniques, such as filtering and feature extraction, are employed to extract relevant information from the EEG signals. Machine learning algorithms, such as support vector machines or deep neural networks, are then utilized to interpret these patterns and translate them into commands that drive device actions.

Challenges of Brain-Computer Interfaces

Developing effective and reliable brain-computer interfaces is not without challenges. One significant hurdle is the variability and complexity of EEG signals. Different individuals exhibit unique brainwave patterns, making it necessary to tailor BCI systems to each user. Training the system to recognize these personalized patterns requires sufficient amounts of annotated data, which can be time-consuming and expensive to acquire.

Another challenge is the low signal-to-noise ratio in EEG recordings. The electrical signals captured by electrodes also contain interference from various sources, such as muscle activity and external environmental factors. Filtering techniques and signal processing algorithms are employed to mitigate these noise sources and enhance the signal quality. However, achieving a high signal-to-noise ratio remains an ongoing challenge for BCI researchers.

Applications of Brain-Computer Interfaces

Brain-computer interfaces have a wide range of potential applications across multiple domains. One of the most important applications is in the field of medicine, particularly for individuals with physical disabilities or neurological conditions. BCIs can enable individuals with paralysis to control robotic limbs or communicate with others using speech synthesis technologies. These interfaces can also assist in neurorehabilitation, allowing patients to regain motor control or restore impaired cognitive functions.

Beyond healthcare, BCIs have the potential to revolutionize various industries. For example, in the gaming and entertainment industry, BCIs can provide immersive experiences by allowing users to control virtual environments using their thoughts. In the field of transportation, BCIs can enhance driver safety by detecting fatigue or distraction based on EEG signals and triggering appropriate alerts or interventions.

Ethical Considerations and Future Directions

As with any emerging technology, brain-computer interfaces raise important ethical considerations. Privacy and security concerns come to the forefront when dealing with direct access to an individual's brain activity. Protecting sensitive information and ensuring the informed consent of users are crucial aspects that need careful attention in BCI development.

In terms of future directions, advances in artificial intelligence and machine learning will continue to propel the capabilities of brain-computer interfaces. The development of more sophisticated algorithms and models will lead to improved accuracy and performance of these systems. Additionally, enhancing the usability and comfort of BCIs by exploring non-invasive techniques and more user-friendly interfaces will be a focus of future research.

Conclusion

Brain-computer interfaces hold immense potential for transforming how humans interact with machines and expanding our cognitive capabilities. The ability to control external devices with our thoughts opens up countless possibilities for individuals with disabilities, as well as for gaming, entertainment, and other industries. However, addressing challenges related to signal variability, noise reduction, and ethical considerations will be crucial to realizing the full potential of BCIs. The future of brain-computer interfaces looks bright, with ongoing advancements offering the promise of new frontiers in human-machine interaction and augmenting our abilities in ways we can only imagine.

AI for Assisted Living

In recent years, the field of artificial intelligence (AI) has witnessed significant advancements, leading to the development of systems and technologies that can assist and enhance various aspects of our everyday lives. One of the most exciting applications of AI is in the realm of assisted living, where it has the potential to revolutionize the way we care for and support individuals with disabilities, aging populations, and chronic illnesses.

The Challenges of Assisted Living

Assisted living entails providing support and care to individuals who may require assistance with activities of daily living, such as bathing, dressing, and eating. Traditionally, these tasks have been performed by human caregivers, but with the aging of the population and the increasing demand for care services, there is a growing need for innovative solutions that can augment human support with AI-driven technologies.

The challenges that arise in the context of assisted living are multifaceted. Firstly, the personalized nature of care and the unique requirements of each individual make it challenging to develop a one-size-fits-all solution. Secondly, ensuring the safety and well-being of individuals is of utmost importance, requiring robust monitoring and emergency response systems. Lastly, promoting independence and autonomy while ensuring quality care is a delicate balance that must be achieved.

AI-Assisted Monitoring and Assistance

AI can play a crucial role in monitoring and assisting individuals in assisted living settings. By employing sensor technologies and machine learning algorithms, AI systems can detect and analyze data related to an individual's activities, behaviors, and health status. For instance, smart wearables can monitor vital signs, sleep patterns, and physical activity, providing real-time feedback and alerts to both the individual and caregivers.

Additionally, AI-powered home automation systems can adapt to the specific needs of residents, adjusting lighting, temperature, and other environmental factors for optimal comfort. These systems can also detect changes in behavior patterns, such as reduced mobility or increased fall risks, and provide timely interventions or alerts to ensure the safety of the individual.

Smart Assistive Technologies

AI-driven assistive technologies have the potential to enhance the independence and quality of life for individuals in assisted living. For example, intelligent virtual assistants (IVAs) can provide verbal reminders for medication adherence, assist with daily routines, and engage in conversation to reduce loneliness and social isolation. These IVAs can be personalized to the preferences and individual needs of residents, offering a human-like interaction that mimics companionship.

Furthermore, robotic devices equipped with AI capabilities can provide physical assistance with mobility, transferring, and other tasks. These robots can adapt to different environments, learn user preferences, and ensure a safe and comfortable experience for the individual. For instance, a robot with computer vision capabilities can guide a visually impaired individual through a room, recognizing obstacles and providing auditory cues for navigation.

AI AND HUMAN AUGMENTATION

Ethical Considerations and Privacy

While the potential benefits of AI for assisted living are immense, there are important ethical considerations and privacy concerns that must be addressed. It is crucial to prioritize the autonomy, agency, and dignity of individuals receiving assisted living services. AI systems should be designed with transparency, ensuring that individuals understand how their data is collected, used, and protected. Informed consent should be obtained, and individuals should have the ability to control their data and personalize the settings of AI systems according to their preferences.

Moreover, robust security measures must be implemented to protect sensitive personal information and prevent unauthorized access. Regular audits and updates should be conducted to ensure the integrity and safety of AI systems and prevent potential biases in decision-making algorithms.

Real-World Examples

Several AI-based assisted living technologies have already been developed and deployed in real-world settings. For example, the OpenVizsla project aims to create an open-source platform that utilizes computer vision and machine learning to provide personalized support for individuals with dementia. The system uses cameras and sensors to detect behavioral patterns and triggers intelligent responses, such as reminders for medication or hydration.

Another example is the KOMP, a communication device designed specifically for older adults by No Isolation. The device uses AI algorithms to simplify communication and connect the elderly with their families and caregivers via video calls, messaging, and photo sharing. The AI-powered features of KOMP allow for intuitive and accessible interaction, ensuring that individuals can easily navigate and utilize the device.

Conclusion

The integration of AI technologies in assisted living holds immense promise to enhance the care and support provided to individuals with disabilities, aging populations, and chronic illnesses. By leveraging AI-powered monitoring, assistive technologies, and personalized support systems, we can promote independence, improve quality of life, and ensure the safety and well-being of individuals in assisted living settings. However, it is crucial to address ethical considerations, privacy concerns, and promote user-centric design to ensure that these technologies truly empower individuals and respect their autonomy. With continued research, development, and collaboration, AI has the potential to revolutionize the way we provide care and support, making assisted living more accessible, efficient, and compassionate.

AI and Creativity

AI-Generated Art

Artificial intelligence (AI) has revolutionized various fields, and art is no exception. With the advancements in machine learning and deep neural networks, AI has the ability to create unique, captivating, and thought-provoking pieces of art. In this section, we explore the fascinating world of AI-generated art, its applications, challenges, and the ethical implications it entails.

Understanding AI-Generated Art

AI-generated art refers to artwork that is created or co-created by artificial intelligence systems. These systems use algorithms and deep learning models to analyze and interpret large datasets of artistic styles and techniques. By learning from existing artworks and patterns, AI can generate new and original pieces of art in a variety of forms, such as paintings, sculptures, music, and even poetry.

Generative Adversarial Networks (GANs)

One of the most popular techniques used for AI-generated art is Generative Adversarial Networks (GANs). GANs consist of two neural networks: the generator and the discriminator. The generator creates new art samples, while the discriminator tries to distinguish between AI-generated art and human-created art. Through an iterative process, these networks compete with each other, ultimately resulting in the generation of highly realistic and visually appealing art.

The Creative Process

The creative process in AI-generated art involves several steps. First, the AI system is trained on a dataset of existing artworks, capturing the essence of different artistic styles and techniques. Then, the system generates new art samples by combining elements from the learned patterns and styles. These samples are evaluated by human experts, who provide feedback and refine the system's output. This iterative process helps in improving the system's artistic capabilities over time.

Applications of AI-Generated Art

AI-generated art has wide-ranging applications in various industries and domains. Here are a few notable examples:

1. **Visual Arts:** AI can generate visually stunning paintings, sculptures, and digital art pieces. It can mimic the styles of famous artists or create entirely new art forms that push the boundaries of creativity.

2. **Music Composition:** AI algorithms can compose original music that resonates with different genres and styles. They can also create unique soundscapes and sound designs for films, video games, and other multimedia projects.

3. **Fashion Design:** AI systems can generate innovative and avant-garde designs, revolutionizing the fashion industry. They can combine different patterns, colors, and styles to create cutting-edge fashion collections.

4. **Literature and Poetry:** AI can generate poems, stories, and even entire novels. These AI-generated literary works are often indistinguishable from human-written ones and offer a new perspective on storytelling.

Challenges and Ethical Implications

While AI-generated art presents exciting opportunities, it also raises important challenges and ethical concerns. Here are a few key considerations:

1. **Originality and Plagiarism:** The issue of originality arises when AI creates art that resembles existing works too closely. The line between inspiration and plagiarism becomes blurred, leading to questions of ownership and attribution.

2. **Human Creativity:** Some argue that AI-generated art lacks the emotional depth and creative intuition that defines human artistic expression. The involvement of AI in the creative process challenges the traditional notion of what it means to be an artist.

3. **Cultural Appropriation:** AI-generated art that imitates specific cultural styles or sources without proper context or understanding can be seen as cultural appropriation. It is crucial to ensure sensitivity and respect for diverse cultural heritage.

4. **Bias and Representation:** The datasets used to train AI systems may contain inherent biases, leading to biased artistic outputs. AI-generated art should be conscious of representation and strive for inclusivity and fairness.

The Intersection of AI and Human Artists

Rather than replacing human artists, AI-generated art has the potential to collaborate and inspire them. Many artists are already using AI tools as a creative medium, incorporating AI-generated elements into their artwork. This collaboration between AI and human artists opens up new avenues for experimentation, innovation, and exploration of artistic possibilities.

Conclusion

AI-generated art is a testament to the power of artificial intelligence to transform and enhance creative industries. It pushes the boundaries of human imagination, challenges traditional artistic norms, and sparks new conversations about the nature of creativity and authorship. As AI continues to evolve, the future of AI-generated art holds endless possibilities, ensuring that art remains a vibrant and evolving part of human culture.

AI in Music Composition

In recent years, artificial intelligence (AI) has made significant strides in various fields, and music composition is no exception. AI algorithms are now capable of generating original music compositions, mimicking the style of different composers, and even collaborating with human musicians. This has opened up new possibilities in the realm of music creation, pushing the boundaries of what is considered possible.

Understanding Music Composition

Before delving into AI in music composition, it is essential to understand the fundamentals of music composition itself. Music composition involves the creation of musical structures, melodies, harmonies, rhythms, and lyrics (if applicable) to convey emotions, tell stories, and evoke particular moods. It combines elements of creativity, technical skill, and a keen understanding of musical theory.

Traditionally, music composition has been the exclusive domain of human composers, who draw on their knowledge, skills, and inherent creativity to craft original compositions. However, with advancements in AI technology, machines can now be used to assist or even independently generate music compositions.

AI Techniques in Music Composition

AI in music composition relies on several techniques to produce compositions that are both technically and artistically sound. Let's explore some of the key techniques employed in this field:

- **Generative Models:** AI algorithms utilize generative models, such as recurrent neural networks (RNNs) or transformers, to generate new musical sequences. These models learn patterns and structures from existing music data and then use that knowledge to create original compositions. By employing generative models, the AI algorithm can produce music that adheres to specific musical styles or follows predefined rules.

- **Pattern Recognition:** AI algorithms excel at recognizing patterns in complex datasets, making them ideal for analyzing and understanding musical patterns. By training AI models on vast amounts of music data, they can identify common patterns in melodies, chords, and rhythms. This enables AI algorithms to compose music that is reminiscent of specific genres or composers.

- **Harmony and Melody Generation:** AI algorithms can generate harmonies and melodies by leveraging knowledge of music theory and composition rules. By analyzing the relationships between notes, chords, and scales, AI models can create harmonically coherent music. These algorithms can also produce melodies that are structurally sound and emotionally engaging.

- **Style Transfer:** AI models can also perform style transfer in music composition. By combining elements from different musical styles, these models can create unique compositions that blend the characteristics of multiple genres or composers. This technique opens up new avenues for experimentation and innovation in music composition.

Challenges and Limitations

While AI in music composition holds immense promise, it is not without its challenges and limitations. Some of the prominent challenges include:

- **Lack of Creativity:** AI algorithms, despite their impressive capabilities, often struggle to replicate the depth of human creativity. While they can generate compositions that follow established rules and patterns, they may lack the nuanced emotional expression and originality that human composers bring to their work.

- **Contextual Understanding:** AI models sometimes struggle to understand the cultural and historical contexts that shape music composition. This understanding is crucial in creating compositions that resonate with human listeners and accurately capture the essence of a particular genre or time period.

- **Integration with Human Musicians:** Collaborations between AI systems and human musicians can be challenging due to the differences in creative processes and modes of expression. It requires effective communication, mutual understanding, and the ability to seamlessly blend the contributions of both the AI system and the human musician.

Ethical Considerations

The use of AI in music composition raises ethical considerations that need careful examination. Some of the key ethical considerations include:

AI AND CREATIVITY

- **Plagiarism and Copyright:** AI algorithms capable of generating music compositions that resemble existing works raise questions about intellectual property rights. It is essential to ensure that AI-generated compositions respect copyright laws and do not infringe on the rights of original composers.

- **Authenticity and Attribution:** When AI algorithms create music compositions, it is important to establish clear guidelines for attribution and recognize the contributions of both AI systems and human creators. This ensures transparency and integrity within the music composition process.

- **Preservation of Human Creativity:** As AI becomes more capable in music composition, it is crucial to preserve and celebrate the unique creativity that human composers bring to their work. AI should be seen as a tool to enhance and augment human creativity, rather than replacing or diminishing it.

Real-World Applications

AI in music composition has found practical applications in various domains. Some notable examples include:

- **Film and Media Industry:** AI algorithms can create original soundtracks and background music for films, television shows, and advertisements. These algorithms can compose music that aligns with the emotions and narrative of a particular scene, enhancing the overall viewing experience.

- **Game Development:** AI-generated music is becoming increasingly prevalent in video game development. AI algorithms can create dynamic and adaptive soundtracks that respond to the player's actions, creating immersive gaming experiences.

- **Personalized Music Recommendations:** AI models can analyze users' listening preferences and generate personalized music recommendations. By understanding individual tastes and preferences, AI systems can introduce users to new artists and genres, enhancing the music discovery process.

- **Assisting Musicians and Songwriters:** AI algorithms can aid musicians and songwriters in the creative process by suggesting chord progressions, melodies, and harmonies. This collaboration between AI and human musicians allows for novel ideas and unique musical expressions.

Conclusion

AI in music composition has opened up new creative possibilities, pushing the boundaries of what is considered achievable in the realm of music creation. Leveraging the power of generative models, pattern recognition, and style transfer, AI algorithms are capable of generating original compositions, mimicking specific styles, and collaborating with human musicians. While challenges and ethical considerations exist, the use of AI in music composition continues to evolve and make a significant impact in various industries, from film and gaming to personalized music recommendations. As technology advances, we can expect AI to play a more prominent role in shaping the future of music composition, augmenting human creativity, and bringing new musical experiences to life.

Resources:

1. Huang, A. (2020). "Deep Learning for Music Composition: A Review." *Journal of Artificial Intelligence Research, 68*, 233-265.

2. Ariza, C. (2021). *Algorithmic Composition: A Gentle Introduction to Music Composition Using Artificial Intelligence.* Independently Published.

3. Gifford, T. (2019). *Composing Music with Artificial Intelligence: Perspectives on Computational Creativity.* Springer.

Exercises:

1. Research and compare the music compositions generated by different AI algorithms. Discuss the similarities and differences in terms of style, creativity, and emotional impact.

2. Choose a popular song and analyze its musical characteristics (e.g., chord progression, melody). Use an AI algorithm to generate a composition inspired by the original song. Compare the generated composition with the original and reflect on the process.

3. Interview a musician or songwriter about their opinion on AI in music composition. Discuss the potential benefits and drawbacks of using AI as a tool in the creative process.

AI in Film and Entertainment

The intersection of artificial intelligence (AI) and the world of film and entertainment has become increasingly captivating and exciting. AI technologies

AI AND CREATIVITY

are revolutionizing the way movies are created, produced, and consumed, leading to entirely new possibilities and immersive experiences. In this section, we will explore the diverse applications of AI in the film and entertainment industry, ranging from scriptwriting and visual effects to personalized content recommendation systems and AI-generated music.

AI-Assisted Scriptwriting

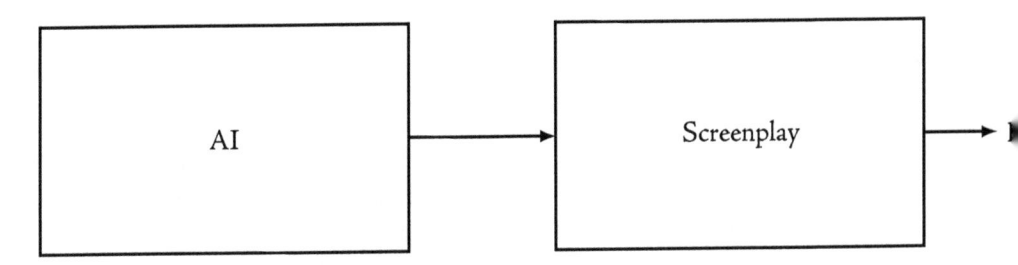

Figure 0.1: AI-assisted scriptwriting process.

Scriptwriting is a crucial creative process in filmmaking, and AI is now playing a significant role in assisting human writers. Using natural language processing (NLP) techniques and deep learning algorithms, AI can analyze vast amounts of existing screenplays, novels, and other narrative content to generate storylines, dialogues, and even complete scripts. AI can provide suggestions, offer alternative plotlines, and help filmmakers refine their ideas. The AI-assisted scriptwriting process (Figure 0.1) offers a collaborative partnership between AI and human storytellers, enhancing creativity and efficiency in the filmmaking process.

However, it is important to maintain a balance between AI-generated content and human creativity. While AI can generate ideas and assist with the writing process, the unique perspective and artistic vision of human filmmakers remain invaluable.

AI-Generated Visual Effects

The realm of visual effects (VFX) has been significantly transformed by advancements in AI. Traditionally, VFX required extensive manual labor and time-consuming processes. Today, AI-powered technologies enable filmmakers to create stunning visual effects more efficiently and cost-effectively.

AI algorithms, particularly deep learning and computer vision techniques, can analyze large volumes of data and generate realistic visual effects that seamlessly integrate with live-action footage. For instance, AI can generate lifelike creatures, simulate natural phenomena, or even recreate historical or fictional environments. Moreover, AI can automate time-consuming tasks like rotoscoping, motion tracking, and green screen keying, accelerating the post-production workflow.

Figure ?? illustrates the AI-assisted visual effects generation process. AI algorithms analyze input data such as motion capture footage, CGI models, and image references to generate realistic visual effects that can significantly enhance the overall cinematic experience.

Personalized Content Recommendation

The vast amount of available content across various streaming platforms presents a challenge for users in discovering what to watch next. AI-powered personalized recommendation systems offer a solution to this dilemma. By analyzing user preferences, viewing history, and social interactions, AI algorithms can suggest movies, TV shows, and other entertainment options tailored to individual tastes.

These recommendation systems utilize machine learning algorithms, including collaborative filtering and content-based filtering, to match users with relevant content. They continuously learn from user feedback and improve their recommendations over time.

Apart from enhancing the viewing experience for users, personalized content recommendation systems also benefit content providers and streaming platforms by increasing viewer engagement, improving customer retention, and facilitating targeted advertising.

AI-Generated Music

AI's impact on the entertainment industry extends beyond filmmaking. In the realm of music, AI has the ability to compose original compositions, replicate the styles of famous musicians, and create unique soundtracks.

AI-generated music leverages deep learning models and generative algorithms to analyze patterns, structures, and rhythms found in music data. By training on vast music databases, AI algorithms can then produce original compositions that mimic specific genres, artists, or even incorporate elements from multiple styles. These AI-generated compositions can serve as a valuable source of inspiration for musicians, a tool for film scoring, or even as standalone compositions.

However, the involvement of AI in the creative process has raised questions about the authenticity and originality of AI-generated music. The debate surrounding AI's role in the music industry is ongoing, with some artists embracing AI as a creative collaborator and others expressing concerns over the loss of human expression and individuality.

AI and Virtual Reality

Virtual reality (VR) has gained significant traction in the entertainment industry. AI and VR can work hand in hand to create immersive experiences that push the boundaries of storytelling and audience engagement.

AI can enhance VR experiences by optimizing real-time rendering, tracking user behavior and preferences, and generating dynamic content based on user interactions. AI algorithms can assist in creating realistic simulations of physical objects or characters, dynamically adapting the virtual environment to the user's preferences and providing an interactive and personalized experience.

Moreover, AI algorithms can analyze user reactions and feedback from VR experiences, enabling filmmakers and game developers to create more engaging and emotionally impactful content for the audience.

AI and Film Restoration

AI has also started to play a significant role in film restoration. Old and damaged film recordings often require extensive manual efforts to repair imperfections, like scratches, dust, and color deterioration.

By using AI-powered computer vision techniques, damaged frames can be automatically restored with minimal human intervention. These techniques leverage deep learning algorithms trained on large databases of historically significant films to identify and repair visual imperfections frame by frame.

AI-powered film restoration not only saves time and resources but also preserves historical film records, ensuring that future generations can appreciate these cinematic treasures.

Conclusion

From scriptwriting and visual effects to personalized content recommendation systems and AI-generated music, AI's influence on the film and entertainment industry is undeniable. However, as AI continues to shape these creative domains, it is important to strike a balance between AI-assisted processes and human creativity. The collaboration between AI and human artists promises to unleash new realms of immersive storytelling and revolutionize the way we experience film and entertainment. As the technology continues to evolve, creative professionals and AI researchers must navigate the ethical and societal implications to create a future that embraces the best of both human and artificial intelligence capabilities.

Index

-up, 18, 25

a, 1–28, 30–32, 35–37, 39–51, 53–59, 61–75, 77–91, 93–96, 98–118, 120, 122–127, 129, 130, 132–143, 145–149, 151, 153, 155–161, 163–170, 175–187, 191–200, 202–206, 209, 211, 213–216, 218, 219, 221, 223–227, 229–243, 245, 248–252, 255–272, 274, 276, 277, 279–285, 287, 289–306, 308–314, 318–322
ability, 6, 16, 32, 54, 62, 69, 73, 75, 80, 96, 111, 125, 166, 206, 225, 237, 256, 264, 266, 292, 309, 311, 320
absence, 81
abundance, 293
acceptance, 267
access, 3, 4, 18, 34, 113, 114, 180, 264, 280, 297, 301, 309, 311
accessibility, 178, 180, 255, 266
accommodation, 26

account, 36, 188, 227, 238, 239, 241
accountability, 4, 7, 9, 240, 241, 268, 280, 296–298
accuracy, 4, 6, 9, 10, 19, 62, 71, 85, 95, 96, 102, 145, 155, 157, 159, 160, 163, 168, 175, 180, 186, 189, 195, 196, 206, 209, 212, 213, 260, 262, 263, 266, 279, 280, 302, 303, 305, 309
action, 57–59, 234, 320
activation, 204
activity, 127, 280, 308–310
ad, 115
adaptability, 166
adaptation, 175, 177
add, 163
addition, 4, 36, 37, 107, 145, 155, 241, 267
address, 2, 4, 6, 9, 12, 17, 18, 23, 64, 71, 101, 118, 119, 122, 134, 174, 177, 180, 182, 185, 187, 198, 213, 218, 229, 233, 240, 241, 245, 261, 264, 266, 268, 270–272, 274, 275, 277, 280, 284, 285, 296–298, 311

addressing, 9, 19, 135, 188, 231, 236, 239, 241, 270, 290, 309
administration, 267
adoption, 6, 296–298, 305
advance, 2, 19, 139, 177, 186, 199, 224, 227, 241, 255, 296
advancement, 17, 242
advantage, 17, 54, 73, 88, 93, 103, 112, 125, 166, 233, 248, 292
advent, 149, 200, 290
adventure, 24
advertising, 17, 49, 320
advice, 6, 255
advisory, 252–255
affinity, 263
age, 22, 77, 135, 149, 169, 240, 260, 281, 291
agency, 311
agent, 57, 58, 61, 231, 234, 236
aggregate, 127
aging, 310, 311
AI, 7
aid, 56, 259
aim, 28, 54, 68, 91, 156, 187, 192, 193, 226, 274, 281, 284, 303
air, 17
alert, 267
algorithm, 2, 3, 7, 8, 53, 54, 58, 63, 67–69, 73–76, 80, 82, 85–90, 93, 136–138, 160, 163, 235, 269, 271, 272, 274, 275
algorithms, 1–4, 6–11, 13, 15, 16, 18, 19, 46, 54, 56–58, 64, 67, 70, 73, 74, 87, 89–91, 110, 111, 117, 118, 136, 140, 148–150, 153, 161, 163, 192, 194, 197, 200, 202, 211, 218, 225–227, 231, 232, 236–241, 245, 248, 249, 251, 252, 255, 256, 258–265, 267, 269–272, 274, 276, 277, 279, 280, 290, 291, 296–301, 305–312, 318–321
Allen Newell, 1
allocation, 300, 306
ambiguity, 158, 164, 168, 186, 188, 189, 199
amount, 17, 42, 55, 91, 99, 111, 118, 163, 165, 204, 259, 305, 320
analysis, 2, 10, 14–17, 19, 24–28, 32, 35, 43, 44, 48, 49, 55, 56, 65, 67, 69, 70, 80, 87, 88, 91, 94, 110, 112, 114, 115, 118, 120, 125, 126, 129, 130, 132–135, 139, 140, 142, 143, 145, 146, 155, 158, 167–172, 192, 197, 213, 244, 255, 258, 260, 272, 291, 295, 306, 307
animal, 77, 84
annealer, 300
annealing, 300
anomaly, 54, 57, 87, 146, 148, 149
anonymity, 114
anonymization, 114
answer, 3, 76, 210
anxiety, 291
Apache Kafka, 114
app, 18
appearance, 194

Index

applicant, 72
application, 23, 32, 64, 108, 115, 116, 119, 126, 133, 175, 177, 200, 215, 216, 219, 255
approach, 1, 4, 8, 9, 56, 87, 89, 90, 93, 99, 102, 103, 113, 136, 149, 156, 182, 186, 194, 209, 226, 231, 233, 236, 243, 250, 255, 256, 263, 270, 276, 293, 300, 301
appropriateness, 188
approval, 263
architecture, 61, 62, 64, 157, 203, 205, 206, 209
area, 3, 6, 10, 176, 188, 189, 218, 227, 233, 261, 266, 270
arrival, 18
art, 11, 12, 62, 198, 199, 312–314
artist, 218
artwork, 216, 312, 314
aspect, 28, 41, 191, 214, 225, 240, 267, 287, 306
assembly, 237
assessment, 70, 100
assistance, 3, 11, 180, 266, 307, 309, 310
assisted, 11, 267, 310–312, 321
association, 136–139
assumption, 70, 81
asteroid, 306
asymmetry, 37
attainment, 27
attempt, 105
attention, 11, 16, 24, 109, 157, 158, 179, 183, 200, 267, 285, 309
attribute, 70, 73
audience, 11, 321

audio, 14, 110, 155, 237
audiobook, 178
audit, 111
auditing, 8
audits, 311
augmentation, 2, 12, 177, 215
Aurélien Géron, 102, 108
authentication, 200
authenticity, 320
authorship, 314
automate, 21, 163, 268, 292, 294, 296, 320
automation, 6, 12, 255, 265, 290–292, 296, 310
autonomy, 8, 305, 310, 311
availability, 2, 149, 183, 277, 280, 288, 301
average, 31, 36, 68, 70, 103, 157
avoidance, 240
awareness, 4, 182, 280
Azure, 115

baby, 123
back, 10, 76, 156, 210, 214
background, 175, 212
backoff, 156, 158
backpropagation, 2, 63, 64
backup, 238
bagging, 104
bail, 297
balance, 4, 58, 61, 105–107, 214, 218, 233, 239, 264, 268, 274, 281, 292, 303, 310, 319, 321
bank, 68, 186
banking, 117
barrier, 177, 266
basic, 30, 67, 235, 291, 292, 299
batch, 115, 125, 129, 131, 132, 209

bathing, 309
bedrock, 48
behavior, 3, 16–18, 43, 54, 87, 89, 107, 117, 118, 129, 146, 227, 234–236, 241, 248, 249, 297, 310, 321
being, 2, 4, 6, 9, 24, 99, 103, 111, 112, 180, 207, 242, 284, 291, 297, 310, 311
belief, 11
Bellman, 58
benefit, 12, 272, 320
Bias, 270, 275, 277
bias, 2, 4, 8, 12, 16, 27, 116, 119, 142, 158, 159, 172, 180, 185, 235, 256, 265, 269–277, 289, 290
bill, 68
Bill Inmon, 125
birth, 1, 2
bit, 262, 299
block, 203
body, 266
book, 102
boundary, 77
bounding, 211
BoW, 163
box, 11, 28, 256, 302
BPC, 158
brain, 12, 60, 61, 308, 309
brainwave, 308
branch, 35, 39, 47, 73
brand, 17
bread, 136
breakthrough, 2
breast, 4
bucket, 187
budget, 26, 89

building, 10, 57, 125, 127, 129, 203, 227, 287, 297, 298
business, 5, 15, 42, 43, 68, 89, 112, 114, 120, 138, 246, 248, 295
buying, 123

caching, 113
calculation, 45
California, 284
camera, 225
cancer, 4, 260, 262
capability, 116, 305
capacity, 157
card, 117, 148, 149
cardholder, 149
care, 3, 11, 117, 262, 265–268, 280, 309–312
career, 295
caregiving, 267
case, 23, 24, 36, 84, 125, 128, 237, 252, 261
Cassandra, 113, 116
cat, 205
categorization, 53, 160, 280
categorizing, 118, 159, 280
Cathy O'Neil, 298
caution, 2, 19, 153
centroid, 87
century, 2
certification, 266
chain, 6, 118, 123
challenge, 17, 48, 64, 91, 112, 125, 129, 148, 158, 164, 165, 169, 185–188, 213, 215, 218, 227, 233, 236, 240, 261, 266, 267, 277, 300–303, 308, 320
change, 32, 124, 292, 298

Index

channel, 308
chapter, 10, 57
character, 157
characteristic, 110, 111, 216, 237
chart, 31
check, 25, 83
checkout, 291
chemical, 263
choice, 40, 75, 78, 82, 84, 85, 101, 102, 104, 107, 116, 133, 159, 160, 163, 204, 281
Christopher M. Bishop, 108
churn, 70, 107
city, 26
claim, 41
class, 70, 81, 82, 84, 86, 100, 156, 211–213
classification, 57, 67, 69, 70, 73, 77, 80, 82, 84–86, 95, 102, 140, 159–163, 204, 205, 209, 212, 260, 280
classifier, 160, 163
cleaning, 19–24, 111
cloud, 115, 116, 301
Cloud Dataflow, 115
cluster, 87–89, 113
clustering, 54, 56, 57, 87–90
co, 312
code, 102
coefficient, 89, 98
coherence, 44, 301
collaboration, 9, 12, 228, 231, 268, 274, 280, 301, 312, 314, 321
collaborator, 321
collapse, 215
collection, 4, 16–19, 120, 147, 244, 275, 280, 281
collision, 240

color, 26, 31, 84, 191, 193, 194, 321
column, 13
columnar, 113, 115
combination, 3, 4, 15, 55, 70, 100, 103, 227, 258
comfort, 267, 309, 310
commerce, 117, 186, 251
commitment, 19
communication, 18, 29, 183, 186, 228, 231, 305, 307, 308, 311
companionship, 11
company, 42, 68, 89, 125, 164, 251, 252, 294
compass, 27
competition, 248
complex, 2, 10, 14, 19, 21, 28, 32, 35, 45, 48, 51, 56, 61, 62, 67, 71, 73, 75, 80, 86, 93, 94, 100, 104–107, 109, 117, 118, 164, 165, 177, 186, 204, 227, 228, 233, 237, 238, 240, 241, 259, 266, 268, 270, 274, 277, 290, 292, 298–303, 305, 307
complexity, 91, 106, 110, 112, 124, 155, 173, 181, 194, 199, 223, 227, 301, 303, 308
compliance, 116, 259, 280
component, 32, 43, 129, 132, 135, 149, 168, 216, 227, 280
composition, 11, 292, 306, 315–318
compression, 92, 157, 193, 194
compromise, 277
computation, 91, 204, 212
computer, 9, 12, 111, 176, 177, 186, 191, 192, 194, 197, 199, 200, 205, 211, 213, 215, 216, 256, 270, 301,

308–311, 319, 321
computing, 2, 10, 12, 112, 113, 218, 235, 299–301, 307
concentration, 9
concept, 44, 64, 73, 77, 80, 86, 98, 102, 120, 123, 125, 129, 132, 143, 149, 159, 211, 216, 231, 255, 273, 274
concern, 240, 261, 297, 306
conclusion, 4, 75, 94, 188, 202, 227, 242, 292, 298, 307
condition, 4
conditioning, 2
conduct, 42, 240, 241, 306
conference, 1
confidence, 27, 42, 136, 137, 157
confirmation, 27, 149
confusion, 157
congestion, 4
conjunction, 98
connection, 293
consent, 8, 17–19, 309, 311
consideration, 4, 42, 161, 240, 268, 277, 297, 303
consistency, 44, 128, 132
console, 265
construction, 70
consumer, 117, 118, 244
consumption, 306
content, 3, 4, 11, 17, 88, 118, 139, 160, 164, 180, 194, 216–219, 243, 319–321
context, 14, 24, 26, 49, 56, 81, 89, 111, 129, 130, 156, 158, 164, 169, 182, 184, 186, 241, 249, 252, 270, 272, 273, 275, 277, 279, 281, 282, 293, 310
contrast, 55, 116, 142, 159, 192

control, 3, 6, 18, 114, 215, 226, 227, 240, 241, 265, 266, 280, 305, 308, 309, 311
convenience, 3
convergence, 11, 208, 214, 215, 235, 301
conversion, 251, 252
convolution, 192, 203
cooking, 248
copyright, 17
cord, 266
core, 9, 49, 61, 67, 70, 73, 169, 181
cornerstone, 158
corpora, 155, 179, 187
corpus, 156, 159, 182, 184
correction, 301
correctness, 206
correlation, 92
correspondence, 187
cortex, 203
cosine, 142
cosmos, 307
cost, 6, 100, 102, 103, 255, 262, 266
council, 280
count, 84, 300
counting, 156
country, 284
course, 295
covariance, 91
coverage, 52
creation, 11, 114, 180, 291, 318
creativity, 11, 218, 292, 314, 315, 318, 319, 321
credit, 68, 70, 117, 148, 149
creditworthiness, 68
crime, 271, 274
critic, 214
cross, 98–104, 107, 183, 204, 209
culture, 314

Index

curiosity, 27, 28
customer, 3, 6, 13, 14, 43, 54, 68, 70, 87, 89, 107, 117–119, 123, 125, 129, 136, 142, 159, 163, 169, 245–249, 251, 252, 291, 295, 320
cut, 264
cutting, 16, 88, 135, 259, 301
cybersecurity, 54, 146

damage, 266
data, 1–4, 6, 8–29, 31, 32, 34–37, 39, 41–44, 48, 49, 51, 53–57, 61, 63–65, 67–73, 75, 77, 79, 80, 84–95, 98–130, 132–136, 138–140, 142–144, 146, 147, 149, 150, 153, 156–160, 163, 165, 166, 168, 169, 172, 177, 180, 182, 184, 185, 187–189, 191, 193, 194, 203, 204, 206, 207, 209, 210, 214, 215, 221, 222, 225, 227, 233, 235, 237, 241, 244, 245, 248, 249, 251, 252, 255, 256, 258–265, 267, 269, 271, 272, 274–281, 283–285, 290, 291, 295–297, 302, 305–308, 310, 311, 319, 320
database, 15, 110, 116
dataset, 19, 20, 22, 23, 26–28, 35–38, 53, 54, 67, 77, 79, 81, 84, 87, 89, 95, 102, 105, 108, 136, 153, 157, 160, 163, 179, 184, 195, 206, 209, 312
date, 13, 116, 205, 259

day, 2, 129, 163
de, 265
deal, 15, 20
debate, 320
decision, 1, 4, 7, 9, 10, 26, 27, 43, 44, 47, 51, 70–73, 75, 77, 94, 111, 120, 124, 125, 129, 132, 138, 139, 153, 233, 236, 238–241, 256, 261, 269, 272–275, 277, 296, 297, 302, 305, 311
decline, 258
decoder, 179, 184
decoupling, 114
Deep, 11, 61, 64, 227
Deep Q-networks, 2
default, 68, 72
define, 77, 109, 216
delivery, 118, 268, 300
demand, 6, 118, 183, 296, 310
dementia, 311
democratization, 293
demographic, 8, 251
dendrogram, 88
density, 90
deployment, 2, 4, 9, 101, 158, 159, 238, 239, 242, 268, 271, 274, 288, 290
depth, 52, 221, 237, 266
dermatology, 260
descent, 63, 68, 209, 218
design, 9, 16, 32, 89, 165, 180, 228, 263–265, 269, 270, 275, 311
designing, 9, 15, 206, 240
destination, 226
detail, 16, 24, 192
detection, 17, 27, 54, 57, 80, 81, 87, 111, 114, 117, 118, 146,

148, 149, 192, 194–197, 205, 211–213, 260, 267, 305
detective, 24
deterioration, 321
determination, 42, 98
developer, 295
development, 1–3, 7, 9, 10, 12, 56, 57, 114, 115, 119, 140, 158, 159, 183, 187, 188, 201, 203, 236, 238–240, 242, 263–265, 267–270, 274, 291, 295–297, 300, 301, 305, 307, 309, 312
deviation, 36–38
device, 308, 311
dexterity, 265, 266
diagnosis, 3, 6, 46, 70, 96, 117, 259–262, 296
diagnostic, 262, 279, 280
dialogue, 274
die, 187
difference, 36, 42, 56, 63, 68, 101, 179, 216
difficulty, 91, 181
dignity, 9, 311
dilemma, 187, 233, 320
dimensionality, 54, 57, 91, 93–95
direction, 9, 51, 57
director, 167
disadvantage, 272
discipline, 146
discovery, 6, 262–265, 305
discrimination, 7, 8, 17, 270, 275, 296, 297
discriminator, 214, 215
discussion, 273
disease, 4, 68, 167, 260, 262
disinfection, 267

disk, 113
dispersion, 36
displacement, 2, 240, 268, 291, 292, 294, 296
disposal, 35
disruption, 290
dissimilarity, 204
distance, 36, 77, 84–86, 89, 92, 225, 227, 299
distraction, 308
distribution, 11, 26, 27, 31, 37, 93, 100, 181, 184, 192, 235, 274
divergence, 93
diversification, 255
diversity, 19, 73, 180, 215
diving, 51, 143, 191, 197, 252
doctor, 261, 268
document, 80, 113, 115, 142
dog, 205
domain, 11, 22–24, 89, 102, 104, 142, 165, 167, 180, 187–189, 192, 255, 259, 303, 315
dominance, 44, 48, 57, 65, 80, 104, 139, 210, 224, 225
dosage, 261
down, 61, 70, 86, 175, 183, 264
downsampling, 204
dream, 1, 16
dressing, 309
drive, 51, 111, 112, 135, 194, 234, 248, 251, 255, 308
driver, 18, 235–237, 308
driving, 2, 4, 6, 7, 12, 44, 56, 138, 149, 183, 197, 205, 211, 213, 235–237, 252, 297
drone, 238
drop, 18, 114

Index 331

dropout, 107
drug, 6, 261–265
dubbing, 180
duration, 178, 306
dust, 321
dynamic, 31, 32, 177, 189, 227, 238, 255, 321

e, 117, 169, 251
Earth, 10, 305
ease, 23, 69
eating, 309
economic, 291
economy, 296
ecosystem, 112, 114, 115
edge, 16, 112, 116, 124, 129, 132, 135, 186, 192, 193, 238, 251, 259, 301
editing, 188, 199
education, 180, 186, 274, 293
effect, 42
effectiveness, 42, 43, 89, 95, 149, 160, 189
efficacy, 264
efficiency, 3, 4, 81, 112, 118, 139, 186, 212, 213, 223, 236, 255, 258, 265, 294, 305
effort, 16, 128, 165, 272
eigenvector, 91
elbow, 87
element, 192, 203
elimination, 291
email, 42, 53, 54, 81, 82, 163
embedding, 92, 142
emergence, 1, 2
emergency, 240, 310
emotion, 178
empathy, 261, 268

employment, 12, 68, 116, 240, 270, 292, 296
encoder, 179, 184
encryption, 114
end, 105, 129
endeavor, 26
energy, 306
enforcement, 114
engagement, 3, 117, 119, 123, 274, 320
engineer, 101, 295
engineering, 1, 15, 70
enhancement, 192, 194
ensemble, 73, 75, 104
entanglement, 299
entertainment, 11, 12, 180, 308, 309, 320, 321
entity, 164–168
entrepreneurship, 291
entropy, 157, 204, 209, 234, 235
entry, 291
environment, 4, 26, 57, 58, 221–227, 234, 237, 238, 241, 267, 288, 290, 321
equalization, 192
equation, 58
equipment, 146
equity, 272
era, 44, 120, 123, 265, 284, 294
eradication, 291
error, 2, 8, 42, 57, 118, 132, 153, 179, 204, 261, 262, 300, 301
essence, 312
estimate, 18, 49, 51, 58, 67, 68, 98–101, 103, 156, 157, 181, 227, 235, 237
estimation, 40, 42, 101, 235
ethnicity, 22

evaluation, 70, 79, 90, 95, 98, 99, 102–104, 143, 145, 146, 149, 153, 157, 163, 167, 188, 209, 274
event, 45, 81, 126
evidence, 41, 45, 81, 261
evolution, 2, 155, 237
examination, 4, 316
example, 3, 8, 9, 11, 13, 14, 17, 18, 22, 32, 36, 49, 51, 53, 54, 56, 59, 67, 73, 77, 81, 84, 87, 89, 96, 101, 105, 108, 113, 115, 117, 118, 123, 128, 132, 136, 142, 148, 153, 155, 164, 165, 167, 175, 186, 187, 209, 223, 225, 237, 238, 241, 245, 248, 258, 260, 261, 264, 266, 267, 269, 271, 274, 276, 279, 291, 296, 303, 305, 306, 308, 311
exchange, 14, 280
execution, 129, 256, 263
exercise, 61, 79, 152, 206
exhibit, 8, 218, 227, 263, 276, 308
existence, 272
expenditure, 49
experience, 2, 3, 6, 12, 17, 89, 175, 238, 248, 251, 259, 295, 310, 320, 321
experiment, 76, 209, 301
experimentation, 65, 89, 210, 314
expert, 1, 76, 234–236
expertise, 187–189, 268, 270, 289
explain, 64, 236, 303
explainability, 7, 10, 262, 297, 302–304
Explainable AI, 10, 261, 302, 304, 305

explanation, 102
exploitation, 58, 61, 233
exploration, 10, 32, 35, 43, 58, 61, 95, 103, 205, 227, 233, 300, 306, 307, 314
explore, 6, 10, 11, 13, 19–21, 25, 26, 28, 31, 32, 45, 47, 48, 53, 56, 57, 59–61, 65, 67, 68, 70, 73, 75, 80, 83, 85, 87, 89, 95, 98, 102, 103, 109, 112, 114, 120, 121, 124, 126, 129, 132, 136, 137, 143, 147, 156, 160–162, 164, 165, 169, 170, 186, 191, 213, 215, 218, 225, 231–233, 238, 251, 253, 263–265, 281, 284, 289, 290, 315
exploring, 28, 54, 64, 90, 153, 187, 188, 205, 211, 219, 236, 248, 263, 309
explosion, 2
exposure, 185
expression, 11, 321
extension, 136
extent, 36, 71
extraction, 92, 160, 163, 164, 167, 168, 308
eye, 48

face, 16, 148, 173, 187, 200–203, 278, 280, 285, 296
fact, 11
factor, 204
failure, 23
Fairness, 273
fairness, 8, 9, 12, 19, 158, 159, 180, 264, 272–274, 296–298
fall, 2, 40, 267, 310

Index

family, 73
fare, 89, 153
fatigue, 308
fault, 114, 126, 128, 238
favor, 8, 41, 272, 296
favorite, 219
favoritism, 275
fear, 291
feature, 15, 54, 70, 73, 75, 77, 81, 84–86, 91, 92, 106, 163, 203, 204, 211–213, 216, 235, 308
feed, 54
feedback, 14, 18, 57, 169, 175, 180, 188, 214, 218, 266, 295, 310, 312, 321
fidelity, 188
field, 1, 6, 10, 17, 28, 30, 32, 47, 48, 50, 51, 53, 64, 69, 75, 90, 139, 143, 158, 159, 163, 164, 172, 175–177, 183, 186, 188, 189, 194, 201, 203, 205, 213, 215, 216, 224, 227, 231, 238, 240, 241, 261, 265, 289, 301, 308, 315
file, 115
film, 11, 12, 318, 320, 321
filmmaking, 320
filter, 127, 137, 192, 203, 204
filtering, 3, 46, 192, 194, 227, 308
finance, 1, 6, 10, 13, 68, 117, 124, 143, 145, 146, 149, 255, 302, 303
finding, 49, 54, 61, 77, 263, 265, 300
fit, 14, 98, 105
flexibility, 85, 132, 165, 238
flow, 114, 125, 284, 285
flowchart, 70, 73

fluency, 155, 159, 181, 188
focus, 32, 54, 62, 64, 92, 96, 106, 115, 182, 217, 291, 292, 296, 309
fold, 99–101, 103
folding, 264
footage, 51, 105, 320
footprint, 179
force, 5, 103, 106, 298
forecast, 3, 144, 249
forecasting, 143, 145, 146
forefront, 309
forest, 73
form, 1, 14, 15, 19, 28, 57, 67, 70, 92, 118, 136, 204
Formant, 178
format, 15
formula, 37
forth, 214
foster, 172, 205, 301
foundation, 1, 19, 25, 39, 45, 57, 80, 120, 125, 228, 281, 282
fraction, 10, 104
frame, 321
framework, 48, 116, 126, 179, 182, 234–236, 280, 281, 285, 303
fraud, 54, 114, 117, 148, 149
frequency, 36, 82, 192, 258
friend, 28, 57
frontier, 10
fruit, 164
fuel, 16, 305
function, 61, 63, 67, 70, 77, 92, 104, 106, 204, 209, 214, 217–219, 231, 232, 234–236, 264
functionality, 266

fundamental, 35, 41, 44, 57, 65, 80, 87, 132, 139, 143, 168, 191, 194, 197, 199, 213, 223, 224
fur, 84
fusion, 2, 15, 111, 227
future, 2, 3, 10, 12, 64, 116–118, 128, 143, 146, 149, 153, 158, 177, 227, 231, 239, 240, 242, 249, 252, 255, 262, 268, 271, 292, 301, 306, 309, 314, 318, 321, 322

gain, 25–27, 31, 35, 37, 43, 51, 83, 110, 112, 116, 119, 124, 125, 129, 135, 138, 155, 169, 248, 251, 295
gait, 11
game, 2, 214, 234, 321
gaming, 59, 308, 309, 318
gap, 301, 304
gathering, 120, 225, 306
gender, 22, 248, 260, 269, 270, 276
generalizability, 165
generalization, 55, 71, 85, 104, 105, 206
generation, 155, 158, 178, 215
generator, 214, 215
ggplot, 35
giant, 245
glass, 24
GloVe, 142
go, 80
goal, 4, 26, 39, 49, 53, 54, 61, 63, 73, 77, 87, 105, 125, 136, 160, 178, 191, 194, 197, 211, 225, 226, 228, 234, 303
good, 85, 109, 226, 264

goodness, 98
governance, 111, 114–116, 124, 264, 277–281, 297
gradient, 63, 68, 209, 218, 231–234
gram, 156, 158, 159, 182
grammar, 181
graph, 113, 115
grasp, 150, 299
grayscale, 191
grid, 103, 191, 203
group, 9, 54, 56, 87, 89, 127, 129, 193, 243
grouping, 127
growth, 124, 128, 251, 265, 291, 293
guesswork, 264
guidance, 24
guide, 3, 44, 48, 51, 61, 153, 185, 266, 298, 310

hailing, 18
hand, 14, 15, 42, 56, 85, 88, 89, 104, 108, 114, 126, 178, 184, 185, 193, 195, 211, 265, 266, 301
handling, 23, 24, 110, 113, 117, 118, 125, 128, 129, 132, 164, 182, 185, 223
hardware, 300, 301
harm, 240, 241, 275
harmony, 292
haystack, 262
health, 11, 117, 118, 259, 263–265, 267, 310
healthcare, 2–4, 6, 10, 13, 22, 68, 117, 118, 124, 138, 146, 149, 197, 228, 235, 236, 259, 261, 262, 264–268, 279–281, 302, 303, 308
heart, 77, 214

heaviness, 37
height, 77, 79, 84
help, 11, 14, 25, 26, 29, 32, 35, 37, 54, 56, 84, 87, 101, 102, 114, 116, 118, 119, 136, 137, 158, 167, 218, 225, 235, 252, 261, 266, 291, 296, 301
herbivore, 84
heterogeneity, 227
hiring, 8, 269, 270, 276, 277, 296, 297
histogram, 192
history, 3, 22, 68, 87, 89, 117, 118, 245, 247, 249, 251, 260, 290, 306, 320
home, 2, 3, 11, 310
hospital, 22, 68
host, 240
house, 51, 67, 105
housing, 51, 105
human, 1, 2, 9–12, 61, 118, 155, 168, 173, 176–178, 187–189, 227, 228, 231, 235, 236, 240, 242, 253, 256, 258, 260, 261, 267–269, 291, 292, 296, 302, 304–306, 309, 310, 312–315, 318, 319, 321, 322
humanity, 10, 12, 307
hurdle, 308
hydration, 311
hyperparameter, 85, 101, 103
hyperplane, 77
hypothesis, 41, 42

i, 169
iceberg, 90

idea, 26, 36, 70, 93, 181, 203, 216, 232, 234, 235
identification, 149, 164, 200, 262, 265
identifying, 19, 54, 56, 146, 164, 167–169, 194, 205, 211, 262, 263, 270, 296
identity, 8, 117
image, 2, 15, 88, 93, 111, 191–194, 197–199, 203–205, 209, 211, 216–219, 225
imagination, 314
imaging, 117, 118, 192, 193, 215, 260
imbalance, 212, 213
impact, 2–7, 12, 19, 49, 64, 100, 116, 119, 185, 196, 199, 240, 242, 252, 261, 263, 266, 268, 271, 283, 296–300, 302, 318, 320
implement, 18, 85, 98, 102, 244, 250, 272, 279
implementation, 69, 172, 261, 265, 267
importance, 18, 19, 22, 24, 25, 31, 32, 104, 115, 123, 124, 142, 177, 238, 241, 274, 279, 280, 294, 310
improvement, 103, 175
imputation, 111
inability, 1
inception, 237
incident, 258
inclusivity, 180
income, 27, 68, 274, 291, 292
increase, 42, 100, 125, 215, 245, 248, 251, 299, 301
independence, 81, 310, 311
indexing, 140

individual, 3, 104, 147, 185, 186, 235, 243, 252, 259, 261, 266, 267, 309, 310, 320
individuality, 321
industry, 4, 6, 11, 12, 56, 117, 123, 132, 180, 213, 252, 255, 265, 268, 279, 281, 298, 308, 320, 321
inequality, 291
inference, 49, 185, 235
influence, 42, 51, 84, 204, 269, 321
information, 3, 8, 10, 13–18, 26, 32, 34, 35, 37, 40, 54, 62, 68, 72, 91, 112, 117, 118, 120, 124, 127, 139, 140, 149, 156, 164, 167–169, 186, 191, 194, 204, 216, 221, 222, 224, 225, 237, 248, 251, 259–261, 297, 299, 308, 309, 311
infrastructure, 110, 115, 133, 259, 267
ingenuity, 12
ingestion, 126
initiation, 262
innovation, 10, 44, 112, 124, 135, 194, 239, 264, 281, 291, 298, 301, 314
input, 53, 61, 63, 64, 67, 91, 155, 157, 160, 178, 179, 184, 203, 204, 207, 260
inspection, 145
inspiration, 320
instability, 215
instance, 3, 10, 11, 51, 88, 112, 117, 118, 123, 164, 205, 213, 215, 251, 260, 270, 271, 292, 296, 306, 310, 320
institution, 186

insurance, 117
integration, 2, 10, 14, 124, 227, 237, 239, 252, 262, 264–268, 300, 307, 311
integrity, 19, 111, 277, 280, 288, 311
intelligence, 1, 5, 13, 16, 19, 24, 28, 30, 32, 44, 48, 50, 51, 53, 57, 61, 75, 86, 90, 104, 120, 129, 130, 132, 135, 139, 149, 159, 168, 186, 188, 189, 194, 197, 199, 200, 210, 224, 225, 227, 252, 265, 281, 301, 309, 312, 314, 322
intensity, 191, 193, 266
interactio, 245
interaction, 176, 177, 228, 229, 231, 235, 267, 309, 311
interest, 27, 39, 64, 68, 194, 197, 211
interestingness, 137, 138
interface, 114
interference, 308
internet, 293
interoperability, 280
interpretability, 64, 69, 70, 91, 93, 149, 261, 303, 304
interpretation, 95, 197, 244
intersection, 10, 237
interval, 40, 42, 127
intervention, 129, 259, 262, 305, 321
intonation, 178
introduction, 2
intuition, 25, 77
invasion, 2
inventory, 13, 118, 123, 129, 213, 280
inverse, 157, 235
investigation, 148, 149

Index

investing, 4
investment, 6, 117, 252, 255, 266
involve, 9, 16, 20, 303
involvement, 320
irony, 172
issue, 71, 87, 100, 218, 236, 240, 268, 272, 274, 296, 301
itemset, 136
iteration, 101, 103

Java, 168
Jerome Friedman, 108
job, 2, 6, 8, 240, 268, 277, 291–294, 296
John McCarthy, 1
journey, 2, 16, 26, 27, 48, 57, 76, 205, 262, 293, 295
jurisdiction, 284
justice, 9, 274, 297

k, 54, 103, 114
Kaggle, 27
Kalman, 227
kernel, 203
key, 2, 7, 10, 23, 25, 32, 53, 54, 61, 65, 70, 93, 95, 112, 113, 115, 121, 126, 128, 134, 143, 150, 158, 160, 173, 176, 203, 216, 223, 224, 228, 232, 234, 237, 245, 248, 250, 253, 256, 257, 262–264, 268, 277, 281, 287, 288, 292, 293, 304, 313, 315, 316
keying, 320
knowledge, 1, 10, 15, 23, 24, 27, 45, 48, 54, 56, 59, 61, 87, 89, 103, 111, 139, 178, 185, 187, 259, 289, 291–293, 315
Kurtosis, 37
kurtosis, 37, 38

lab, 118
label, 81, 82, 84
labor, 6, 181, 290
lack, 7, 10, 42, 182, 187–189, 240, 266, 280
landing, 306
landscape, 6, 80, 114, 116, 248, 255, 258, 264, 268, 287, 290–292
lane, 241
language, 2, 3, 15, 93, 111, 139, 155–159, 163, 168, 169, 172, 175, 177, 180, 181, 183, 185–189, 215, 244, 276, 301
latency, 128, 132
law, 270
layer, 61, 62, 64, 184, 203, 204
lead, 8, 9, 42, 71, 85, 87, 91, 99, 104, 105, 158, 180, 187, 212, 227, 240, 259, 262–264, 268, 270, 275, 291, 296, 301, 309
leaf, 70, 73
learn, 1, 2, 11, 13, 32, 56, 57, 61, 65, 72, 104, 140, 160, 166, 179, 181, 185, 187, 204, 233, 234, 236–238, 260, 292, 293, 310
learning, 1–4, 7, 8, 11, 46, 53–65, 67, 69, 70, 73–75, 78, 80–82, 85–87, 91, 94, 95, 98, 99, 101, 102, 104, 105, 107, 108, 111–113, 136,

                    138–140, 142, 149, 152,
                       160, 161, 163, 165, 166,
                       168, 169, 172, 177, 180,
                       183, 185, 187, 197, 199,
                       200, 209, 211–213, 215,
                       216, 219, 225, 227,
                       231–236, 238, 244, 249,
                       251, 252, 255, 259–264,
                       290, 292, 293, 295, 296,
                       301, 305–312, 319–321
length, 82
level, 40, 42, 68, 88, 113, 197, 204,
        248, 266, 274, 284, 303
leverage, 3, 17, 18, 32, 69, 80, 112,
        115, 132, 149, 186, 213,
        261, 292, 295, 299, 321
lexicon, 172
liability, 241, 297
library, 168
lidar, 225, 241
life, 2–4, 11, 48, 59, 266, 293, 296,
        311, 318
lifeblood, 13, 19
lifecycle, 275, 276
lifestyle, 118
light, 17, 28
lighting, 213, 227, 310
likelihood, 235, 248, 251
limitation, 71, 72
line, 11, 31, 105, 294
lineage, 111, 114
linearity, 70
listing, 26
literature, 259, 261
living, 11, 240, 292, 309–312
loading, 26
loan, 7, 68, 72
localization, 211, 213, 227

location, 17, 18, 26, 51, 67, 105,
        120, 165, 191, 211,
        225–227, 238, 283
log, 125, 235
logic, 113
logistic, 67–70, 107
look, 59, 62, 105, 108, 255, 265
lookout, 248
loop, 100, 101
loss, 63, 104, 106, 128, 179, 204,
        209, 214, 216–219, 291,
        321
lot, 16
Lower BPC, 157
loyalty, 246
luck, 76
lung, 262
luxury, 89

machine, 1–4, 8, 46, 53, 56, 57, 61,
        65, 67, 69, 70, 73–75, 78,
        80–82, 85–87, 91, 94, 95,
        98, 99, 101, 102, 104, 105,
        108, 111–113, 136, 138,
        139, 142, 149, 155, 158,
        160, 161, 163, 165, 168,
        169, 172, 181–183,
        186–188, 215, 227, 244,
        249, 251, 252, 255, 259,
        260, 263, 290, 295, 296,
        301, 306, 307, 309–311
magic, 194
magnitude, 104
mainstream, 11
maintenance, 266
majority, 70, 84
makeup, 261
making, 1, 4, 6, 7, 9, 10, 13–15, 27,
        28, 37, 39, 42–44, 47, 48,

Index   339

    51, 56, 67, 68, 71, 85, 86, 88, 93, 94, 98, 111, 113, 114, 120, 124–126, 129, 132, 138, 139, 149, 153, 156, 157, 159, 179, 187, 204, 215, 230, 233, 236–241, 251, 256, 261, 263, 264, 266, 269, 270, 272–275, 277, 296, 297, 302, 305, 306, 308, 311, 312
mammography, 4
management, 6, 10, 15, 110, 112, 114, 121, 123, 124, 126, 129, 132, 213, 255, 258, 277, 280, 306, 307
manager, 252
manipulation, 215
manner, 6, 61, 129, 214, 248, 277
manufacturing, 6, 146, 149, 228, 237, 291, 294
map, 26, 31, 70, 179, 203, 204, 225, 227
mapping, 227, 300
margin, 77
marginalization, 270
market, 6, 17, 117, 125, 132, 169, 246, 248, 258, 264, 291–293
marketing, 42, 68, 87, 89, 92, 117, 119, 123, 125, 149, 243–246, 248, 252, 295
Marvin Minsky, 1
mask, 192
masking, 114
Matplotlib, 35
matrix, 91
Max, 204
maximum, 91, 204, 235

maze, 25, 27, 61
mean, 35–38, 96, 153, 167, 179, 204, 291
meaning, 120, 164, 178, 186, 187
means, 54, 81, 87, 89, 90, 187
measure, 36, 89, 92, 95, 96, 102, 136, 142, 158, 167, 225, 240
mechanism, 84, 185
media, 14, 17, 18, 88, 110, 117–119, 125, 169, 186, 200
median, 35–38
medication, 261, 267, 311
medicine, 1, 41, 199, 261, 308
medium, 314
memory, 113, 115, 156, 179
Meredith Broussard, 298
messaging, 114, 115, 311
metadata, 114
meteorology, 143, 145
method, 16, 17, 86, 87, 186, 293
metric, 84, 85, 92, 95, 98, 102, 103, 157, 167
militarization, 307
milk, 136
mind, 30, 34, 75, 87, 131, 254
mindset, 293
minimum, 137
mining, 93, 136–142
Minkowski, 84
minute, 262
mishandling, 8
misinformation, 215
misrepresentation, 180
mission, 238, 306
misuse, 8, 215, 297
mitigation, 4, 277
mix, 16, 71
Mobile, 17

mobile, 17, 18
mobility, 266, 310
mode, 35–38, 215
model, 49, 51, 53–55, 63–65, 67,
	68, 70, 91, 93, 95, 96,
	98–108, 113, 145, 149,
	153, 155–157, 159, 160,
	163, 175, 180, 182, 184,
	185, 195, 209, 226, 236,
	262, 269, 290, 293, 303
modeling, 15, 19, 48–52, 140,
	142–144, 146, 149–153,
	155–159, 172, 178
moment, 146, 287
monitor, 11, 13, 18, 209, 280, 310
monitoring, 17, 54, 111, 114, 125,
	126, 149, 241, 260, 266,
	267, 280, 310, 311
Moses, 182
motion, 193, 226, 227, 266, 320
motor, 266, 308
move, 7, 12, 61, 87, 104, 225, 239
movement, 17, 18
movie, 167
multicollinearity, 70
multiplication, 192, 203
muscle, 308
music, 3, 11, 12, 215, 312, 315–318,
	320, 321
myriad, 249

n, 182
Naive Bayes, 46, 80–83, 163
name, 73, 132
naturalness, 179, 181
nature, 40, 56, 148, 153, 279, 310,
	314
navigation, 6, 10, 180, 225, 227, 228,
	305, 307, 310

need, 17, 64, 77, 87, 89, 111–114,
	126, 128, 175, 186, 201,
	213, 227, 234–236, 240,
	241, 250, 258, 261–268,
	272, 291, 292, 297, 298,
	300, 303, 306, 309, 310,
	316
needle, 262
negation, 172
negative, 37, 61, 118, 163, 166, 169,
	291, 296
neighboring, 217
network, 61–64, 88, 104, 204, 206,
	212, 214, 217, 232, 305
neuron, 204
neurorehabilitation, 308
New York City, 165
news, 117, 159
NLTK, 168
node, 70, 73
noise, 85, 92, 104, 105, 111, 175,
	177, 191, 192, 199, 214,
	236, 301, 308, 309
norm, 146
note, 23, 37, 98, 100, 291
noun, 164
novel, 11, 263
number, 26, 31, 32, 36, 51, 64, 67,
	84, 87–89, 91, 95, 100,
	102, 103, 105, 148, 156,
	157, 204, 206, 263, 301

Obama, 164
object, 115, 192, 194, 195, 197, 199,
	204, 205, 211–213, 223,
	227
objective, 77, 92, 211, 218, 219, 232,
	273
observation, 36, 146

Index

observer, 16
occurrence, 96
odd, 84
odometry, 227
off, 18, 156, 303
offer, 3, 4, 68, 78, 89, 113, 126, 166, 251, 252, 255, 291, 320
offering, 80, 89, 123, 189, 309
office, 11
one, 23, 49, 58, 61, 64, 65, 67, 87, 88, 95, 99, 116, 120, 156, 165, 186, 214, 216, 219, 224, 225, 232, 292, 293, 310
online, 16, 17, 169, 247, 249, 251, 252, 293, 295
OpenVizsla, 311
operating, 227
operation, 128, 203, 204, 238, 240
opinion, 169
optimization, 10, 63, 68, 77, 103, 104, 184, 209, 214, 218, 231, 232, 263, 265, 300, 301, 307
optimum, 300
option, 255
order, 36, 126, 129, 156, 225
ordering, 3
organization, 62, 164, 277, 279, 280, 284
orientation, 194
origin, 114, 284
original, 11, 193, 215, 303, 312, 315, 318, 320
originality, 320
other, 14, 15, 27, 42, 56, 73, 74, 81, 84, 85, 87–89, 92, 98, 104, 105, 107, 109, 114, 117, 118, 126, 129, 143, 164, 178, 184, 185, 193, 195, 199, 213, 214, 225, 227, 237, 240, 248, 281, 284, 291, 307, 309, 310, 320
out, 26, 31, 36, 48, 68, 83, 95, 96, 101, 102, 104, 126, 129, 137, 166, 176, 258
outbreak, 32
outcome, 73
outlier, 27, 111, 146
output, 53, 54, 61, 63, 64, 192, 203, 204, 214, 312
overfit, 71
overfitting, 73, 75, 91, 101–108, 204, 206, 208
overload, 27
overview, 205
ownership, 17, 18, 280, 293

pace, 293
padding, 204
pain, 265
pair, 58
pandemic, 31, 267
paper, 182
paradigm, 1
paradigms, 2, 53, 55, 57
parallel, 113, 115, 132, 179, 182, 184, 187–189, 218, 300
parallelism, 300
parallelization, 183
paralysis, 308
parameter, 40, 107
park, 84
parole, 9, 297
part, 4, 80, 314
particle, 227
partitioning, 70, 192, 197
partner, 11

path, 61, 225–227, 238
patient, 3, 6, 22, 68, 117, 118, 146, 167, 235, 259–265, 267, 268, 279, 280, 302
pattern, 2, 87, 172, 203, 318
pedestrian, 241
penalty, 104
people, 11
percentage, 32
perception, 221–225, 227, 239, 266
performance, 2, 19, 42, 55, 60–62, 69–71, 79, 80, 85, 89, 91, 93, 95, 98–105, 107, 108, 113, 117, 118, 129, 142, 145, 149, 153, 157, 158, 163, 165, 166, 168, 177, 184, 185, 187, 205, 206, 208, 209, 212, 214, 215, 228, 248, 251, 252, 272, 303, 307, 309
period, 1
perpetuation, 9
perplexity, 93, 157–159
person, 11, 164
personalization, 248
personnel, 114
perspective, 59, 109, 319
Peter Toma, 181
phase, 1, 4
phenomenon, 299
philosophy, 9
phone, 16
photo, 218, 311
photography, 192
phrase, 181, 182, 187
physics, 301
pick, 18
picture, 16
piece, 160, 164, 169

pipe, 16
pipeline, 128
pixel, 191, 192, 203
place, 129, 290
plan, 125, 225, 238, 252
planet, 306
planning, 26, 226, 227, 239
platform, 311
play, 9, 11, 16, 46, 53, 57, 87, 111, 120, 139, 148, 176, 183, 184, 199, 211, 221, 238, 240, 255, 260–262, 281, 291, 310, 318, 321
playing, 2, 3, 234
poetry, 312
point, 36, 40, 77, 79, 84–89, 105, 147
polarity, 169
police, 271, 274
policing, 271, 274
policy, 58, 114, 231–234, 270, 272, 297, 298
polysemy, 164
pooling, 203, 204, 206
popularity, 3, 62, 82, 166, 175, 182, 216
population, 16, 17, 39–41, 49, 310
pose, 112, 187, 213, 227
position, 226, 305
positive, 37, 96, 102, 118, 163, 166, 169, 298
post, 182, 188, 302, 303, 320
potential, 1, 2, 4, 6, 8, 10–12, 16, 18, 23, 24, 35, 51, 54, 64, 80, 101, 104, 111, 116–119, 122, 124, 135, 139, 158, 159, 168, 170, 171, 189, 199, 202, 215, 219, 226, 236, 239, 240, 248–252,

Index

258, 261, 263–265, 268, 272, 274, 275, 287, 290–292, 295–302, 304, 307–309, 311–313
power, 2, 7, 9, 10, 12, 13, 17, 18, 42, 48, 59, 69, 80, 104, 112, 116, 119, 121, 124, 128, 129, 132, 149, 163, 186, 188, 194, 210, 225, 227, 248, 251, 265, 274, 293, 299, 301, 314, 318
practice, 23, 60, 65, 76, 81, 89, 95, 152, 210, 225
practitioner, 163
precision, 40, 42, 96, 102, 163, 167, 209, 258, 261, 265, 266
prediction, 54, 57, 70, 73, 84, 105
preparation, 71, 143, 184
preprocessing, 15, 111, 206, 207, 209
presence, 81, 82, 164, 182, 194, 225, 269, 271, 272
preservation, 93, 218
president, 164
pressure, 258
prevention, 213, 267
price, 13, 26, 51, 105
principle, 49, 67, 84, 160, 234
prison, 9
privacy, 2, 4, 6, 8, 9, 12, 17–19, 112, 114, 116, 119, 158, 159, 172, 180, 213, 227, 241, 261, 262, 264, 265, 267, 277, 280–285, 288, 290, 297, 311
probability, 35, 39, 44–48, 68, 70, 80, 81, 156, 157, 181, 182, 184
problem, 54, 56, 73, 77, 89, 90, 102, 104, 105, 107, 153, 160, 164, 199, 212, 213, 227, 232, 234–236, 292, 300
process, 4, 6, 9, 13, 18–25, 35, 39–41, 49, 57, 63, 68, 70, 71, 85, 87, 89, 91, 103, 104, 110, 111, 113, 120, 125–127, 129, 140, 149, 159, 160, 164, 186, 192, 194, 195, 203, 210, 214, 215, 218, 225, 232, 235, 237, 238, 240, 251, 256, 259, 261–263, 266, 269, 272, 283, 290, 293–295, 299, 302, 312, 319, 320
processing, 2, 3, 10, 14–16, 93, 109–116, 125–132, 139, 149, 168, 172, 175, 177, 178, 180, 182, 191–194, 215, 224, 225, 244, 281, 300, 301, 308
product, 13, 119, 142, 163, 247
production, 6, 178, 294, 320
productivity, 6, 251, 294
professional, 295
profiling, 271
profitability, 245
program, 294
programming, 30, 113, 241, 294, 295
progress, 2, 31, 183, 197, 201, 227, 228, 231, 266, 270, 292, 301
progression, 260
project, 311
prominence, 179
promise, 10, 183, 187, 233, 260, 300, 309, 311, 316
pronunciation, 180

propagation, 63
property, 136, 299
proportion, 95, 96, 98, 102, 166
propose, 64
prosody, 178, 179
protection, 12, 17, 119, 248, 281, 282, 284
protein, 264
proximity, 54, 86, 225
proxy, 269
pruning, 70, 72
psychology, 92
public, 9, 14, 27, 32, 169, 172, 180, 268, 270, 297
publish, 114
purchase, 54, 87, 117, 123, 136, 247, 249, 251
purchasing, 54, 87
purpose, 72, 204

quality, 6, 11, 17–19, 23, 25, 89, 98, 111, 124, 142, 179, 184, 187, 188, 191–193, 218, 261, 262, 266, 280, 296, 308, 310, 311
quantity, 13
quantum, 2, 10, 12, 299–301, 307
qubit, 300
querying, 113, 115, 140

race, 248, 269
radar, 241
radiology, 261, 262
Rakesh Agrawal, 136
Ralph Kimball, 125
Ramakrishnan Srikant, 136
randomness, 73, 75
range, 20, 36–38, 40, 42, 47, 56, 59, 63, 66, 67, 70, 74, 88, 110, 127, 146, 148, 158, 167, 170, 172, 179, 180, 183, 194, 196, 197, 205, 227, 238, 251, 259, 266, 292, 308
ranging, 2, 16, 18, 30, 79, 86, 138, 149, 168, 169, 178, 199, 213, 234, 305, 313
rate, 61, 96, 112, 166, 209, 262
ratio, 166, 308
rationale, 240
reading, 6, 180, 205, 295
readmission, 22
reality, 6, 81, 211, 213, 227, 239
realm, 3, 24, 48, 120, 172, 211, 215, 318, 320
reason, 109, 237
reasoning, 1, 64, 261, 302, 303
recall, 96, 102, 163, 167, 209
recognition, 2, 8, 15, 17, 87, 93, 155, 164–168, 172, 177, 193, 194, 196, 197, 199–204, 211, 223, 224, 227, 270, 318
recommendation, 2, 4, 93, 113, 302, 320, 321
record, 126
recovery, 258, 265, 266
recruiting, 297
redistribution, 291
reducing, 4, 6, 91, 93, 95, 106, 176, 192, 204, 262, 264, 266, 267, 291
reduction, 6, 54, 57, 91, 93–95, 99, 177, 233, 309
redundancy, 92, 238
refinement, 89
region, 193, 195, 197, 204, 212

Index

regression, 49, 51, 57, 65–70, 73, 80, 98, 104, 105, 107, 153, 204, 260
regularization, 70, 102, 104, 106–108, 209, 217–219
regularizer, 217
regulation, 12
rehabilitation, 266
reinforcement, 2, 58–61, 185, 231, 233–235, 238, 301
relationship, 22, 26, 27, 49, 51, 65, 67, 260, 261, 268
reliability, 4, 19, 137, 145, 149, 196, 238, 268, 307
reliance, 306
religion, 248
reminder, 3
renaissance, 2
rendering, 321
reoffending, 9
repeat, 248
reporting, 120
repository, 120
representation, 71, 88, 93, 178, 180, 187, 204
representative, 8, 17, 18, 39, 40, 100, 261, 264, 271
representativeness, 17, 262
research, 1–4, 10, 12, 16, 17, 40, 49, 90, 92, 158, 159, 176, 179, 188, 189, 201, 203, 205, 213, 218, 227, 233, 236, 259, 264, 266, 267, 270, 291, 307, 309, 312
Reskilling, 291–293
reskilling, 292, 294, 296
resolution, 213, 218
resonance, 179
resource, 10, 132, 175, 185, 306, 307

respect, 17, 63, 172, 213, 217, 218, 234, 311
response, 214, 260, 267, 310
responsibility, 8, 19, 240, 268, 274
rest, 114
restoration, 321
result, 99, 100, 158, 204, 270, 271, 292
resume, 128, 276
resupply, 306
resurgence, 1
retail, 13, 123–125, 129, 136, 138, 213, 252
retailer, 123, 247
retention, 320
retrieval, 113, 120, 139, 140
return, 232
revenue, 49, 246, 248, 251
review, 167, 261
reward, 57–59, 61, 185, 231, 234–236
ride, 18
rider, 18
right, 7, 22, 29, 32, 35, 37, 44, 57, 61, 106, 107, 118, 126, 129, 214, 218, 233, 248, 303
rise, 2, 112
risk, 11, 68, 70, 73, 75, 118, 240, 252, 258, 267, 291, 296
river, 186
road, 4, 7, 56, 57
Robert Tibshirani, 108
robo, 252, 254, 255
robot, 221, 223–228, 231, 235, 240, 267, 310
robotic, 228, 265–268, 306–308, 310

robustness, 71, 75, 176, 227, 238, 306
role, 9, 11, 16, 23, 37, 42, 46, 53, 56, 87, 102, 111, 114, 117, 124, 125, 129, 138–140, 143, 146, 148, 155, 158, 159, 167–169, 176, 177, 183, 184, 191, 194, 199, 211, 214, 221, 224, 240, 255, 260, 262, 266, 281, 291, 295, 304–306, 310, 318, 320, 321
room, 310
root, 36, 70
route, 300
routine, 291
routing, 18, 118
rover, 305
row, 13
rowing, 60
rule, 1, 73, 117, 136–139, 165, 168, 169, 181
run, 87
running, 115

safeguard, 149, 262
safety, 4, 6, 213, 227, 238, 240–242, 263, 264, 268, 291, 297, 308, 310, 311
sale, 13
sample, 37, 39–42, 49, 214, 236, 306
sampling, 39, 40, 42, 73, 75, 100, 184, 185, 235
San Francisco, 165
San Francisco Bay Area, 165
satisfaction, 3, 6, 123, 125, 228, 245, 246, 248, 251, 291
scalability, 124, 126, 301
scale, 110, 112, 113, 128, 165, 183, 194, 263
scaling, 70, 85
scatter, 26, 89
scenario, 302
scene, 194, 227
scheduling, 3, 118, 132
schema, 113
science, 9, 47, 270
scientist, 101
scope, 57, 291
score, 68, 85, 96, 157, 163, 167, 209
scoring, 320
scraping, 14, 17, 18
screen, 320
screening, 4, 262, 263, 265, 276
scriptwriting, 321
sea, 24, 27
search, 13, 103, 175, 231
searching, 103, 262
seasonality, 143
second, 7
section, 2, 7, 13, 15, 16, 18, 19, 24, 28, 32, 35, 39, 44, 48, 53, 56, 61, 65, 67, 70, 76, 80, 87, 90, 91, 95, 98, 102, 104, 109, 112, 115, 120, 123, 129, 132, 136, 143, 149, 159, 164, 165, 172, 177, 186, 189, 191, 210, 211, 225, 231, 240, 248, 252, 255, 265, 281
sector, 3, 6
security, 4, 6, 8, 18, 112, 114–116, 124, 180, 241, 261, 262, 264, 267, 277, 280, 287, 288, 290, 297, 309, 311
segment, 89, 197, 246, 260

segmentation, 87, 88, 192–194, 197–199, 245–248
selection, 70, 73, 75, 87, 101–104, 106
self, 2, 4, 7, 157, 179, 183, 205, 237, 291, 293, 295, 297
selling, 67, 258
semantic, 142
sense, 32, 67, 111, 114, 159, 163, 169, 222, 237
sensing, 225, 240
sensitivity, 70, 96, 166, 218, 280
sensor, 14, 18, 56, 57, 110, 117, 125, 192, 221, 227, 237, 310
sentence, 159, 164, 165, 181, 182, 184
sentencing, 297
sentiment, 14, 15, 17, 80, 114, 117, 118, 140, 142, 155, 158, 159, 167–169, 171, 172
separation, 89
sequence, 143, 155, 157, 179
series, 129, 143–146, 191, 226, 263
service, 68, 163, 291
session, 127
set, 16, 39, 44, 63, 68, 82, 85, 99–101, 103–105, 109, 113, 127–129, 157, 159, 181, 202, 203, 209, 231, 234, 281, 292
setback, 1
setting, 3, 16, 41
severity, 31
shape, 12, 27, 37, 177, 194, 231, 242, 321
share, 26, 114
sharing, 212, 280, 311
shelf, 213, 223
shift, 268
shipping, 117
shot, 195
show, 31
shuffling, 100
side, 37
sigmoid, 67
signal, 172, 175, 308, 309
significance, 95, 120, 123, 281
silhouette, 87
similarity, 89, 93, 142, 193
simplicity, 81
Siri, 175, 180
site, 266
situation, 302
size, 22, 37, 42, 67, 99, 127, 184, 193, 204, 209, 310
skewness, 37, 38
skill, 292, 296
skin, 260
sleep, 310
slide, 203
smoothing, 156, 158
society, 2, 7, 116, 272, 291, 292
sociology, 9, 92, 270
softmax, 184
software, 30, 295
soil, 306
solution, 64, 187, 310, 320
sonar, 225
sorting, 159
sound, 315
source, 17, 23, 27, 155, 167, 181, 182, 184, 187, 188, 311, 320
space, 10, 54, 70, 77, 84, 86, 91, 92, 103, 142, 175, 215, 263, 305–307
spacecraft, 305, 306
SpaCy, 168

spam, 46, 53, 54, 80, 81, 159, 163
span, 117
sparsity, 104, 106
speaker, 175–177
specific, 4, 11, 13, 15, 16, 22, 32, 56, 87–89, 95, 99, 101, 102, 105, 125–127, 133, 142, 167, 168, 187–189, 191, 203, 207, 211, 223, 235, 238, 246, 252, 260–263, 266, 281, 300, 302, 303, 310, 318, 320
spectroscopy, 306
speech, 2, 155, 164, 172, 173, 175, 177–180, 186, 308
speed, 10, 18, 213, 218, 237, 241, 258, 263
spiral, 258
split, 7, 73, 103
splitting, 85, 99–101
spread, 32, 36, 37
spreadsheet, 13, 30
square, 36, 51, 105
stage, 178, 195, 212
stagnation, 1
stake, 240
standard, 36–38, 146, 292
star, 305
start, 26, 61, 67, 70, 89, 219
starting, 136, 172, 290
state, 57, 58, 62, 126, 156, 198, 199, 234, 235
status, 22, 269, 292, 310
stemming, 142
step, 19, 25, 57, 61, 91, 125, 184, 192, 204, 252, 263, 272, 290
stock, 117, 125, 258
stocking, 123

stone, 86
stop, 209, 240
stopping, 104, 209, 237
storage, 110, 113, 115, 120, 193, 280
store, 58, 164, 299
storytelling, 321
strategy, 61, 107, 231, 245, 248, 251
stream, 114–116, 125–129, 194
streaming, 115, 116, 127, 245, 320
strength, 41, 51, 73, 107, 136, 137, 266
stress, 92, 178
stride, 204
structure, 14, 27, 49, 54, 56, 61, 62, 70, 73, 88, 120, 155, 187, 203, 206, 214, 263, 264
study, 1, 23, 40, 42, 125, 178, 252, 261, 305
style, 215–219, 318
subfield, 61
subject, 283
subjectivity, 172
subscribe, 114
subset, 39, 73, 99, 100, 106, 136, 260
success, 2, 12, 23, 61, 64, 86, 124, 138, 149, 158, 182, 185, 194, 215, 248, 252, 259, 262
sum, 166, 217
summary, 67, 112
summation, 192
summing, 203
superposition, 299
supplier, 118
supply, 6, 118
support, 11, 77, 136, 137, 261, 266, 268, 291, 308–312
surface, 306

Index

surgeon, 265
surgery, 265, 266
surrounding, 186, 241, 266, 296, 298, 320
surveillance, 8, 192, 200, 205, 213
survey, 16
synergy, 265
syntax, 164
synthesis, 2, 178–180, 308
system, 7, 9, 11, 17, 54, 114, 115, 126, 128, 129, 142, 164–166, 175, 178, 228, 237, 238, 264, 269, 272, 274, 279, 280, 302, 308, 311, 312

t, 76, 93, 94, 105, 135, 215
table, 58
Tableau, 35, 114, 115
tail, 37
tailor, 11, 89, 235, 246, 308
target, 9, 11, 16, 17, 53, 70, 87, 98, 123, 179, 181, 184, 185, 187, 204, 238, 260, 262–264
targeting, 267
task, 14, 19, 21, 23, 32, 53, 64, 95, 108, 148, 164, 165, 168, 181, 186, 194, 197–199, 211, 223, 259, 300, 305
taste, 3
teacher, 185
technique, 17, 29, 32, 40, 49, 60, 65, 87, 91, 98, 100, 101, 103, 104, 136, 138, 139, 153, 156, 192, 193, 216, 260
technology, 2–4, 8, 9, 17–19, 47, 164, 175–177, 180, 201, 202, 215, 224, 227, 255, 268, 290, 292, 296, 309, 315, 318, 321
telecommunications, 68
telemetry, 305
temperature, 17, 310
tendency, 35–37, 71
tenure, 68
term, 104, 106, 109, 217, 218
terrain, 19
test, 42, 48, 49, 56, 61, 76, 79, 99–101, 103, 157, 159, 209, 210, 260
testament, 314
testing, 4, 41–43, 100, 238, 262, 263, 268, 277
text, 14, 93, 110, 111, 118, 139–142, 155, 157–164, 166–169, 172, 175, 178–182, 186, 188, 215
texture, 193, 194
the AI Winter, 1
the United States, 164
theft, 8, 117, 213
theorem, 45, 80, 81, 232, 234
theory, 39, 44–48, 52, 80
therapy, 261, 266, 267
think, 101
thinking, 292
thought, 204
threshold, 137, 193
thresholding, 193
throughput, 262
throw, 86
tick, 125
tie, 84
time, 4, 6, 10, 14, 16–18, 21, 23, 31, 32, 42, 57, 58, 61, 76, 86, 110, 113–118, 125–129, 132–135, 143–146, 149,

164, 165, 175–177, 184,
194, 210, 214, 218, 224,
226, 227, 232, 237, 238,
240, 260–264, 266–268,
305, 308, 310, 312, 320,
321
timestamp, 126
tip, 90
title, 167
today, 10, 16, 112, 116, 124, 135, 169, 175, 246
tokenization, 114, 142
tolerance, 126, 238, 252
toll, 291
tomorrow, 135
tone, 172
tool, 22, 41, 42, 44, 45, 48, 50, 51, 67–69, 75, 80, 86, 94, 101, 114, 115, 138, 142, 146, 149, 163, 218, 236, 248, 255, 263, 300, 307, 320
toolbox, 139
toolkit, 86, 101, 182
topic, 108, 140, 251
total, 64, 89, 95, 102
touch, 261, 266–268
track, 13, 18, 114, 237, 266
tracking, 111, 320, 321
tract, 178, 179
traction, 255
trade, 104, 133, 195, 303
tradeoff, 58
trading, 6, 117, 255–258
traffic, 4, 18, 56, 88, 118, 213, 237, 241
train, 53, 56, 61, 68, 99–101, 103, 105, 107, 166, 179, 187, 206, 209, 231, 269, 271, 297

training, 8–10, 53, 54, 56, 57, 61, 64, 68, 71, 73, 85, 99, 100, 103–105, 107, 153, 155, 156, 158, 160, 165, 166, 168, 179, 180, 182–185, 205, 206, 209, 210, 214, 215, 234, 261, 264, 268, 269, 271, 272, 276, 277, 280, 290, 291, 294, 296, 297, 320
trajectory, 12, 31, 226, 237, 305
transaction, 117, 149
transcription, 172, 177
transfer, 209, 218, 284, 318
transferring, 217, 218, 285, 310
transform, 94, 127, 194, 305, 314
transformation, 125, 291
transformer, 157, 158
transit, 114
transition, 240, 291, 294–296
translation, 2, 155, 158, 177, 181–183, 185–189
transmission, 192, 193
transparency, 4, 7, 9, 10, 240, 241, 255, 261, 262, 268, 280, 297, 298, 302–304, 311
transportation, 4, 6, 118, 308
travel, 89, 226
treatment, 18, 117, 118, 158, 235, 259–262, 266, 270, 275, 302
tree, 70–73, 88
trend, 17
Trevor Hastie, 108
trial, 2, 57, 262, 263
Trifacta Wrangler, 23, 24
trip, 18, 26, 89
trust, 10, 18, 86, 172, 180, 267, 268, 272, 275, 280, 297, 302,

Index

305
trustworthiness, 111
tumor, 260
tune, 100, 153
tuning, 85, 101, 168
type, 15, 53, 57, 84, 103, 113, 116

U.S., 258
ubiquity, 17
uncertainty, 40, 42, 44, 48, 157, 224, 235, 236, 291
understanding, 3, 10, 11, 13, 15, 23, 28, 35, 37, 47, 48, 56, 67, 69, 75, 76, 79, 80, 83, 87, 92, 94, 103, 132, 143, 146, 149, 153, 155, 158, 159, 163, 164, 168, 172, 183, 191, 193, 205, 206, 209, 210, 213, 219, 225–228, 231, 234–236, 246, 252, 277, 287, 290, 293, 297, 307
unemployment, 291
unfairness, 17
universe, 10, 24
up, 3, 7, 11, 12, 18, 25, 41, 44, 57, 61, 87, 104, 105, 116, 136, 185, 203, 205, 231, 234, 259, 263, 268, 292, 295, 301, 309, 314, 318
update, 63, 81, 89, 149, 218, 292, 297
upskilling, 268, 291–294, 296
usability, 228, 277, 280, 309
usage, 280, 305, 306
use, 3, 4, 9, 17, 18, 23, 34, 42, 49, 51, 54, 56, 64, 68, 72, 79, 81, 84, 100, 108, 110, 112, 113, 117–119, 123, 127, 128, 142, 153, 157, 158, 162, 179, 180, 186, 187, 193, 209, 215, 218, 223, 225, 231, 234, 235, 241, 249, 252, 256, 260, 264, 266–268, 271, 274, 280, 281, 299, 302, 305, 307, 312, 316, 318
usefulness, 149
user, 3, 17–19, 89, 114, 117–119, 129, 169, 172, 175, 177, 180, 218, 228, 245, 308–311, 320, 321
utilization, 101, 121, 306

validation, 19–24, 85, 98–104, 107, 209, 238, 268
value, 35–37, 40, 58, 70, 84, 85, 87, 89, 96, 111–113, 115, 156, 163, 203, 204, 231, 258, 260, 274, 280, 292
variability, 36, 37, 42, 100, 173, 175, 177, 194, 224, 266, 308, 309
variable, 27, 49, 51, 65, 67, 70, 98, 204, 235, 260
variance, 36–38, 85, 91, 98, 233
variant, 100, 101
variation, 26, 98
variety, 110–113, 133, 215, 312
vastness, 305
Vaswani, 182
vector, 184, 308
vehicle, 18, 56
velocity, 112, 305
veracity, 111, 112
verification, 149, 200
versatility, 14, 59, 68
version, 42

video, 14, 93, 110, 111, 194, 211, 311
view, 120
viewer, 320
viewing, 3, 12, 245, 320
virus, 32
vision, 111, 186, 191, 192, 194, 197, 199, 200, 205, 211, 213, 215, 216, 225, 227, 301, 310, 311, 319, 321
visitation, 235
visual, 28, 35, 88, 145, 191, 192, 194, 203, 211, 213, 216, 225, 227, 237, 319, 321
visualization, 27–29, 31, 32, 35, 55, 91, 92, 112, 114, 115, 266, 295
vocabulary, 176, 181, 184
vocoder, 179
voice, 3, 4, 175, 177, 178, 180
volume, 55, 111–113, 116, 132, 169
voting, 84

wake, 267
warehouse, 120–125, 223
warehousing, 115, 120–125
warm, 25
water, 306
way, 2, 4, 5, 12, 13, 16, 27, 32, 67, 80, 114, 134, 158, 176, 177, 180, 192, 224, 237, 248, 255, 265, 283, 301, 312, 321
weather, 3, 118, 175
web, 14, 17, 18, 125
week, 129
weight, 63, 77, 79, 84, 204

well, 9, 12, 13, 19, 48, 81, 82, 89, 91, 95, 98, 101–103, 105, 107, 113, 157, 166, 175, 215, 238, 242, 265, 291, 309–311
whole, 2, 7, 116, 291
wisdom, 86
word, 142, 156, 163, 181, 182, 184, 186, 187
work, 8, 11, 54, 121, 125, 129, 194, 231, 240, 292, 296, 299, 301
workflow, 320
workforce, 291, 292, 294, 296
working, 9, 15, 64, 81, 89, 91, 99, 100, 183, 194
workload, 128, 262
workout, 25
world, 5, 10, 12, 15–17, 23, 26, 28, 32, 44, 47, 48, 51, 56, 57, 60, 61, 64, 65, 67, 73, 76, 80, 86, 87, 89, 90, 101, 104, 105, 108, 112, 116, 123–125, 135, 141, 146, 149, 151, 159, 160, 162, 177, 185, 186, 189, 191, 194, 197, 201, 209, 211, 213, 219, 223, 224, 230, 231, 234, 237, 238, 247, 248, 252, 255, 258, 265, 270, 274, 280, 294, 300, 305, 311
write, 113
writing, 319

yield, 42, 184
yourself, 28

zip, 269